I0810702

IMAGES
of America

PORT WASHINGTON

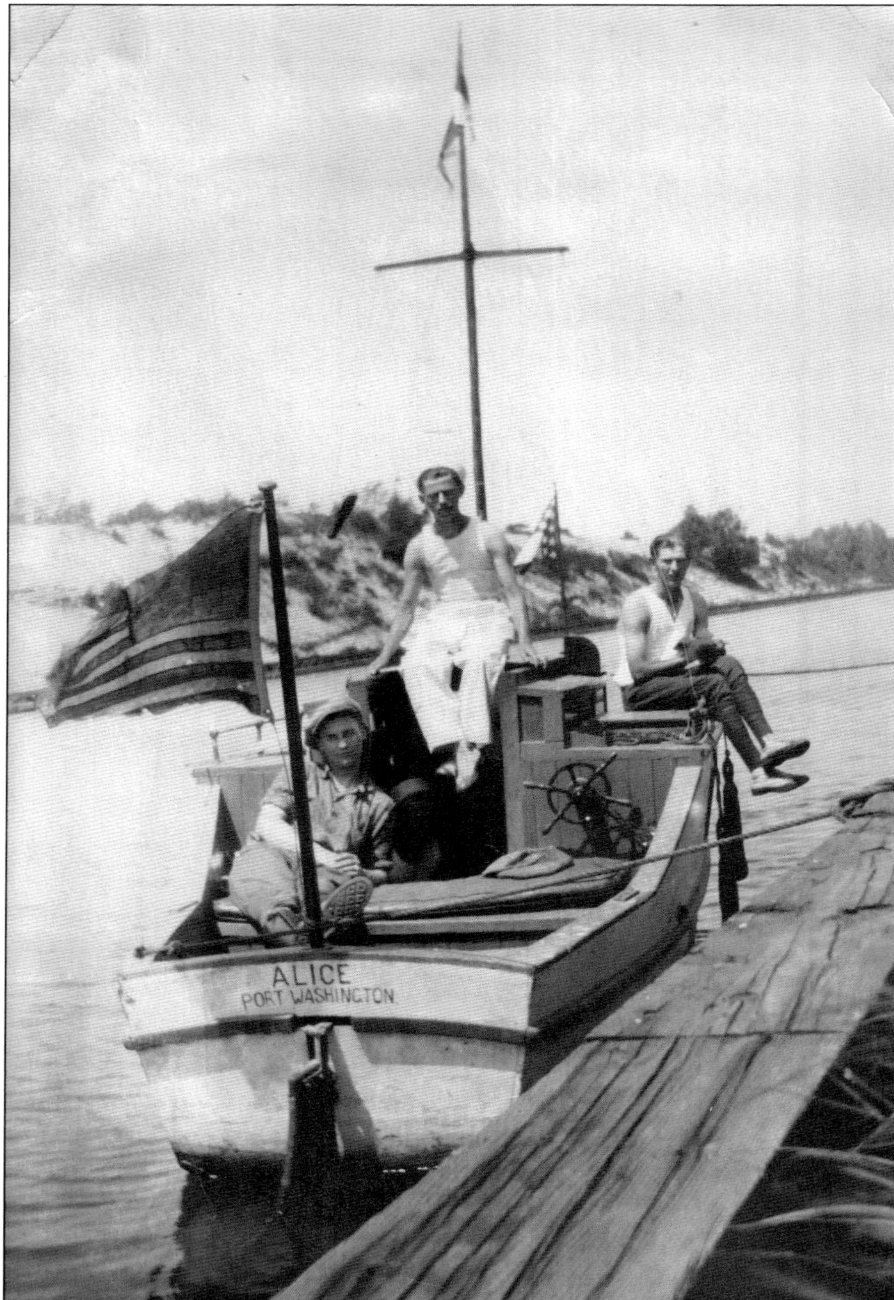

Aboard *Alice*, these three patriotic young men are out for a leisurely day of sailing in Port Washington harbor. This photograph was taken in the 1920s or 1930s. (Courtesy of the Port Washington Historical Society.)

On the Cover: The breakwater causeway is seen here jutting out into Lake Michigan in the winter. (Courtesy of the Port Washington Historical Society.)

IMAGES
of America

PORT WASHINGTON

Richard D. Smith with
Kathie U. Gordon

ARCADIA
PUBLISHING

ISBN 978-0-7385-8365-5

Published by Arcadia Publishing
Charleston, South Carolina

Printed in the United States of America

Library of Congress Control Number: 2010942241

For all general information, please contact Arcadia Publishing:
Telephone 843-853-2070
Fax 843-853-0044
E-mail sales@arcadiapublishing.com
For customer service and orders:
Toll-Free 1-888-313-2665

Visit us on the Internet at www.arcadiapublishing.com

Contents

ACKNOWLEDGMENTS

Different than my other publications, I sought out the help and support of people and their knowledge of the history of Port Washington for this project. Thank you to my daughter, Sarah, for her encouragement. Thanks also to the Port Washington Historical Society, Linda M. Nenn, Geri Zehren, Angela Cope, Jackie Oleson, and Mary Flierl for their invaluable assistance and research, and to Kathie Gordon for her editing and computer skills.

The following individuals are acknowledged for their contribution of artwork or photographs: Lawrence Bruecher, John Enright, Chris Hurst, Ambrose Mayer photograph collection, Linda M. Nenn photograph collection, Port Publications and the *Ozaukee Press*, Port Washington Historical Society photograph collection, Gerald Lee Smith artwork, Richard D. Smith photograph collection, and Paul G. Wiening photograph collection published in The History of Port Washington Harbor, Passages.

—Richard D. Smith

Introduction

The small city of Port Washington, Wisconsin, is located on the shores of Lake Michigan, 25 miles north of Milwaukee. The population is a little more than 10,000, and it was once a city of many industries. Today, like many other small towns, Port Washington is rapidly becoming a bedroom community for its larger neighbor to the south.

Going back into the past about 100 years or so and standing in the downtown where there are shops and restaurants, one would have witnessed the clay rock and pebble stratum, which had been deposited by the Wisconsin glacier, slowly being eroded. This glacier created an outwash and ground moraine, covered with a clay stratum, the erosion of which caused the formation of several small streams and one larger one that would become Sauk Creek.

The early Native Americans found this a favorable spot to camp and fish during the warmer spring, summer, and fall. There is evidence that the Sioux, Fox, Sauk, Potawatomi, Menomonee, Sac, and Chippewa tribes once coveted the area. When French explorers and missionaries landed at this opening between the bluffs, they found many Native American encampments. There is evidence that Fathers Marquette, Marest, Hennepin, and Rene-Robert Cavalier, Sieur de La Salle also landed here, because it is about 25 miles from Sheboygan to Port Washington and 25 miles from Port Washington to Milwaukee—and 25 miles is one day's worth of good canoeing.

The first permanent settlers were land speculators who had become familiar with the area during the Black Hawk Wars. When the government opened up the area in 1835, Wooster Harrison, James Daly, and Solomon Juneau platted what they called "Wisconsin City." Juneau later sold out to Solon Johnson. Wisconsin City was abandoned during the financial panic of 1837 and then was resettled in 1842. From that point on, the little city began to grow rapidly. Johnson and Harrison built the first pier for the landing and loading of schooners and steam ships. Barnum Blake later built a 1,000-foot pier at the end of Pier Street and Lion Silverman built one at the end of Second Pier Street on the south side.

In 1870, the mouth of Sauk Creek was dug out to form the first artificial harbor on the Great Lakes. It was notoriously unsafe, so another strip was built running north to absorb the wave action. This also was a failure until an 800-foot-long set of piers was built and in 1889 a lighthouse was constructed on the north pier. Previously there had been a lighthouse on the north bluff in 1849, which was rebuilt in 1860. The 1860 lighthouse still exists; it was restored and serves as a museum. In 1935, a new, bigger harbor was built to accommodate large steamers that carried in coal for the new power plant. This, too, proved to be an unsafe harbor during southeastern storms. Finally, in 1980 a new, small boat harbor was successfully built.

The Town of Port Washington—encompassing an area that included the present towns of Fredonia, Saukville, and Belgium—was incorporated on January 21, 1846, two years before Wisconsin achieved statehood. Town officials were elected at the first town meeting held in April in the newly constructed schoolhouse. The first board of supervisors included Solon Johnson, Col. William Teall, and John McLean. Wooster Harrison was named a town assessor. Seventy-six names were registered on the first poll list.

One of the greatest controversies at that time was the selection of a town to serve as the county seat. An Act of the Territorial Legislature passed in 1836, divided Washington County (which included Ozaukee County) from Milwaukee County and named Wisconsin City (now Port Washington) as the seat of justice. But after the town was abandoned, Hamburg (now Grafton) was chosen as the seat of justice in a vote held in 1840.

In 1847, Wisconsin City, having been renamed Port Washington, was again made the county seat, a decision which generated animosity among the citizens of other rapidly developing communities including Mequon, Cedarburg, West Bend, Belgium, and Newburg—all within the county boundaries. The battle raged on for eight years. Many plans for solutions were submitted and rejected by the voters. In 1852, the legislature, desperate to end this matter, pushed a bill through, which divided the area into two counties—Washington County to the west, having the county seat at West Bend, and Ozaukee County to the east, with Port Washington named as county seat.

Port Washington was incorporated as a village on July 20, 1848, with boundaries designated as section 28 and the southeast one-quarter of section 29 in the town of Port Washington. Thirty-three years later, in 1882, the village was officially incorporated under a city charter using a mayor-aldermanic form of government. James W. Vail was elected the first mayor of the city. In 1917, a commission form of government—which is currently in use—was formally adopted.

In the early 2000s, the power plant converted from coal-powered to natural gas-powered, so the big steamers that used to haul coal no longer came to Port Washington. This along with the sale and relocation of the town's major industries started a chain of events that changed the nature of Port Washington.

There have been a number of short histories written about what some people call the "quaint little city" along the shores of Lake Michigan. My intent here is not to repeat these stories but to present a photographic journal of our town.

—Richard D. Smith

One

Native Americans and Explorers

When the first Europeans landed at the mouth of Sauk Creek, they found Native American villages of the Sauk, Potawatomi, and Fox tribes. These Native Americans fished from various watercraft with seines, weirs, hooks, and spears.

Sauk Creek is named for the Sauk or Osaukee, a tribe that at one time lived in the Port Washington area prior to being moved westward by the federal government in the 1840s and 1850s. Legend has it that a raiding party of Chippewa attacked the Sauk near the location of the present Port Washington High School football field. The victorious Sauk drove the aggressive Chippewa from the area. At different times the Menominee camped at the mouth of Sauk Creek if other tribes were not present.

In 1879, Fr. Louis Hennepin and Rene-Robert Cavalier, Sieur de La Salle camped at the first landing north of the Milwaukee River to replenish supplies at a Potawatomi village at the mouth of a small stream—probably Sauk Creek.

September 1862 brought about the great Native American scare in Ozaukee County. Although most of the Native Americans were moved west of the Mississippi by the Treaty of 1821, a few remained around the Waubeka area. A report from unknown sources stated that Native Americans came in large numbers and killed men, women, and children. People panicked and rushed to Milwaukee for safety, passing each other while coming and going. Troops were called out and found nothing but a couple of very frightened berry pickers and a bunch of very embarrassed citizens trying to find many of their buried belongings.

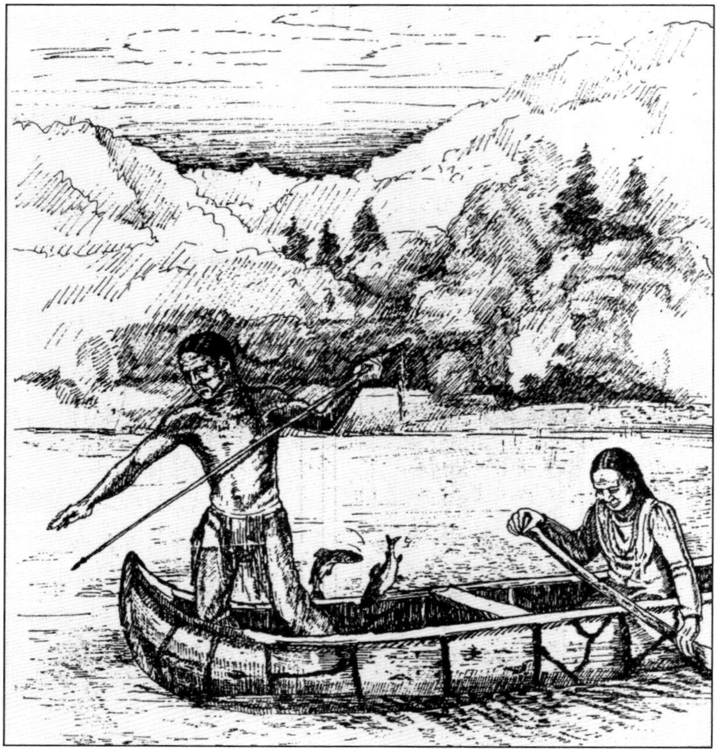

The Potawatomi were the last Native Americans to live in the Sauk Creek area. As late as the 1850s, chief Waubeka traveled from Waubeka to the shores of Port Washington. Most tribes had been moved westward to "Indian Country," but some came back to live peacefully with the whites.

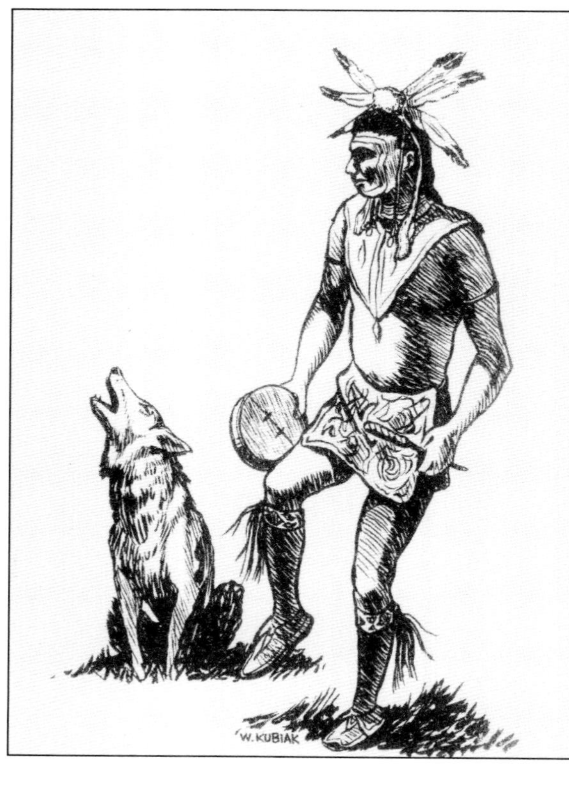

The Sauk and Menominee were also among the last tribes to live in the area before removal westward by the federal government. Previously chief Waubeka moved inland for the winter and toward the lake for the summer. There is a small city west of Port Washington named after chief Waubeka.

Sauk Creek is named for the Sauk or Osaukee, a tribe that lived in the Port Washington area prior to being moved westward by the federal government in the 1840s and 1850s. At one time, the Sauk battled the Chippewa near the location of the present Port Washington High School football field. The victorious Sauk drove the aggressive Chippewa from the area.

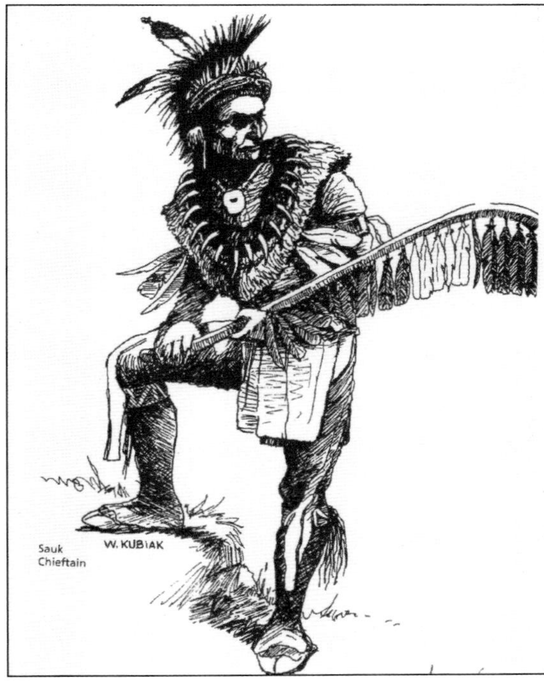

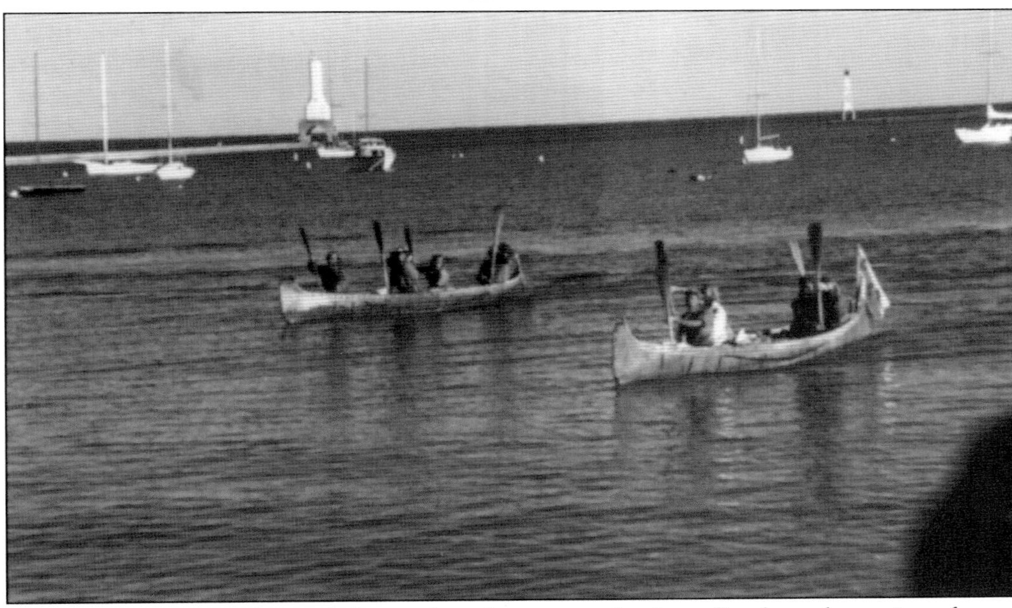

Due to inclement weather and the need to obtain more food supplies from the natives, for two and a half days, Fr. Jacques Marquette's party was forced to camp one day's canoe ride north of Milwaukee at the mouth of a small rivulet under the bluffs. Much evidence indicates this was Sauk Creek and the Native American encampment was that of the Potawatomi. In 1879, Fr. Louis Hennepin and Rene-Robert Cavalier, Sieur de La Salle camped at the first landing north of the Milwaukee River to replenish supplies at a Potawatomi village at the mouth of a small stream—probably Sauk Creek. Here is the 1976 reenactment of their landing at Port Washington as they searched for the Mississippi River.

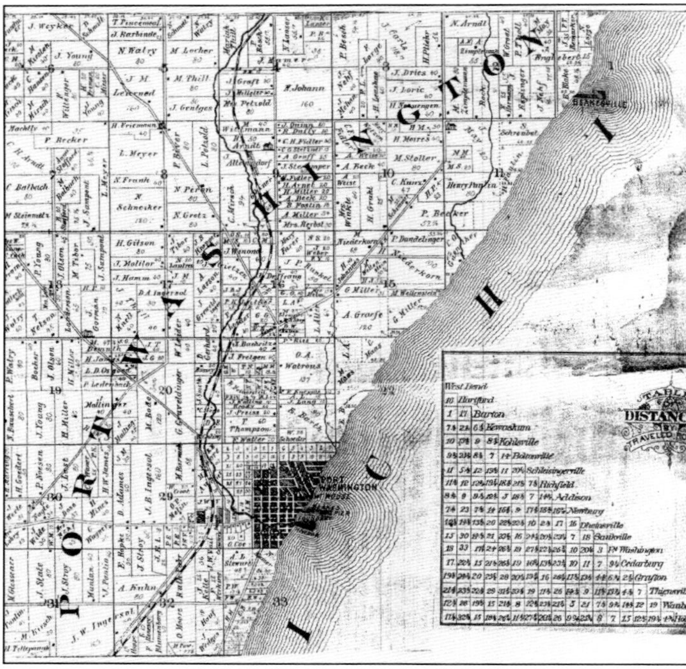

This plat map of Port Washington dates to 1873–1874. The first military road, which was surveyed after the Menomonee Treaty of 1821, extended from Dekorra (now Decorah, Iowa) east to Port Washington and was opened by General Dodge in 1832. The Green Bay-Lake Shore road from Chicago to Green Bay was surveyed between 1832 and 1833. This road, passing through Port Washington, met the Dekorra Road so that even before any white man had settled on the Port Washington site the place had become a rather important spot in the wilderness.

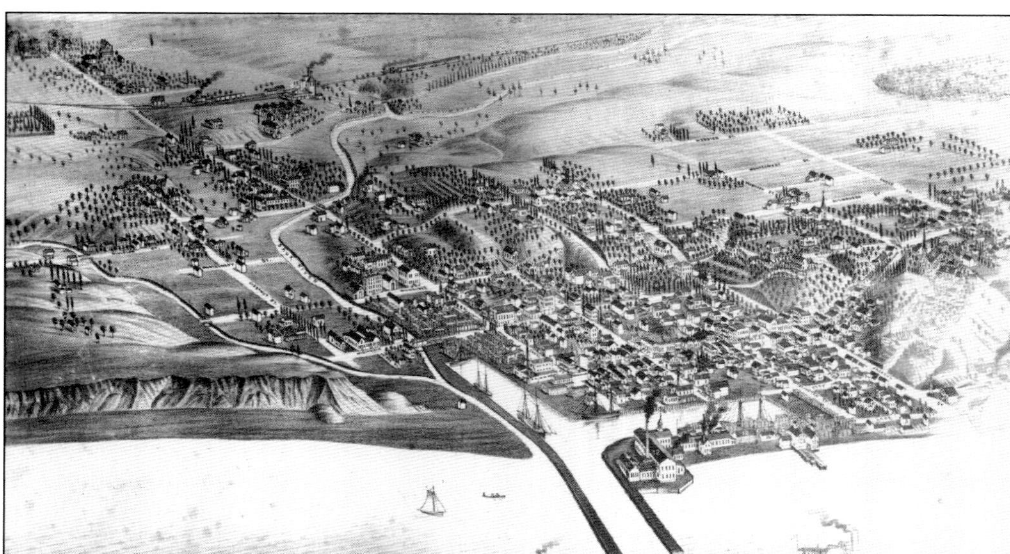

Pictured here is Port Washington in 1883. Note that there is no lighthouse on the end of the north pier. That was added in 1889.

Two

The First Businesses of Port Washington

For the 1908 homecoming, the Business Men's Club of Port Washington sponsored a booklet of Port Washington and its businesses. It was felt that part of this booklet should be reproduced in order to familiarize the community with the vibrancy of its little city since so many of the people living here today are not native Port Washingtonites. The Business Men's Club no longer exists and was superseded by the chamber of commerce. The Business Men's Club building, located on Franklin Street, still stands and was incorporated into the former First National Bank, which later became part of the Marshall and Ilsley bank system. These buildings, slated to have been torn down in 2012, have been given new purpose. The original First National Bank has been incorporated into a new commercial development of businesses and condominiums. The Business Men's Club, located at 118 North Franklin Street, was weeks away from being razed when a generous anonymous donor gave the Port Washington Historical Society the funds to purchase, restore, and develop the building into an interactive museum dedicated to local and maritime history. It is now called the Port Exploreum. The booklet is reproduced here with the permission of the Port Washington Historical Society.

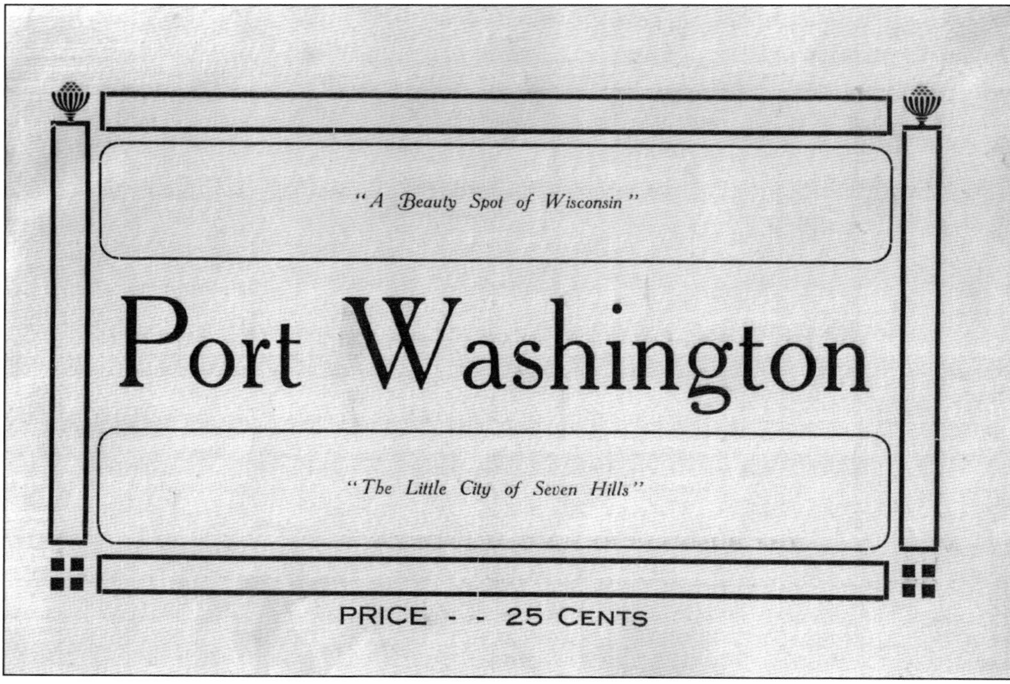

"A Beauty Spot of Wisconsin"

Port Washington

"The Little City of Seven Hills"

PRICE - - 25 CENTS

Shown here are inserts from the Business Men's Club of Port Washington booklet, which was printed just 70 years after the founding of Port Washington and shows the progress of this industrious little city.

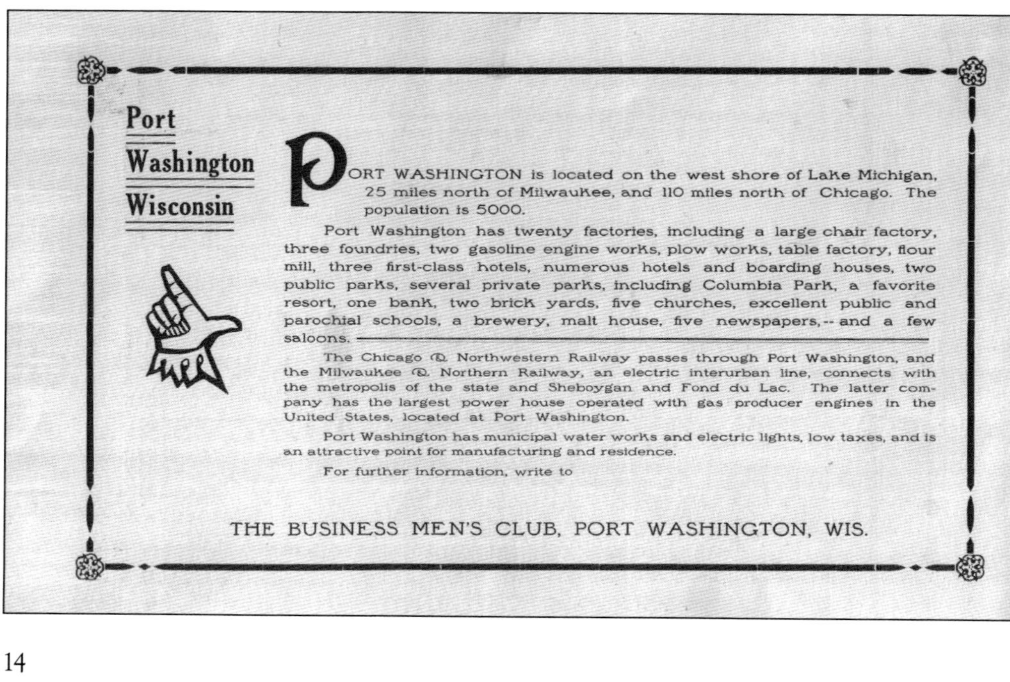

Port Washington Wisconsin

PORT WASHINGTON is located on the west shore of Lake Michigan, 25 miles north of Milwaukee, and 110 miles north of Chicago. The population is 5000.

Port Washington has twenty factories, including a large chair factory, three foundries, two gasoline engine works, plow works, table factory, flour mill, three first-class hotels, numerous hotels and boarding houses, two public parks, several private parks, including Columbia Park, a favorite resort, one bank, two brick yards, five churches, excellent public and parochial schools, a brewery, malt house, five newspapers,-- and a few saloons.

The Chicago & Northwestern Railway passes through Port Washington, and the Milwaukee & Northern Railway, an electric interurban line, connects with the metropolis of the state and Sheboygan and Fond du Lac. The latter company has the largest power house operated with gas producer engines in the United States, located at Port Washington.

Port Washington has municipal water works and electric lights, low taxes, and is an attractive point for manufacturing and residence.

For further information, write to

THE BUSINESS MEN'S CLUB, PORT WASHINGTON, WIS.

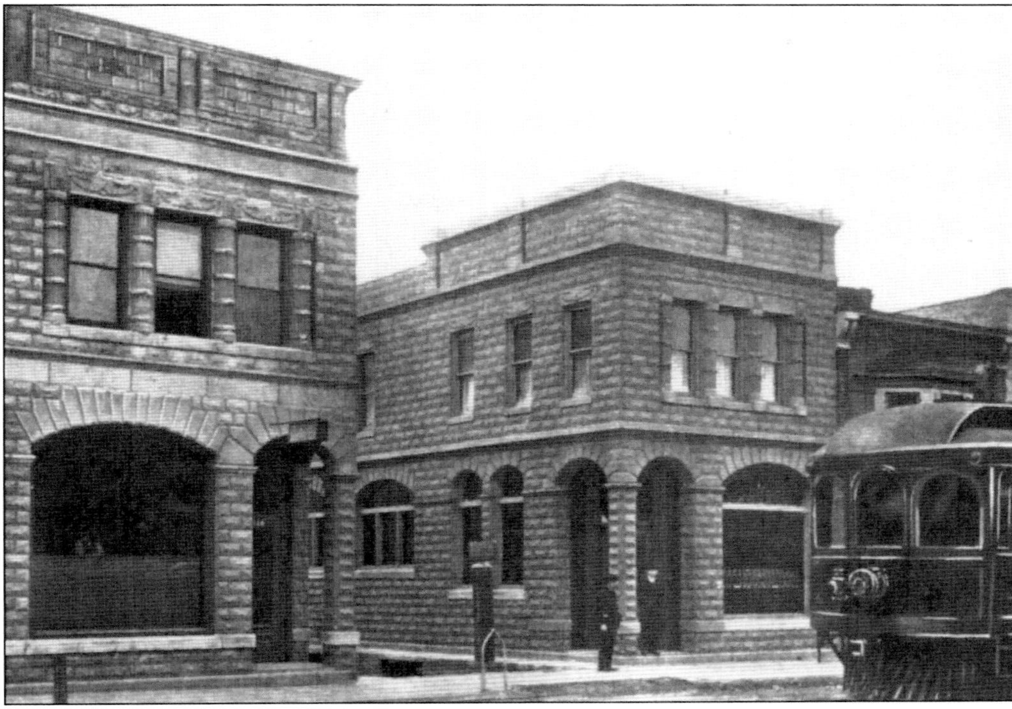

The building on the right was once Zimmerman's Sample Room. It is still a saloon, now called the Schooner Pub. The building on the left, a near mirror image, was the Business Men's Club, referred to on the previous page. It is now the Port Exploreum.

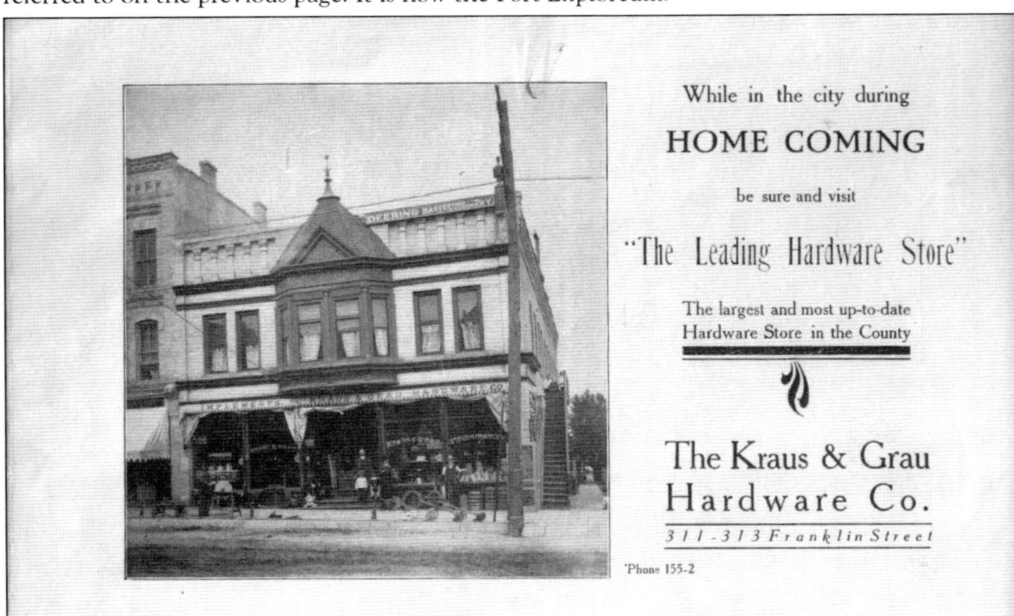

Before the advent of chain stores, Port Washington had several hardware stores. They carried just about everything, and if a customer wanted only one of something he or she didn't have to purchase a prepackaged amount.

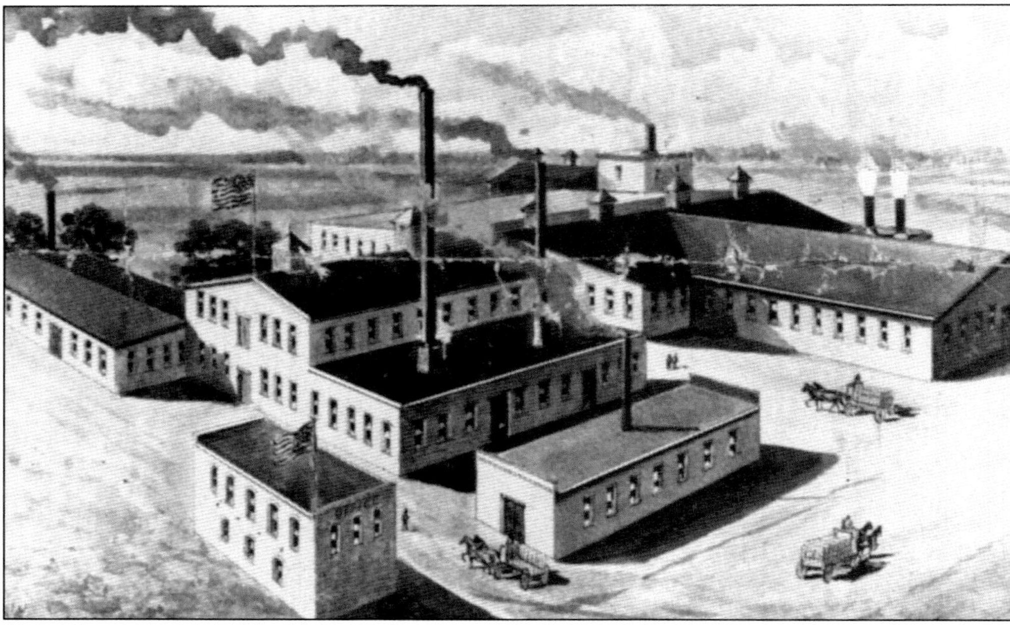

The Gilson Company first made gasoline engines for industrial and commercial use and eventually became the Gilson Bolens Manufacturing Company, which merged with Troy-Bilt of New York and has since moved to New York state.

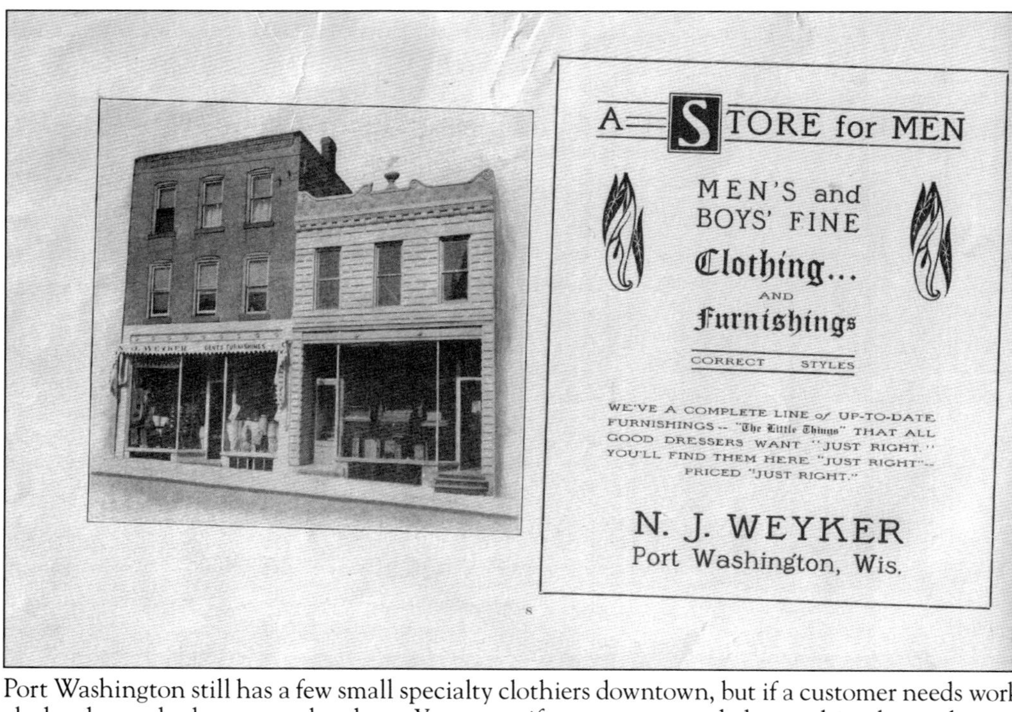

Port Washington still has a few small specialty clothiers downtown, but if a customer needs work clothes he or she has to go elsewhere. Years ago, if a customer needed something he or she just went downtown to purchase it and probably enjoyed lunch or a refreshment while there.

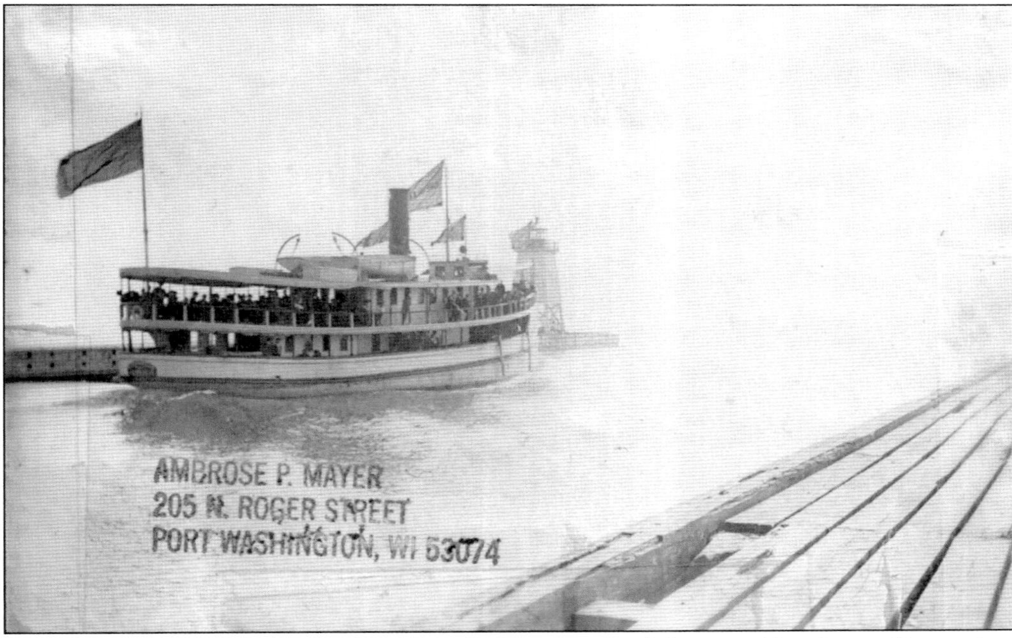

Steamboats often brought people to Port Washington and they would either walk or take a carriage ride up the hill to Columbia Park and the saloon. The saloon still exists, but the park has decreased in size. At times, due to too much partying, the walk downhill was longer than the walk uphill! Pictured here is the *Pabst* boat from Milwaukee around the late 1920s.

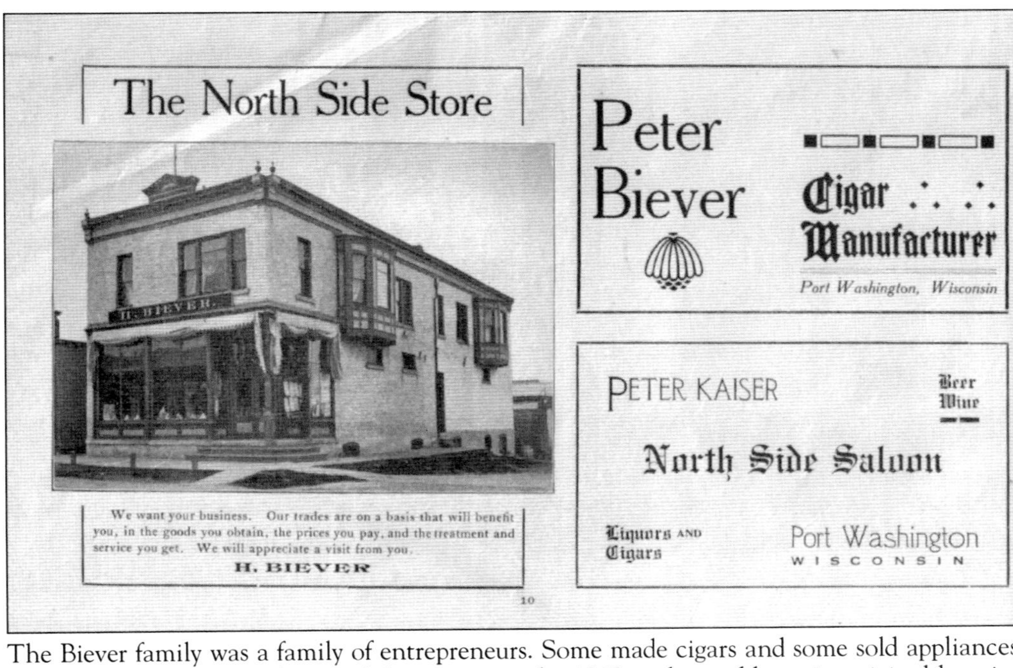

The Biever family was a family of entrepreneurs. Some made cigars and some sold appliances. Ironically the store, which moved downtown in the 1940s, relocated here, its original location on Wisconsin Street, after Joe Biever scaled down the business.

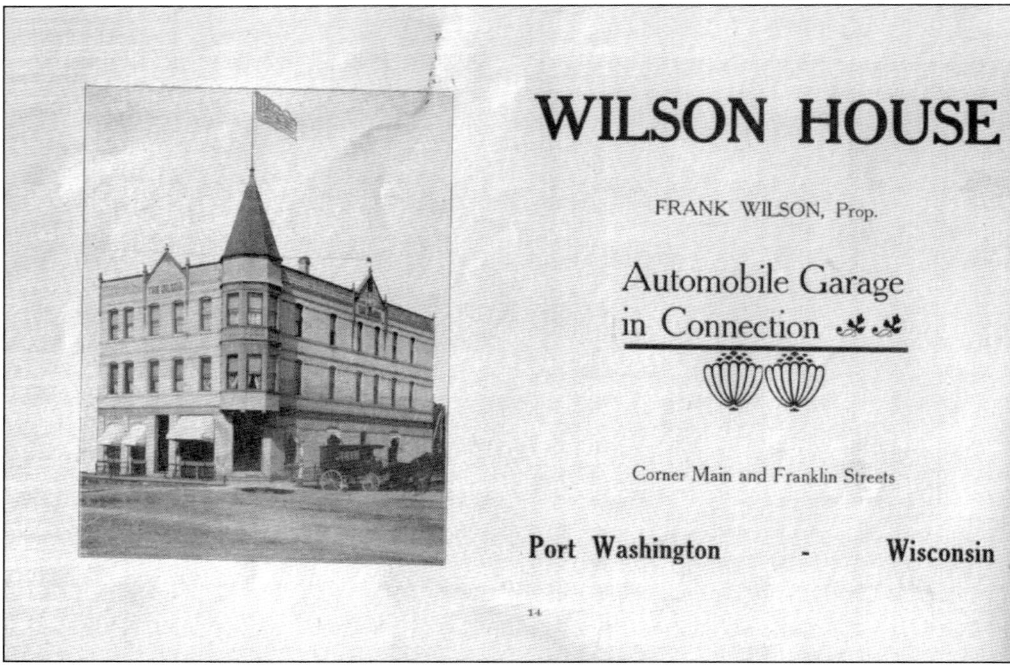

The 1901 *Industrial Review* of Port Washington called the Wilson House "strictly a first class hotel." Frank Wilson, the owner, had been a steward on the Goodrich Steamship Line. He obtained a small tonnage captain's license for Lake Michigan and was politically active. The Wilson House is now part of the Port Washington State Bank.

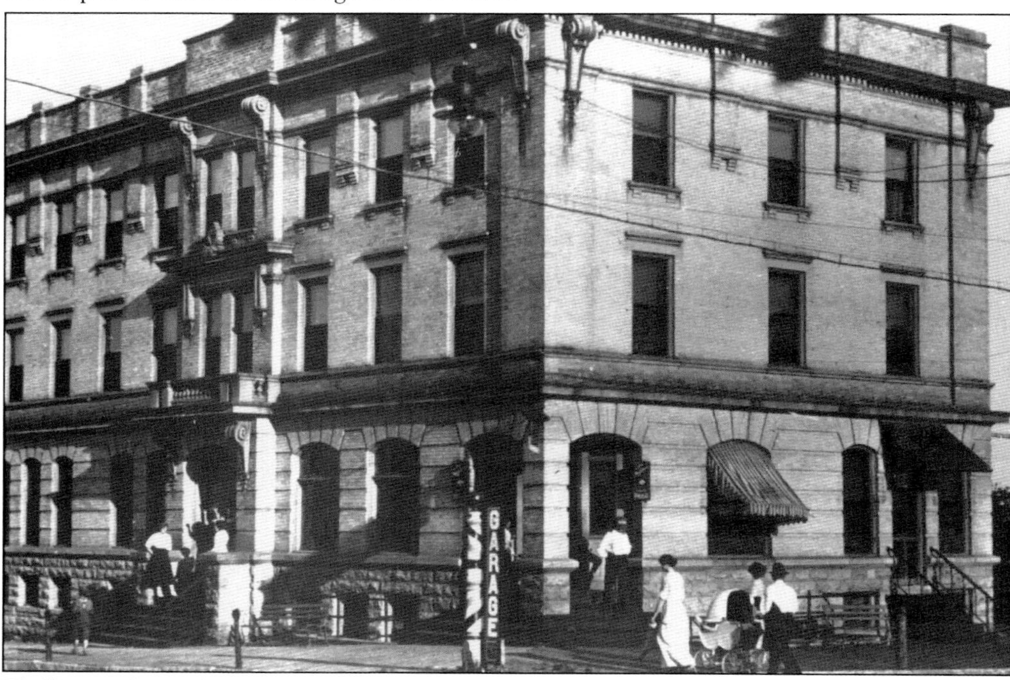

Thill's Hotel, now known as the Port Hotel, has had many owners. It was converted from rooms into suites. The building itself retains a restaurant and maintains its original charm.

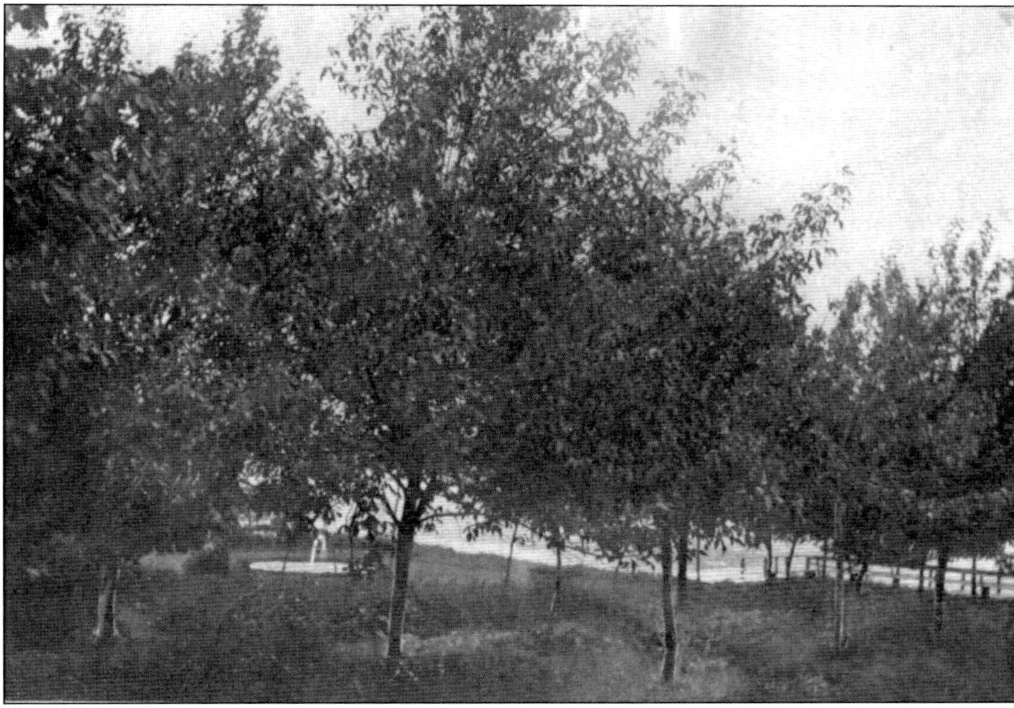

Gilson Park was donated to the City of Port Washington by the John Gilson family for the pleasure of lakeside visitors. The park's artesian well has since been capped, and the area serves the marina and those who visit the lakeshore.

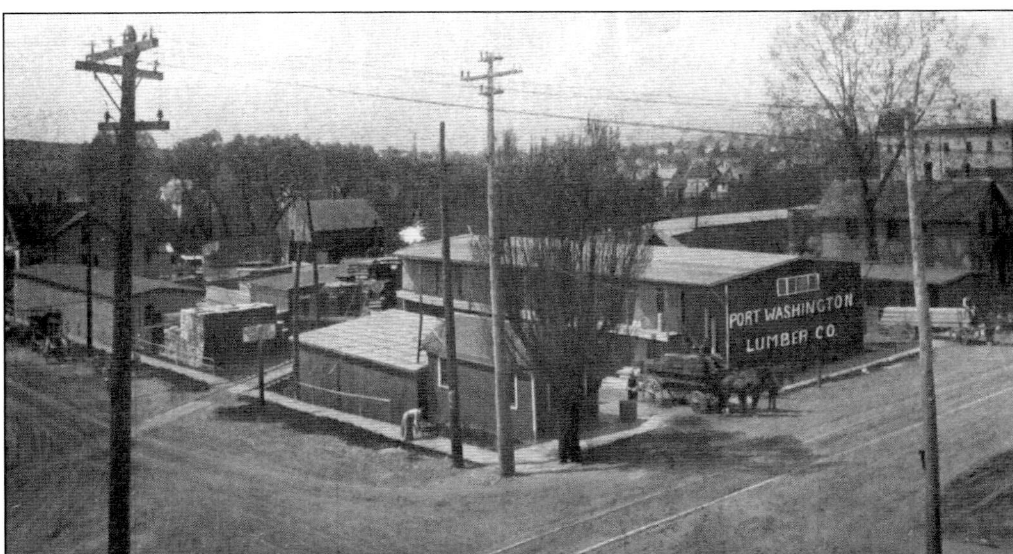

Schooners and small steamers once delivered large amounts of lumber and other wood products to Port Washington. Located right downtown, the Port Washington Lumber Company was very convenient for townspeople. Note the horse-drawn delivery wagon.

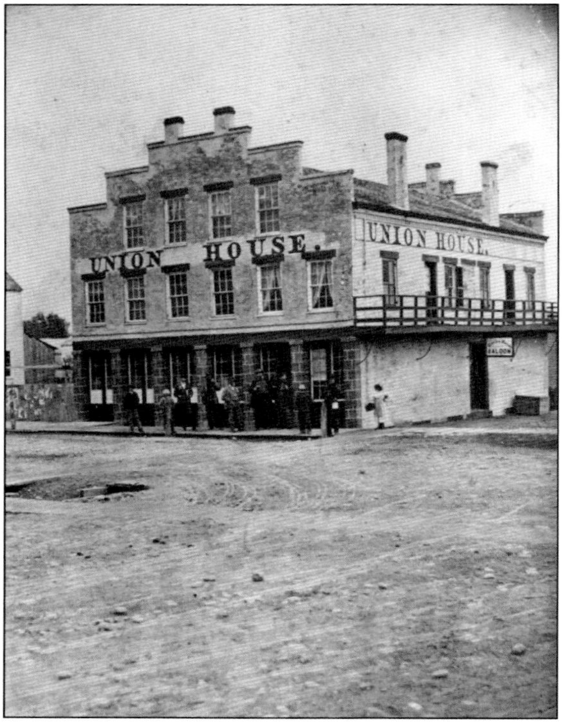

The Exchange Block building was built by Barnum Blake, an early land speculator and businessman. Located on the northeast corner of Franklin and Main Streets, in 1868 it became the Union House Hotel, replacing an earlier saloon. Maj. John C. Schroeling, the owner, later sold it to Sievers and Schwin. In 1891, the Wilson House was built, replacing the Union House on this site.

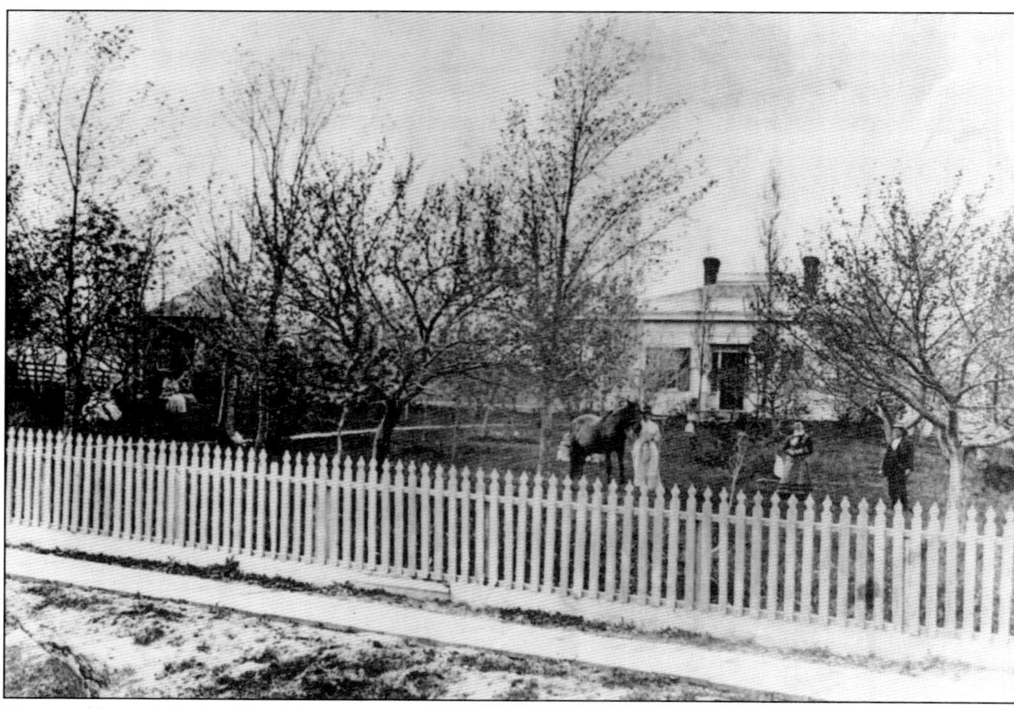

Pictured here is Judge Pors's house, owned by William A. Pors, who acted as a draft commissioner in 1862. During the Civil War draft riots, his house was ransacked and vandalized. Pors and his family escaped to Milwaukee.

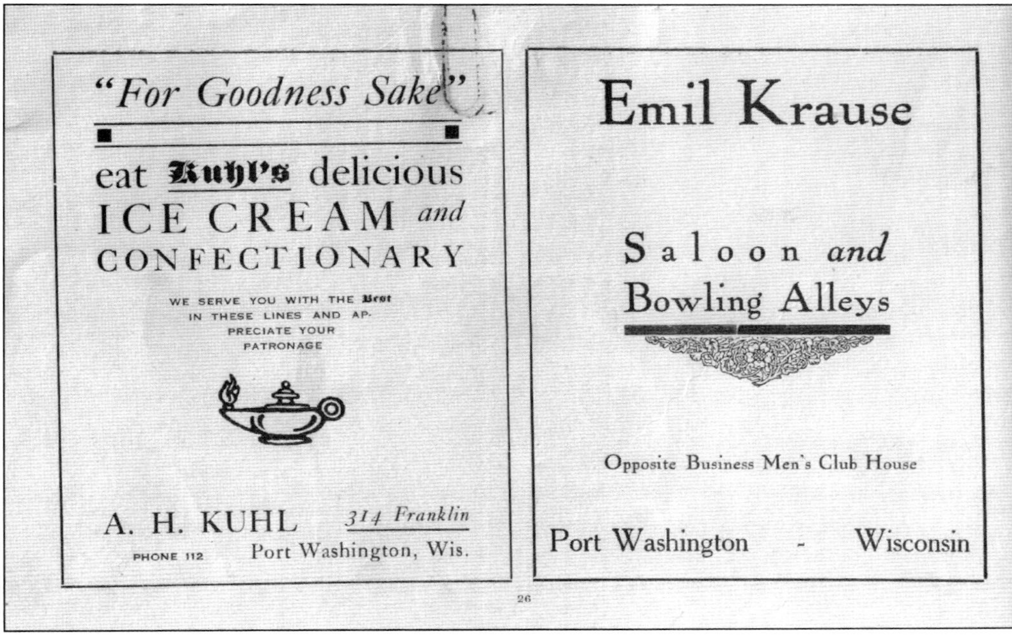

Bakeries, bars, bowling alleys, and ice cream parlors—Port Washington had it all and actually still does, but a scaled-down quantity. With confectioneries, cigars, saloons, a theater, and blacksmiths, Port was a civil little place with a vibrant downtown area of privately owned businesses that kept the town alive.

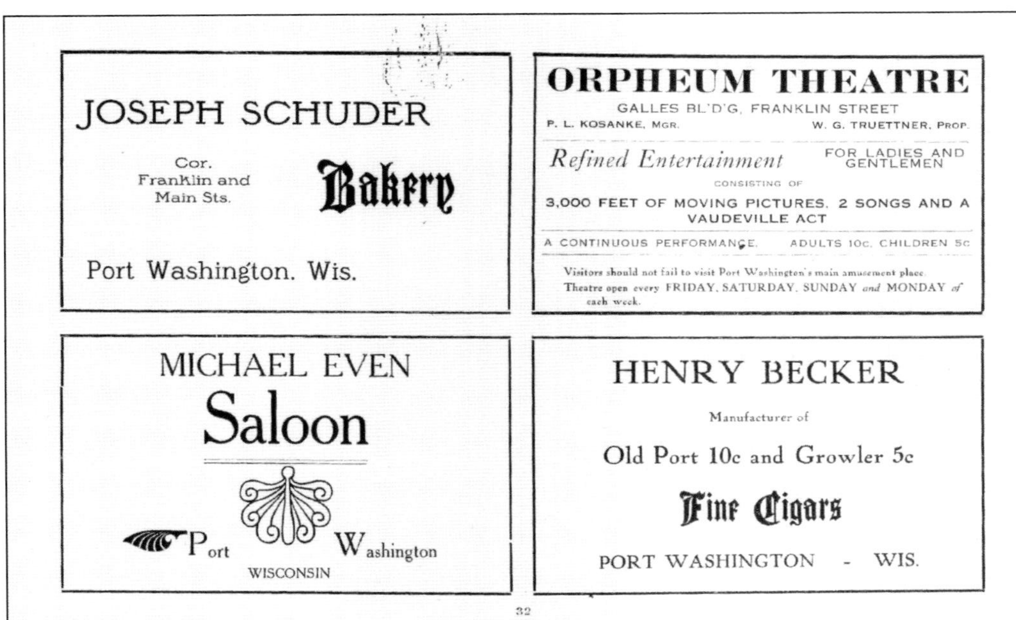

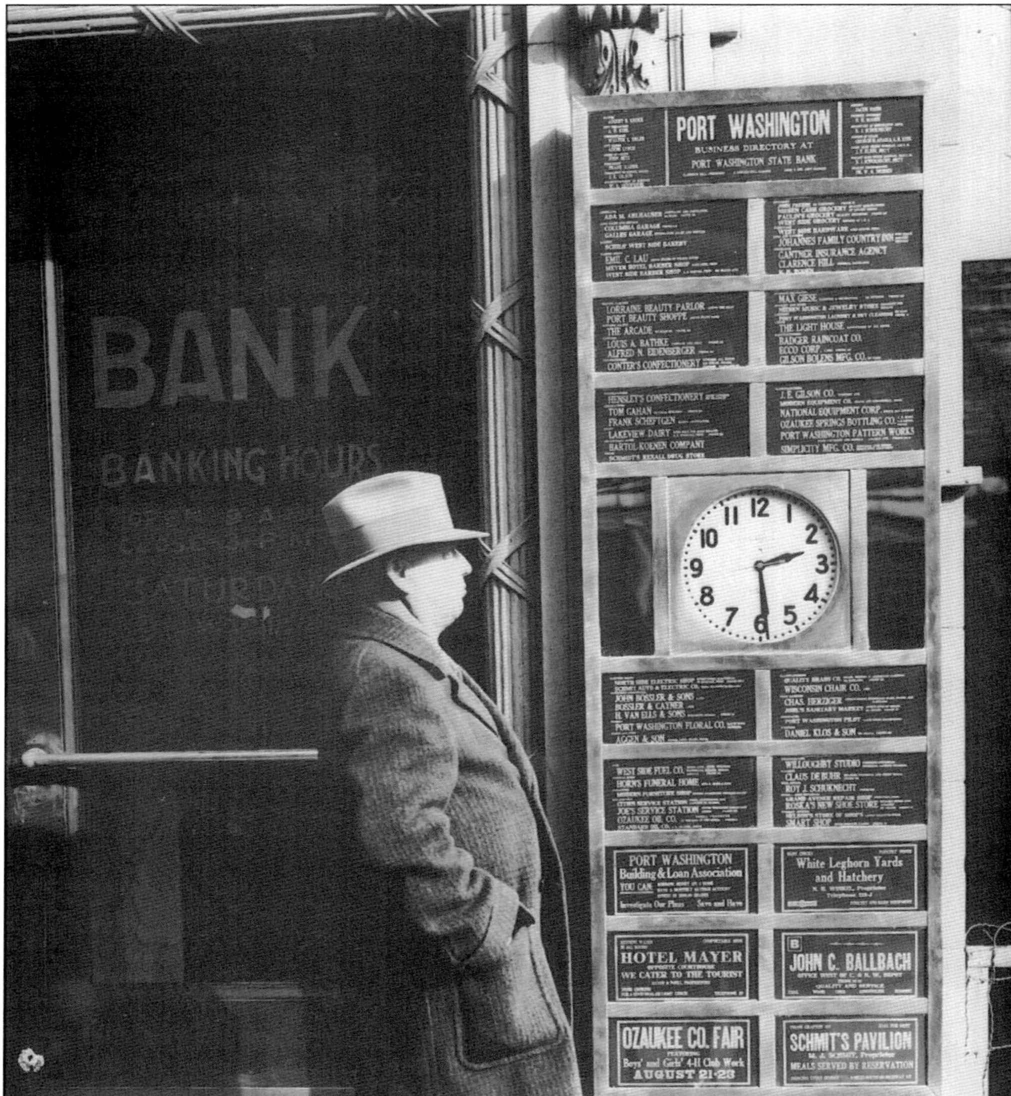

Clarence Hill, one of the founders of Port Washington State Bank, looks at a business directory at the bank around 1930.

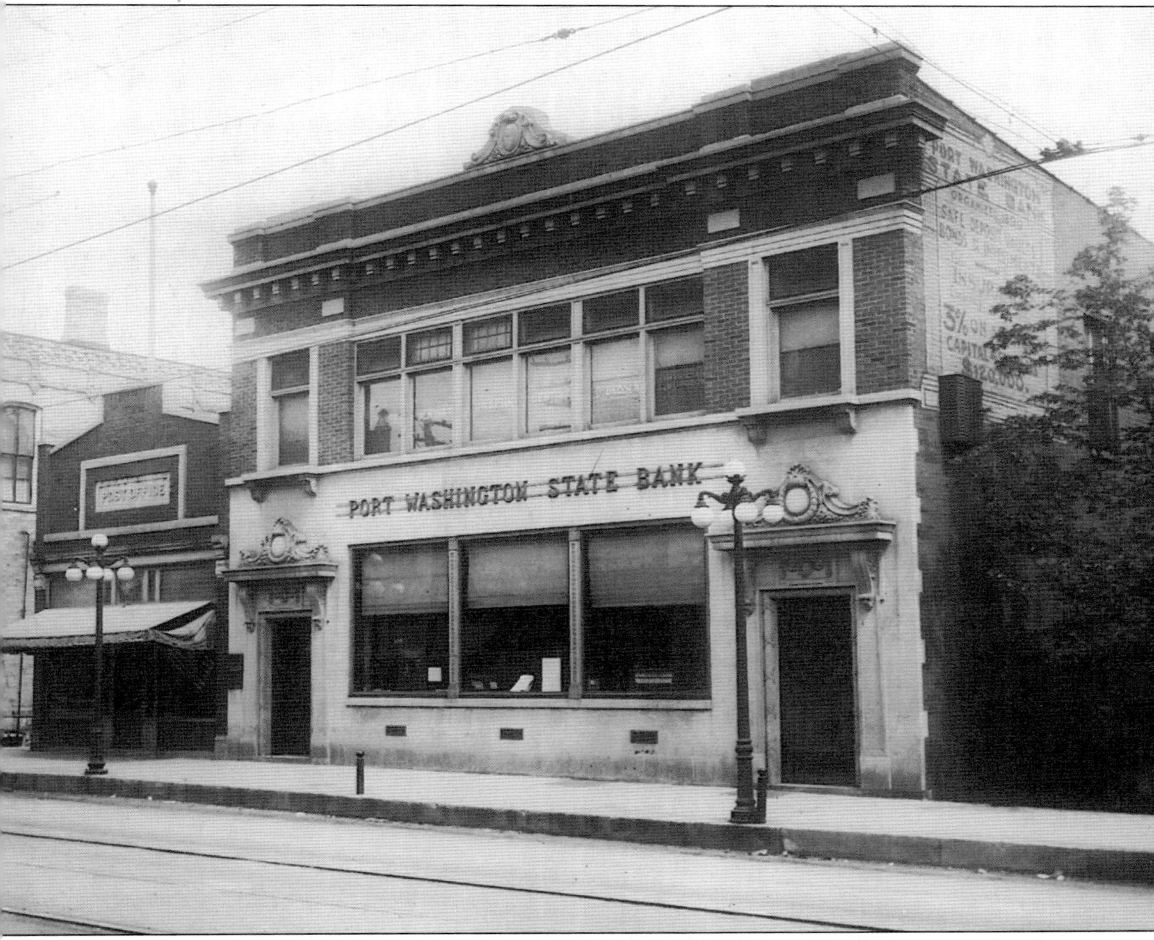

The late 1800s found Port Washington and most of Ozaukee County without proper banking services and with many previously failed ventures. Two partners, Clarence Hill and Dr. George Henry, both of Manitowoc, got together to purchase a site and organize a bank on September 11, 1899. Hill, one of the original organizers of the First National Bank of Manitowoc in 1895, and Henry, a local dentist with Port Washington ties, capitalized the bank with $25,000 in personal and investor monies. This photograph from the middle to late 1920s is of the second bank building, erected in 1921 on the original bank site.

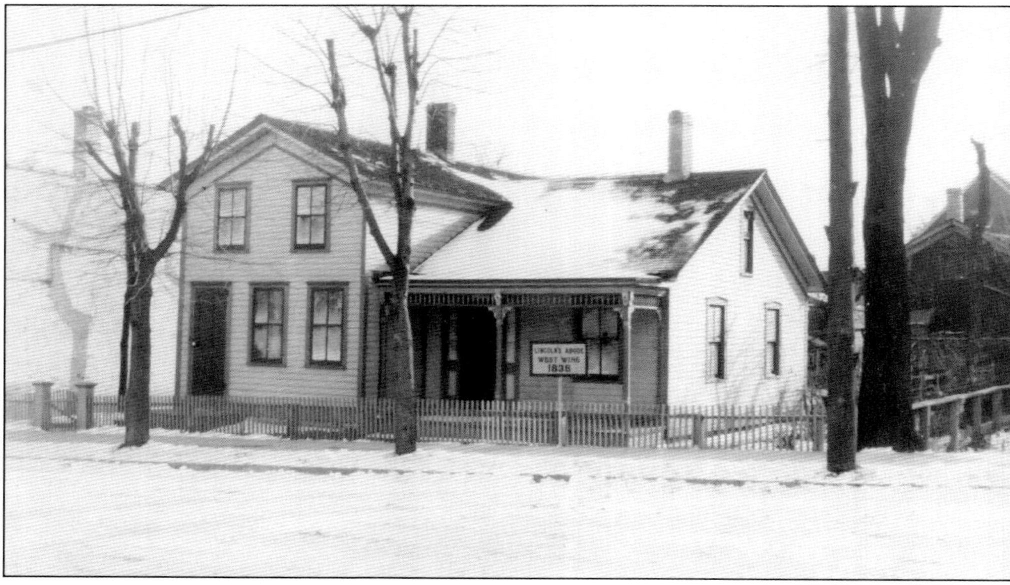

One of the city founders was Gen. Wooster Harrison. Here is a photograph of his home, which was located just off Franklin Street. It is rumored that during his travels in the early 1830s, Abraham Lincoln stopped in Port Washington and spent a day or two at Harrison's home.

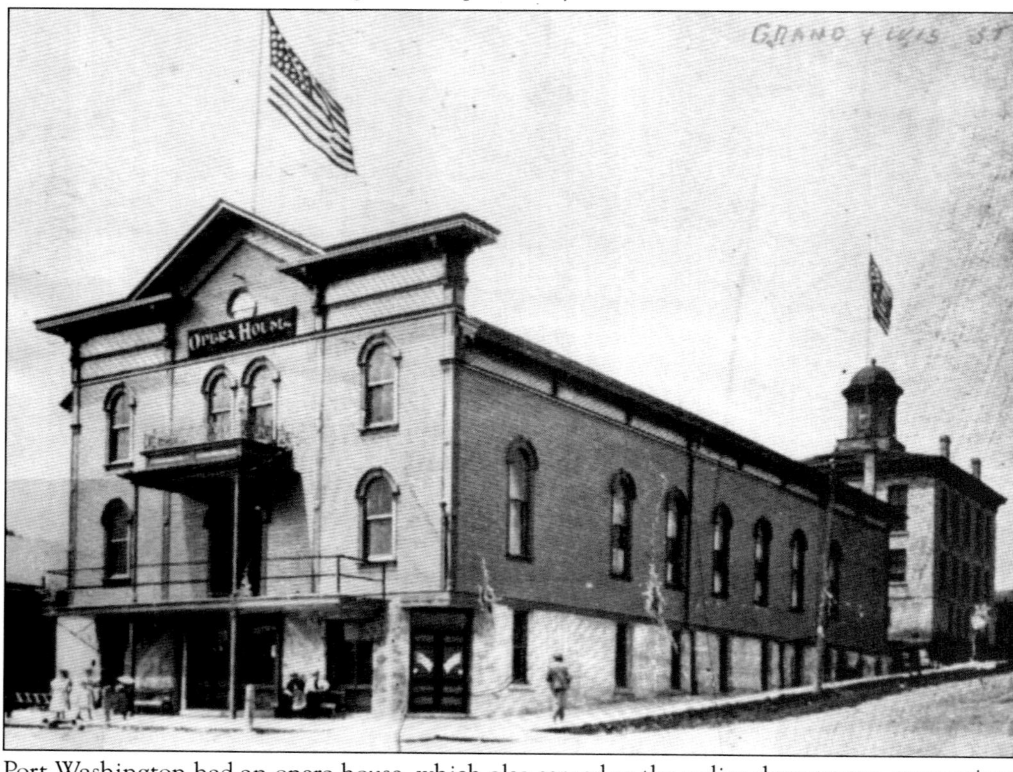

Port Washington had an opera house, which also served as the police department, gymnasium, community center, and—in the basement—the U.S. Army Reserve armory. The opera house was located on the site of the present city hall.

Three

The Harbor, Piers, and History

There is a large creek that flows into Lake Michigan between two bluffs 25 miles north of Milwaukee, Wisconsin. This was once the camping site of Native Americans, the landing point for missionaries and explorers, a point of departure inland for many immigrants, and the lifeblood of Port Washington. Where once there were just bridge piers jutting into the lake, there grew the first artificial harbor on the Great Lakes and a center of commerce. The large ships are now gone but the harbor and the city remain.

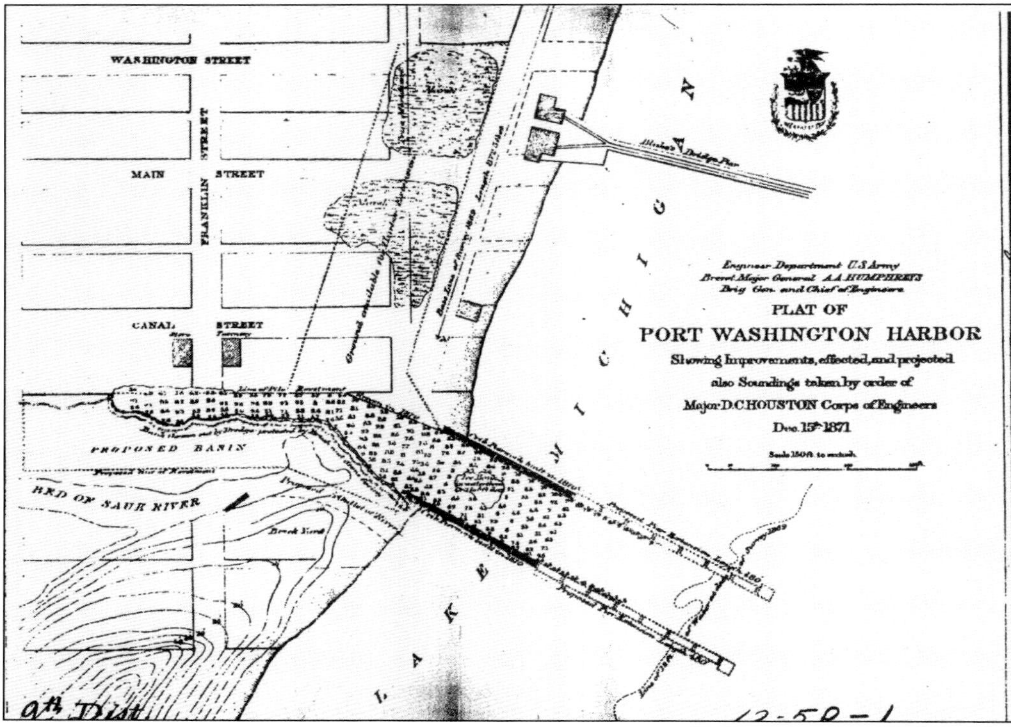

This U.S. Army Corps of Engineers map shows the projected improvements to the 1870 man-made harbor, which was basically a failure. The north slip helped, but did not solve the problem. The later additional pier length helped.

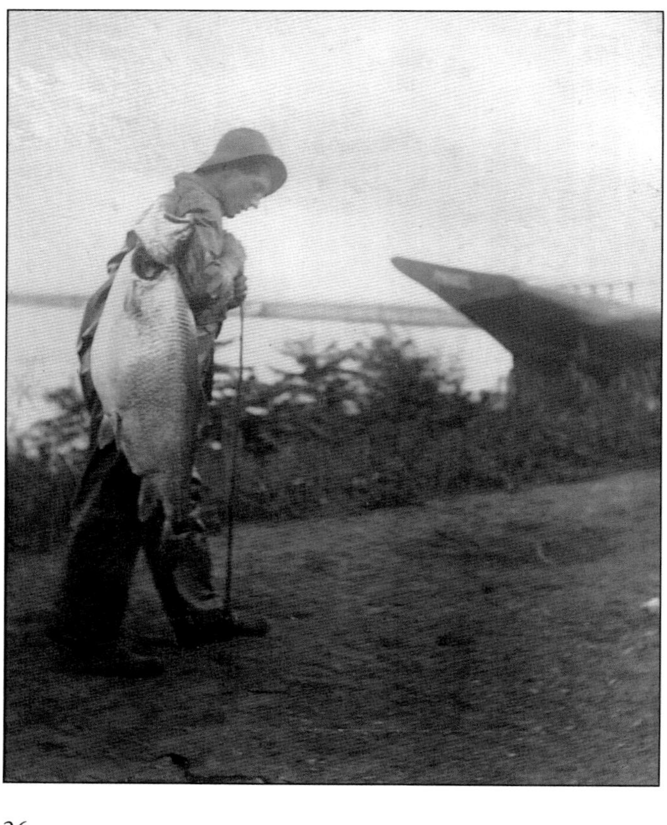

A photograph similar to this c. 1900 one became the logo for Smith Brothers Fisheries, Restaurant, and wholesale operations. A statue of this can be seen today at the Fishermen's Memorial at Rotary Park in the harbor.

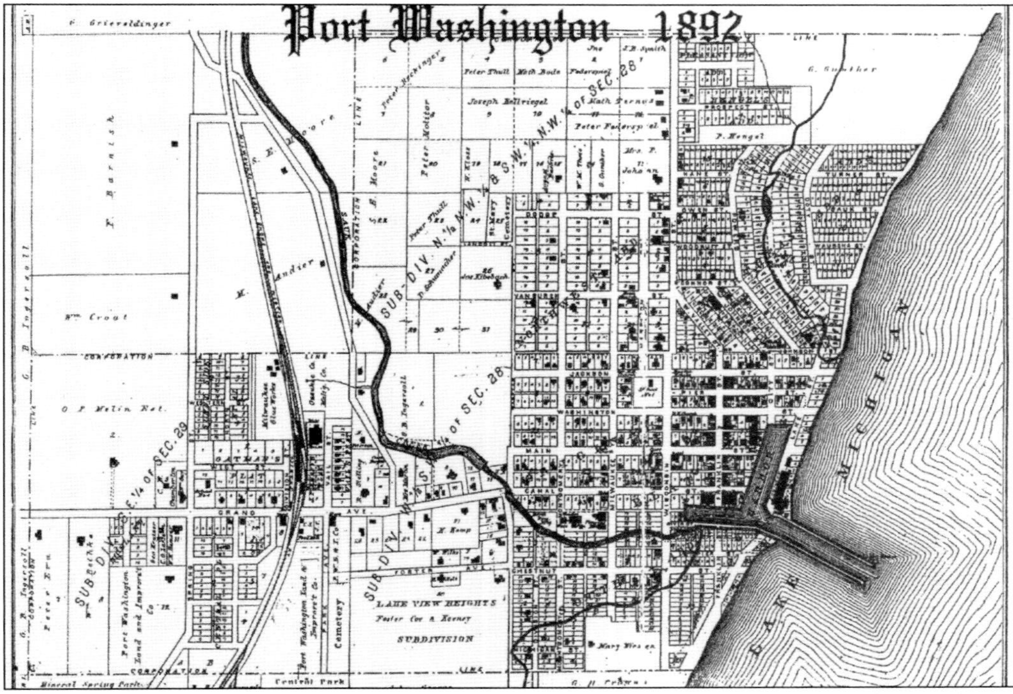

This 1892 plat map shows the west slip, north slip, 1889 piers, and lighthouse on the north pier. Looking closely, one can tell that the mouth of the Sauk Creek was dug out to form the west slip and was diverted to the south to form the initial harbor.

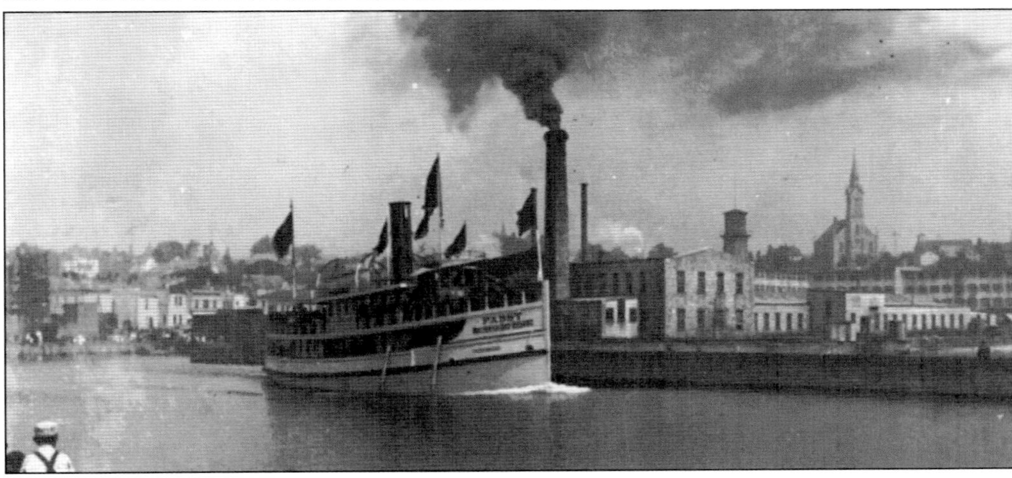

The vessel *Chequamegon* was built as a cruise and passenger boat used around Chequamegon Bay and Lake Superior. It was later used by Capt. Fred Pabst to take passengers from the Milwaukee River to his Whitefish Bay resort and to Port Washington's Columbia Park. The vessel was later converted to a tugboat named the *Robert Pringle* and in 1922 it sank off Sheboygan, Wisconsin. In 2008, it was relocated in 300 feet of water. Many businessmen were introduced to the city of Port Washington while on a summer excursion trip from Whitefish Bay. The Pabst Whitefish Bay Resort ran regular excursion trips to the city, where visitors were greeted by a band. Visitors then went along Franklin Street to Columbia Park on Wisconsin Street where food and refreshments were served.

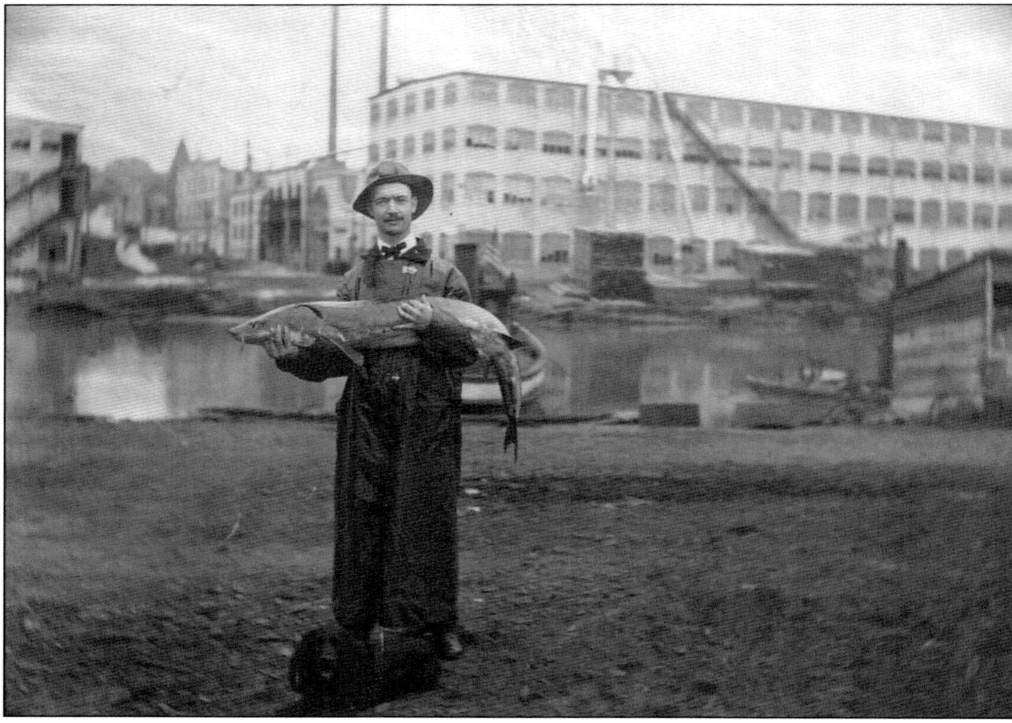

This photograph of Port Washington's north slip shows the chair factory in the background. This fisherman poses with his loyal dog and the day's big catch sometime around 1910.

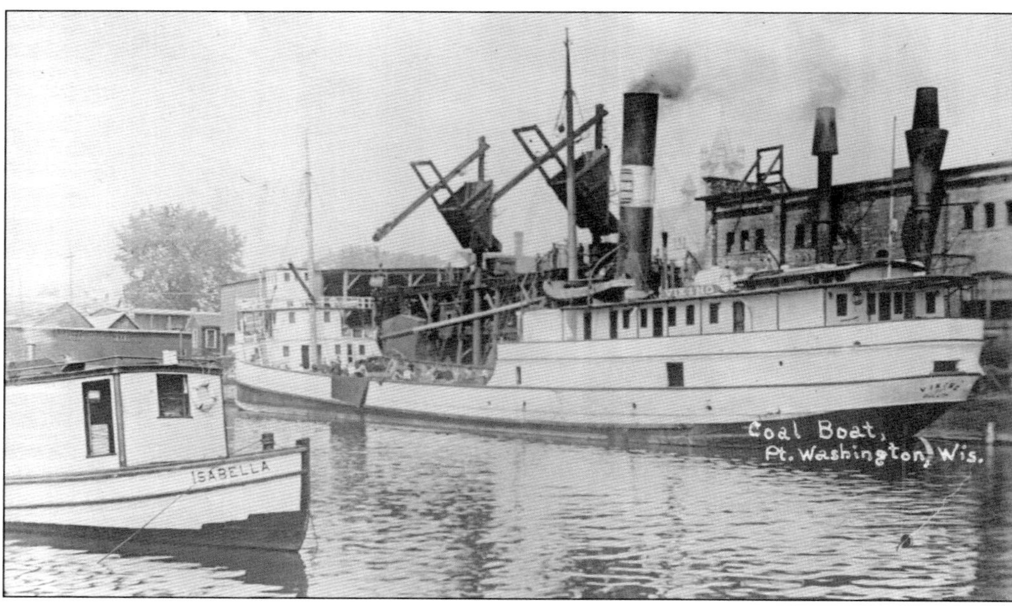

The small cargo steamer *Viking* normally hauled lumber but occasionally carried other cargo. Here it is seen in Port Washington's west slip unloading coal at Ubbink Coal Company's dock. The small fish tug *Isabella*, once owned by Smith Brothers, is in the foreground.

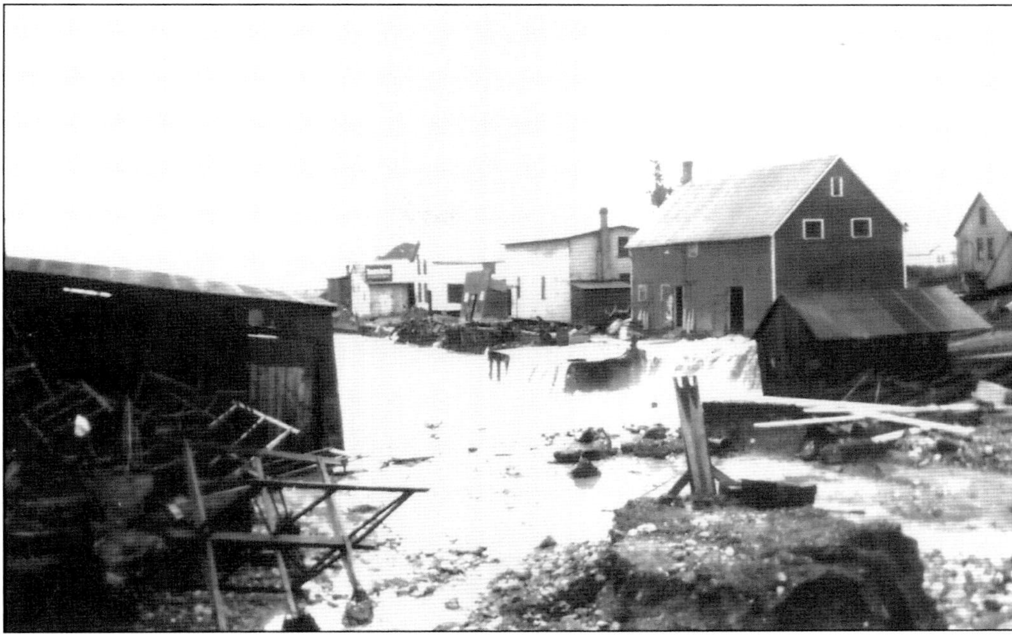

When the harbor in Port Washington was built, the mouth of Sauk Creek was diverted to the south. During a period of heavy rains, Sauk Creek and Mother Nature decided to take back the waterway's original course. This occurred in 1915, 1924, again in the 1940s, and almost happened again in the 1980s. The area is now surrounded with condominiums. This view of the 1924 flood shows the damage to the Van Ells' dock and shed at the west end of the west slip. The Van Ells ceased fishing soon after.

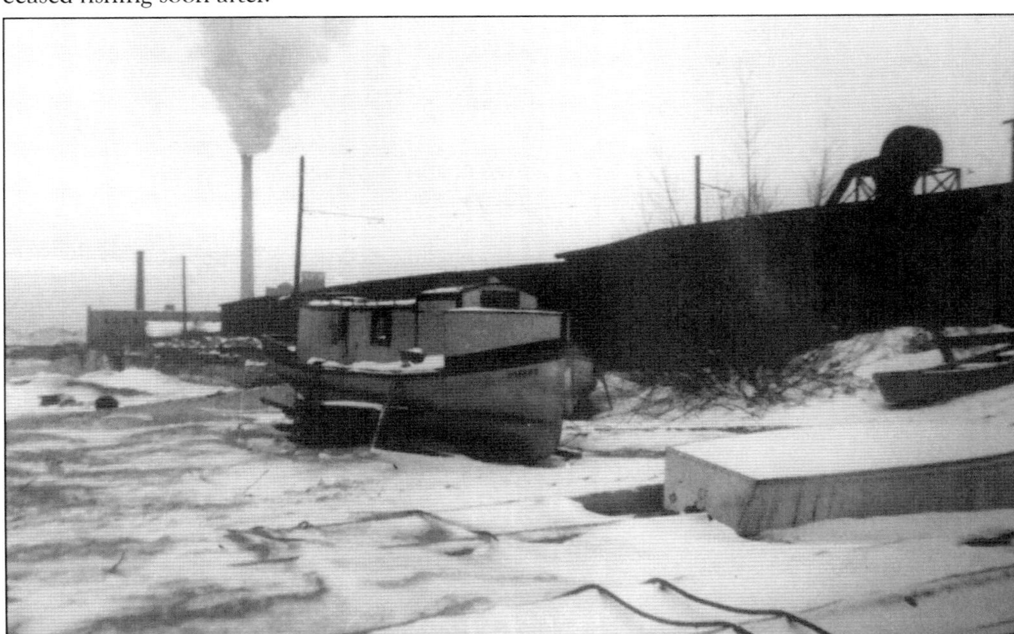

At one time, Port Washington's boatyard was located in the present-day marina. Seen here are fishing boats pulled up on the beach for the winter season and needed repairs.

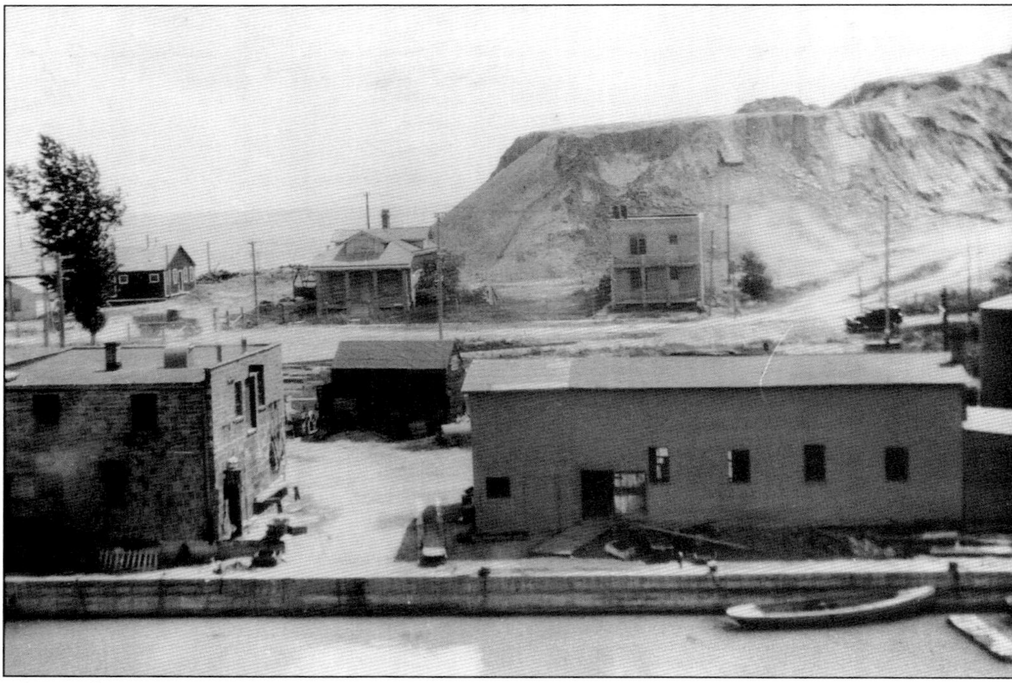

This early-1900s photograph shows the south bluff, the area known as the "Canada side" before the power plant was built in 1930. The houses and fish shanties were on the second pier street, which once lead to Silverman's pier.

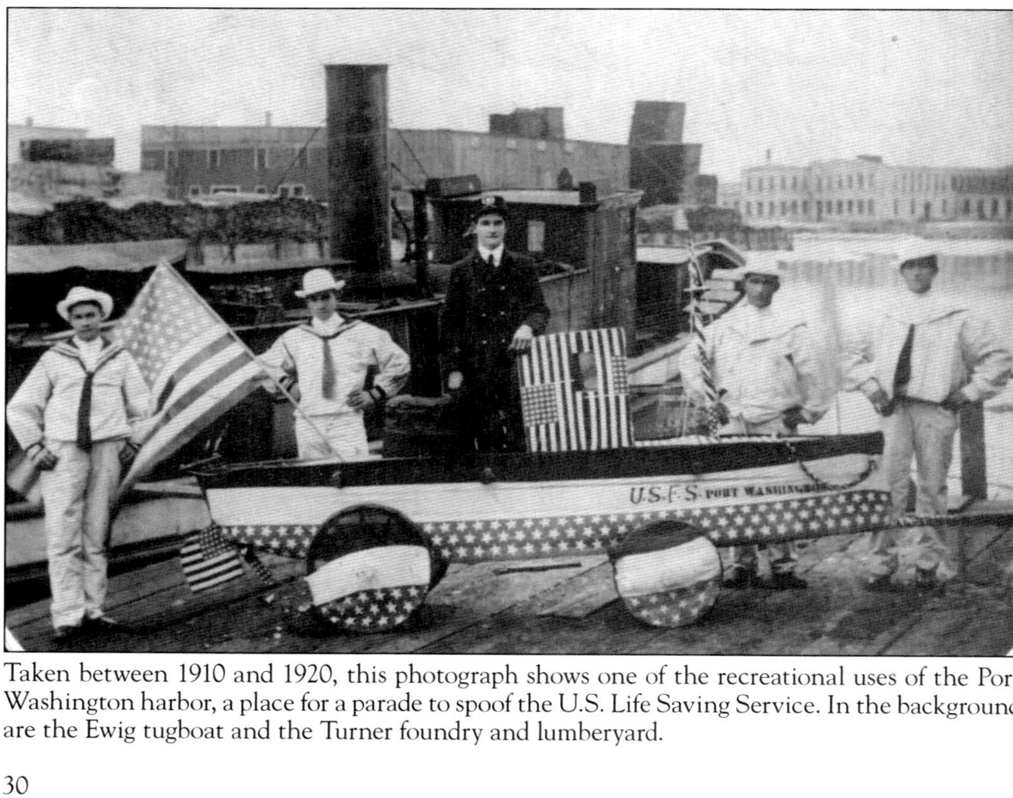

Taken between 1910 and 1920, this photograph shows one of the recreational uses of the Port Washington harbor, a place for a parade to spoof the U.S. Life Saving Service. In the background are the Ewig tugboat and the Turner foundry and lumberyard.

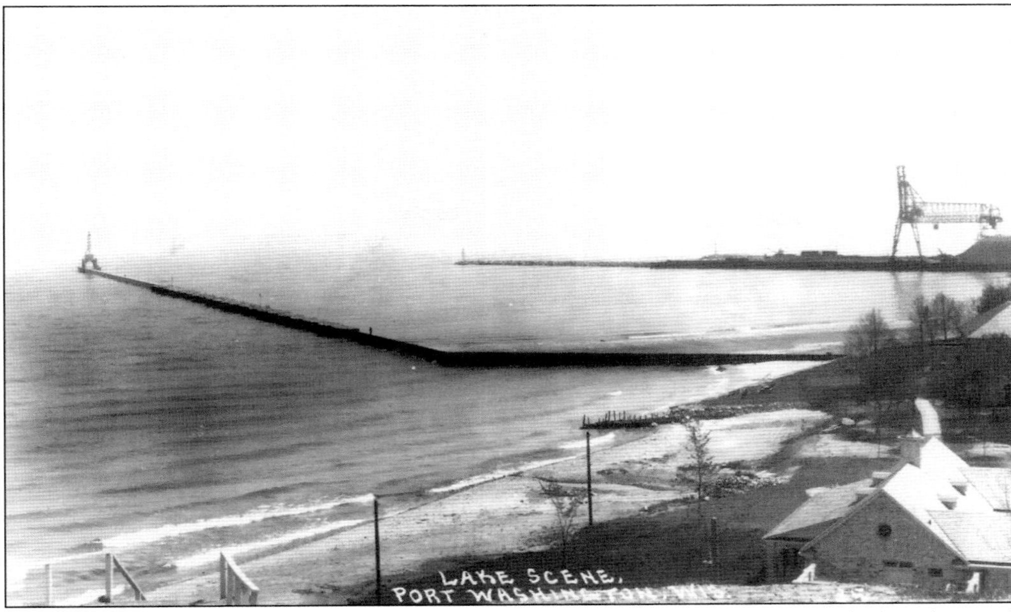

This photograph shows Port Washington's harbor after it was built in 1934 but before the south pier was extended. Note the old pier jutting out from where today's water treatment plan is located. This is possibly the remains of the location of the first pier built by Wooster Harrison, Solomon Juneau, and Solon Johnson.

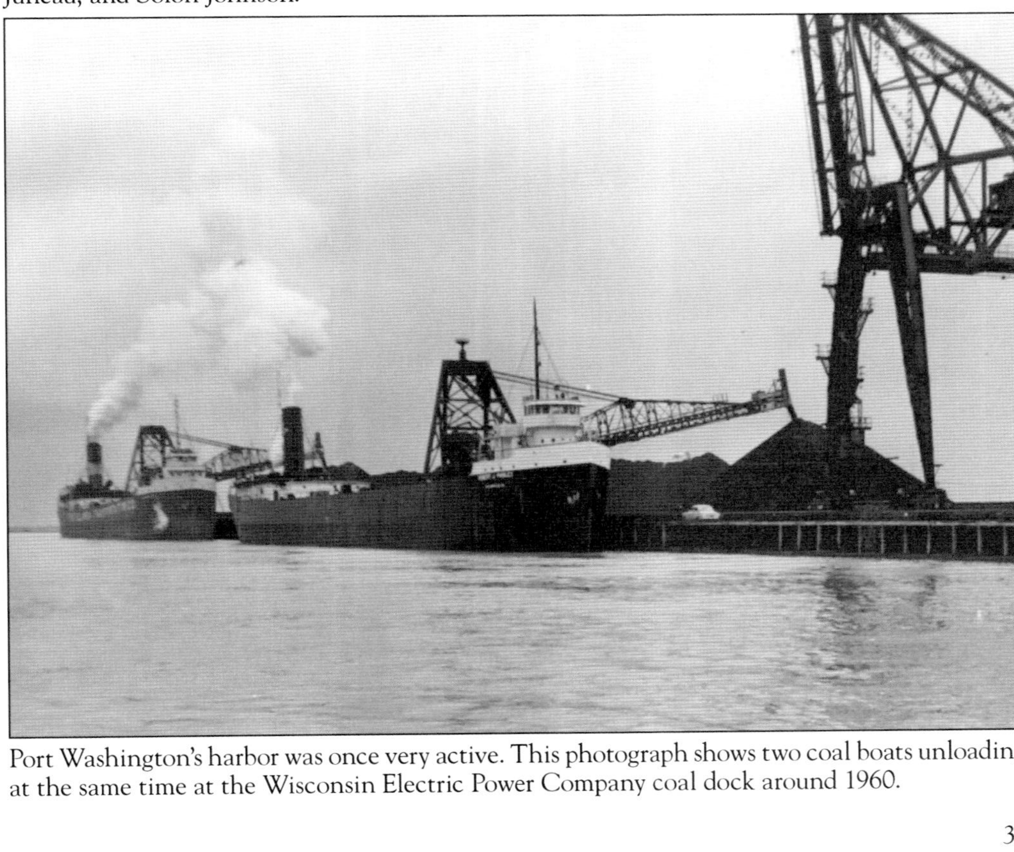
Port Washington's harbor was once very active. This photograph shows two coal boats unloading at the same time at the Wisconsin Electric Power Company coal dock around 1960.

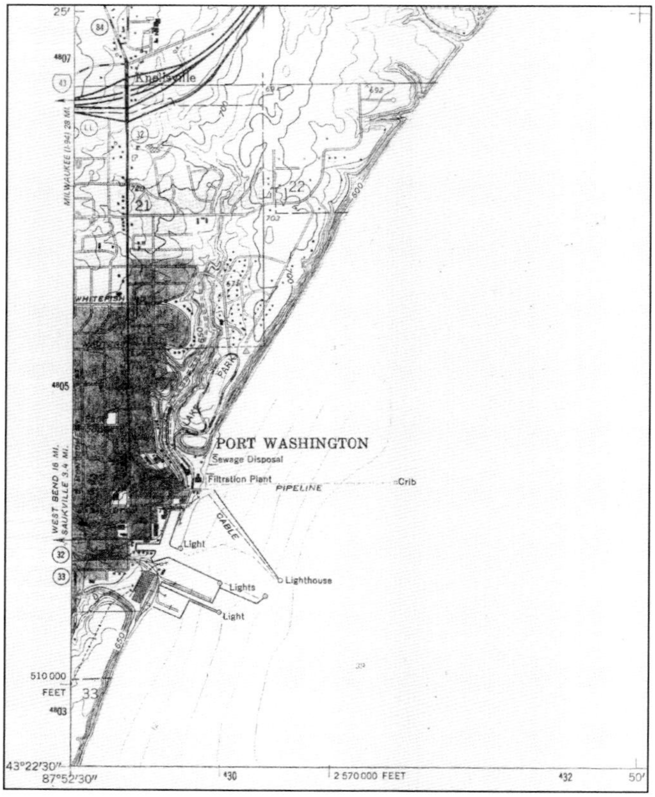

This map gives an aerial view of Port Washington's 1934 harbor, which allowed an easy entry for coal boats servicing the Wisconsin Electric Power Plant; the harbor failed, however, to offer protection when the wind came from the southeast.

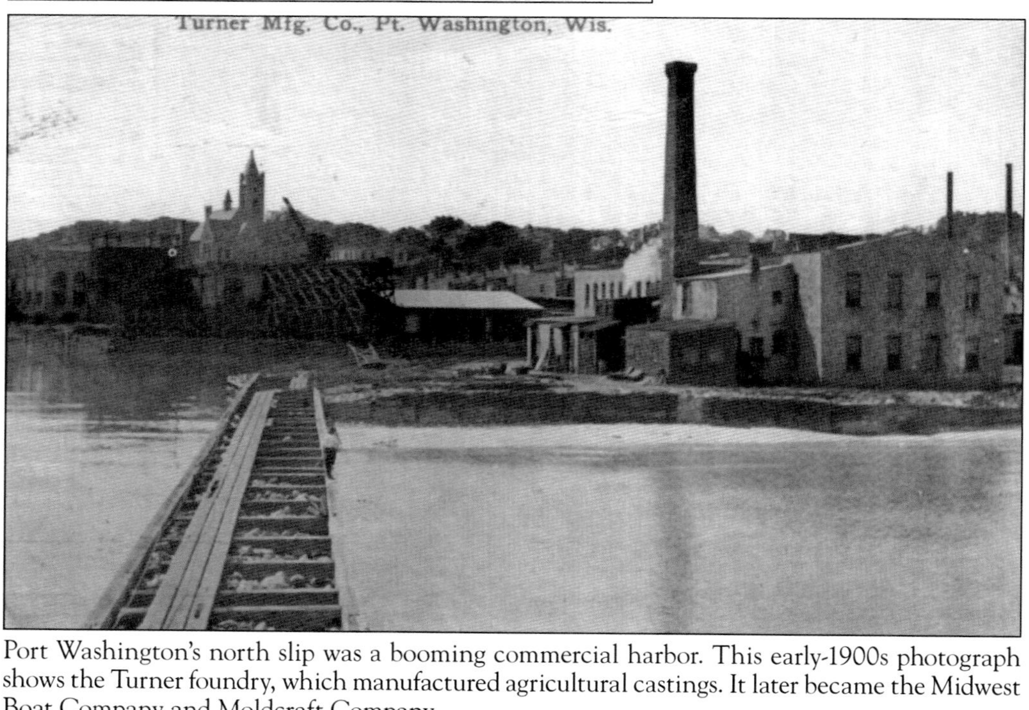

Port Washington's north slip was a booming commercial harbor. This early-1900s photograph shows the Turner foundry, which manufactured agricultural castings. It later became the Midwest Boat Company and Moldcraft Company.

Four

LIGHTHOUSES

Lighthouses were once the signposts along the highway that was the Great Lakes. Port Washington has had four lighthouses, built in 1849, 1860, 1889, and 1934. Two of them remain—one as a functioning aid to navigation, and the other as a museum spotlighting a bygone era. The first lighthouse built in Port Washington atop what was originally called Lighthouse Hill had a tower that was 35 feet high, with a diameter at the base of 20 feet and 10.5 feet at the top. The walls were 2 to 3.5 feet thick. The separate one-story dwelling had a loft. At the top of the tower was an octagonal lantern with 15 lights (or windows) per octagon. The house was 34 feet by 20 feet. It was poorly constructed and had to be rebuilt in 1860.

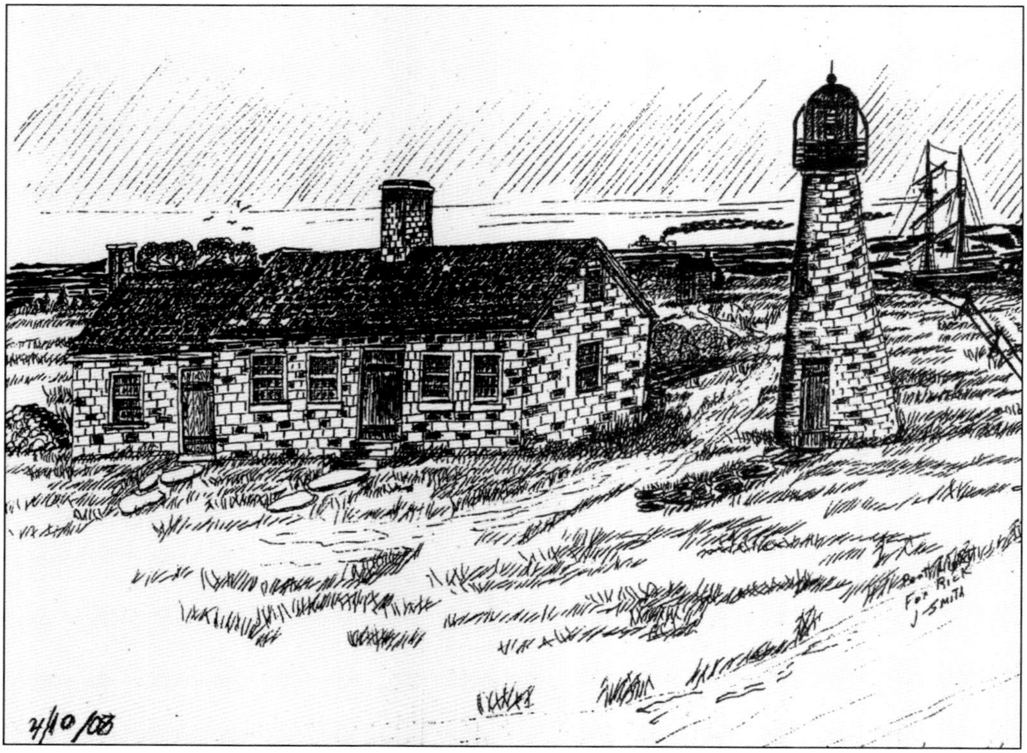

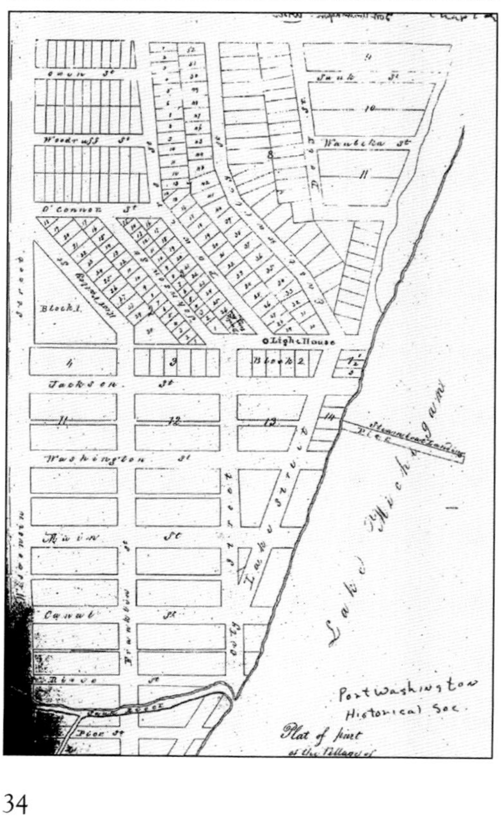

The first Port Washington lighthouse, built in 1849, is depicted in this sketch above by Gerald Lee Smith. Because of shoddy construction, it had to be rebuilt within approximately 10 years. The west wall, which was the leeward wall and therefore in good condition, was incorporated into the 1860 building.

This early plat map of the city of Port Washington shows the original course of Sauk Creek, one of the early piers, and the location of the original 1849 lighthouse on the top of the north bluff. Many of these lots were actually in a ravine on the edges of the bluffs.

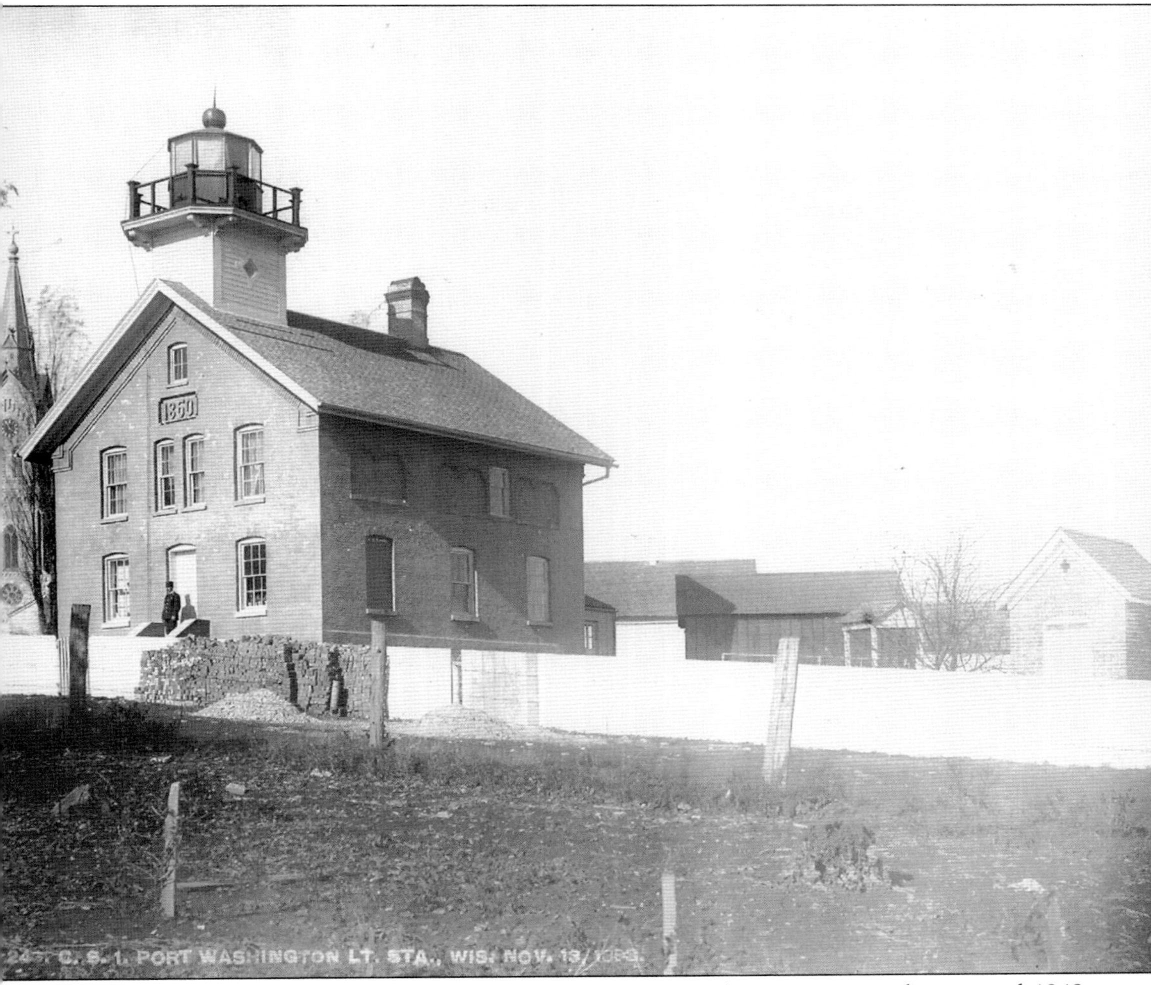

Port Washington's second lighthouse was built in 1860 on the same site as the original 1849 lighthouse. The new lighthouse's tower was constructed with a focal plane 128 feet above Lake Michigan. There is conclusive evidence that part of the 1849 keeper's cottage was incorporated into the 1860 lighthouse, which has been restored and now serves as an interpretive museum.

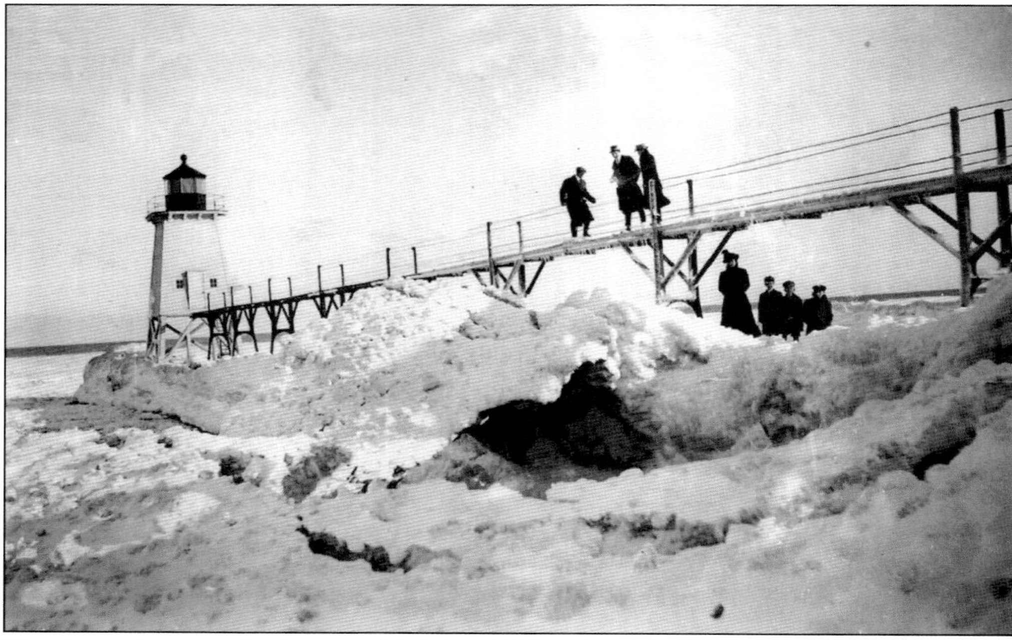

The elevated storm walk that was added after 1889 made it a little safer for the lighthouse keeper to tend the pierhead light, but it was still hazardous. Winter storms often iced up the walkway and even with cables to use as a railing, it was very slick.

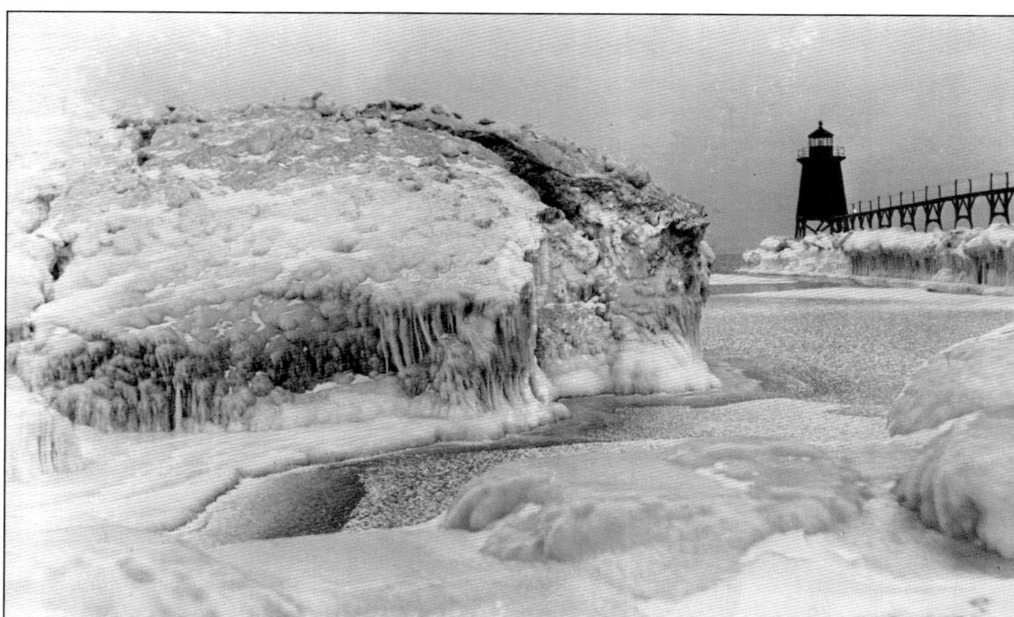

After 1889, an extra 50 feet was added to the north pier and an elevated storm walk was added. This greatly decreased the hazards of tending the lighthouse, although walking the storm walk 920 feet out into the lake was still hazardous, as this photograph shows. Port Washington's lighthouses operated 12 months of the year due to the area's large fishing fleet.

Port Washington's lighthouse has had numerous keepers since 1849. The Charles Lewis family comprised a father and son lighthouse-keeping duo. The first, Capt. Charles Lewis (at right), had been a whaler and a Great Lakes sailor until he took over the Port Washington light station in 1874. He managed the lighthouse for six years, and after he passed away, his wife looked after it until their son Charles Jr. came off the lake and took over.

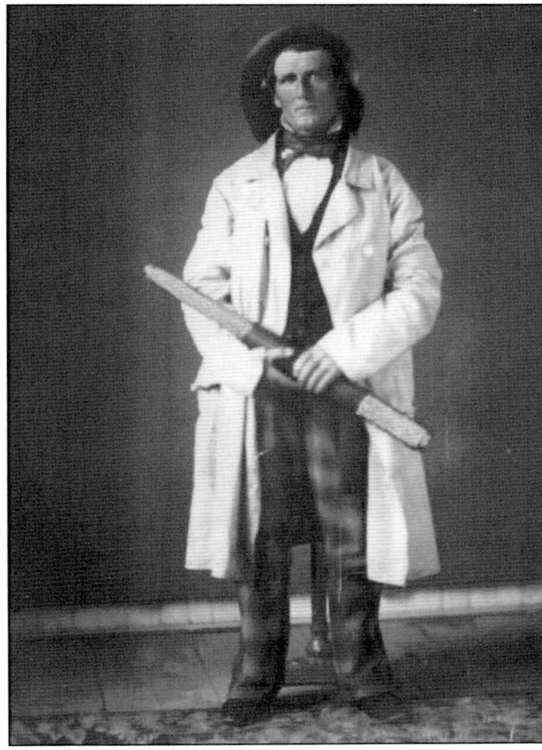

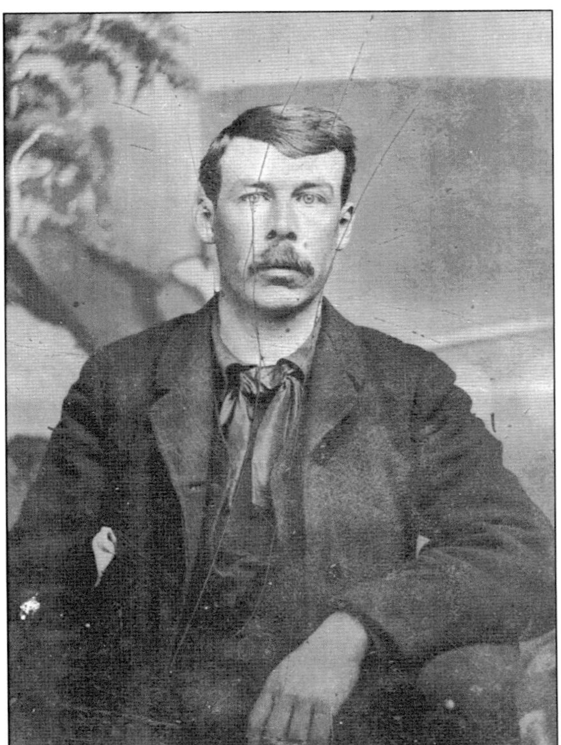

Charles Lewis Jr. took over the Port Washington light station in 1880 with the passing of his father. He continued maintaining the lighthouse until his official retirement in 1924. He stayed on as caretaker until 1934. A young Lewis is show in this photograph.

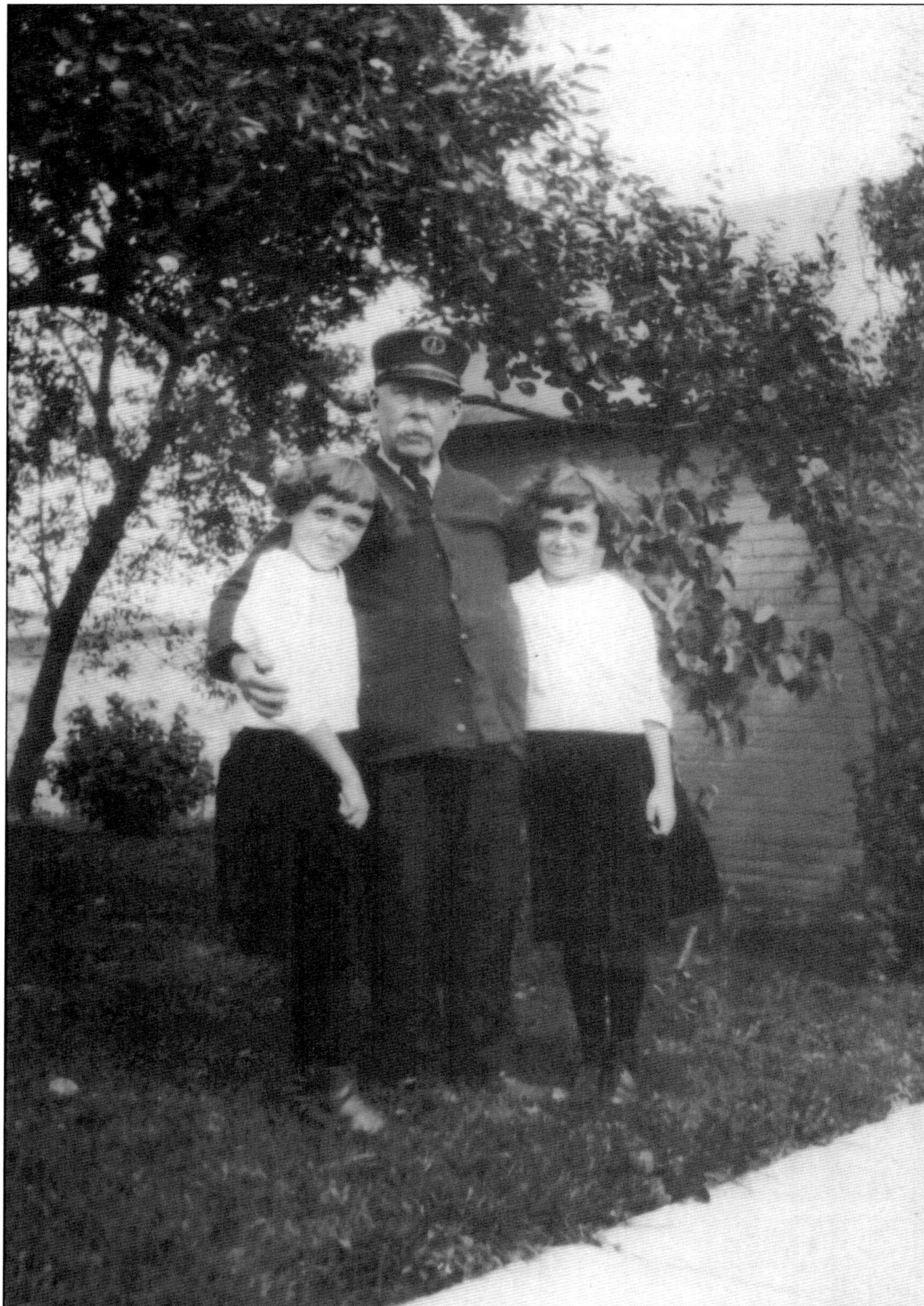

This photograph shows retired Captain Lewis and his two grandchildren—Janette and Genevieve—who lived with them for six years.

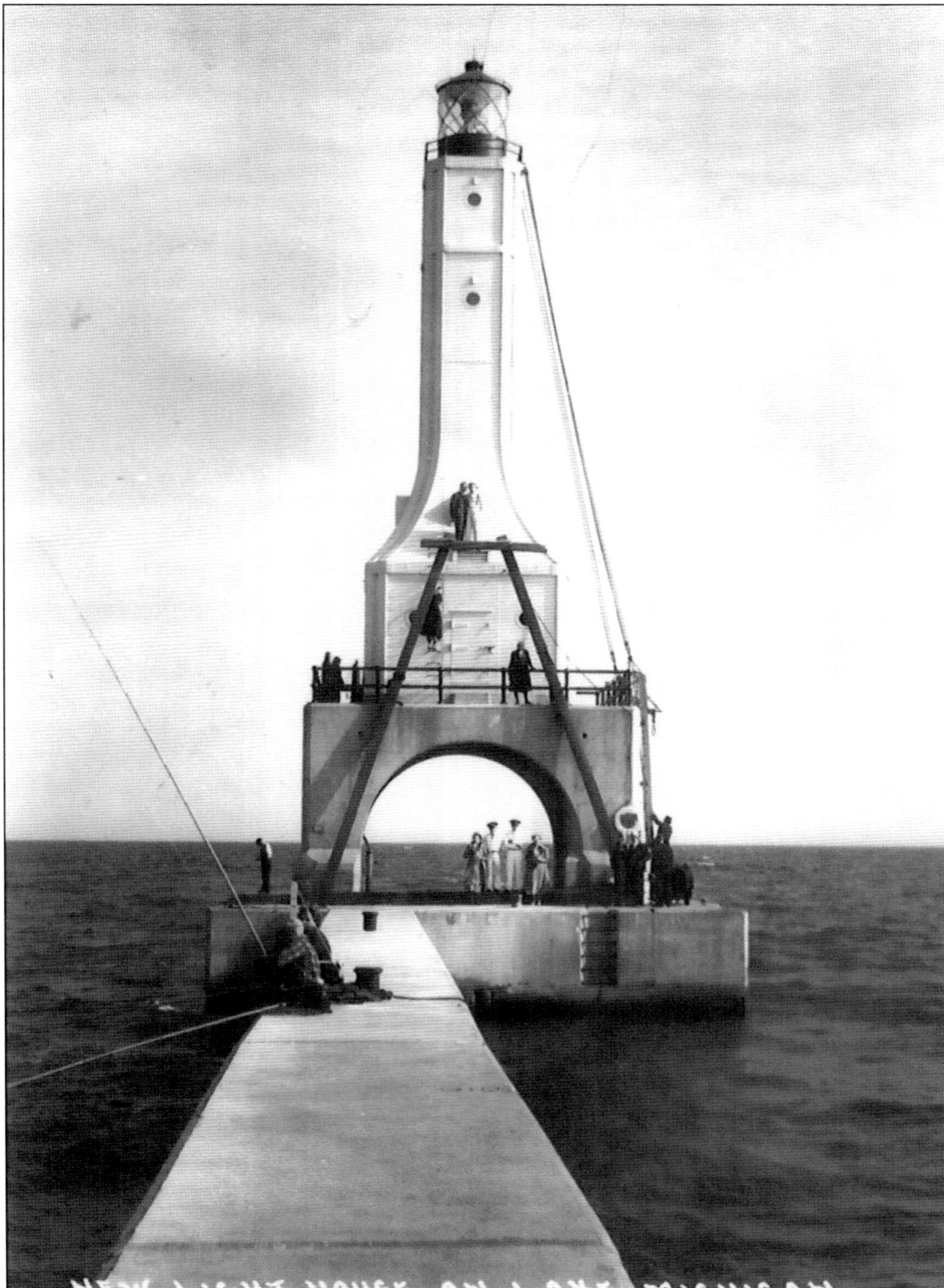

A federally funded breakwater project began in 1931 and was finished in 1935. The new breakwater cost about $1 million. At its completion, a 71-foot, art deco–style steel light tower was built on a cement foundation with four legs and arches. An identical lighthouse was built at Indiana Harbor, Indiana. This lighthouse still stands today, minus its helical lantern.

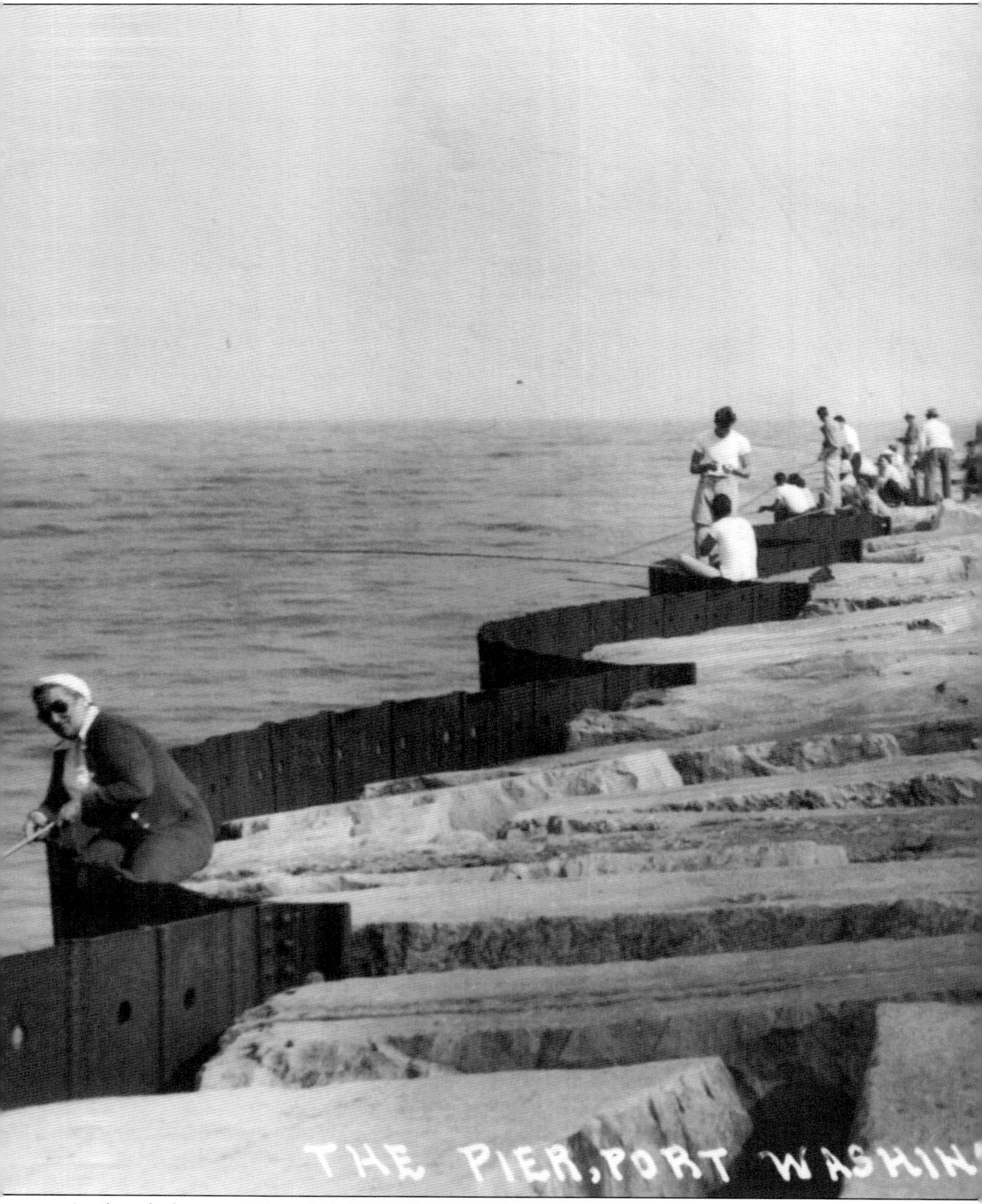

A relaxed afternoon of perch fishing off Port Washington's north breakwater is seen here, around 1940. Notice the cane poles being used. Notice, also, the rough, unfinished surface and lack of a safety rail on the breakwater. Fishing from the north pier was and still is "at your own risk" and

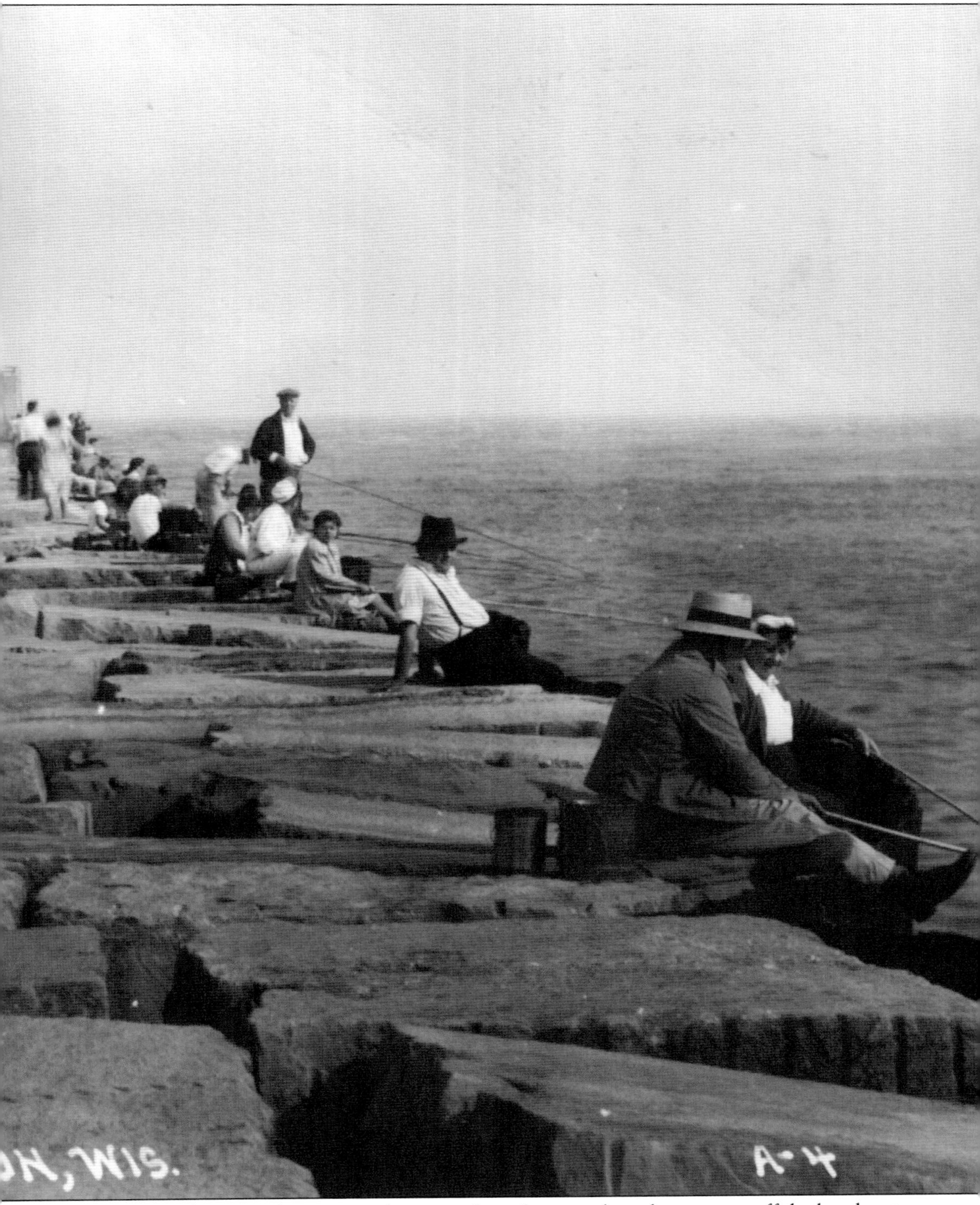

over the years during inclement weather a number of persons have been swept off the breakwater and drowned.

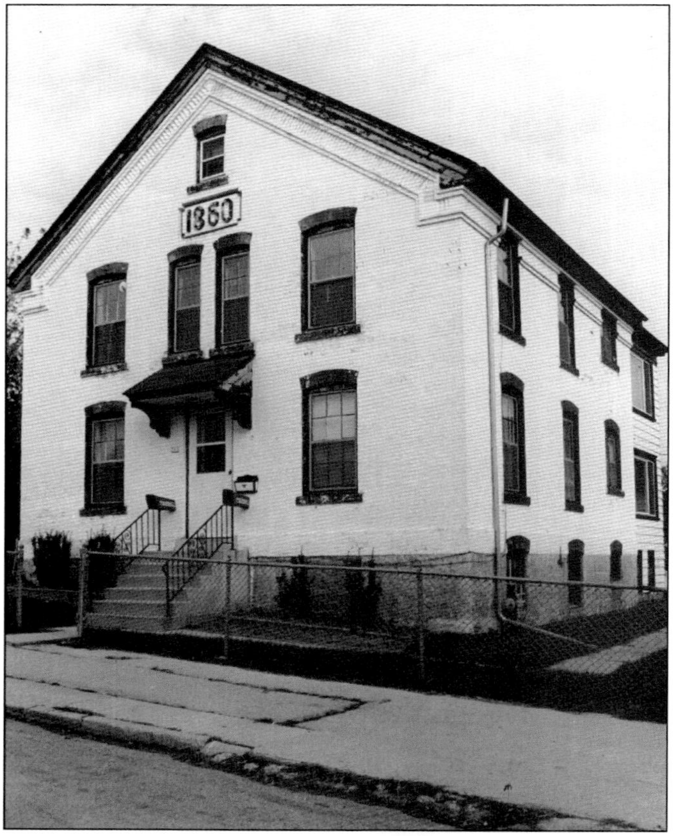

Pictured is the light station structure as it appeared in 2001. The restoration project, as approved by the U.S. National Park Service and the Wisconsin State Historical Society, encompassed cleaning and repairing the exterior masonry and rebuilding the infrastructure, walls, roof, tower, and lantern room. The exterior bears the scars of a 1934 renovation, but the dwelling once again stands as a complete light station. The first floor was completely gutted and rebuilt to the original specifications. The second-floor rental unit was completely remodeled. A new access ladder for the tower and lamp room, as well as a restored landing for the stairway from the first floor, was added in anticipation of visitors and tours. Below is the beautifully renovated light station as it appears today.

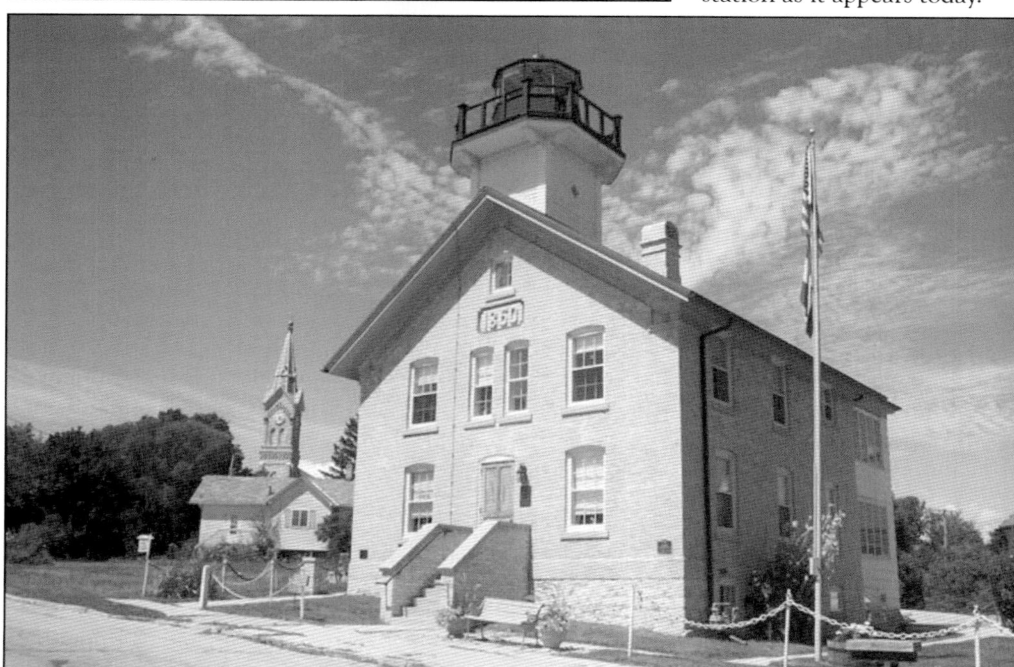

Five

Ships and Shipwrecks

Since the time of the voyageurs' canoes and the arrival of the first recorded schooner, the *Charles Hibbard,* many ships have visited Port Washington. Most have come and gone doing their business and passing away after serving their owners well. Some have left their bones on the beaches and lake bottom near Port Washington, along with their cargoes of merchandise and passengers.

After the St. Lawrence Seaway opened, the Great Lakes had a large influx of deep draft ocean vessels. There were numerous collisions, strandings, and a few direct sinkings caused by the disdain of deep-sea sailors for the Great Lakes "ponds." In time, a respect for these largest of freshwater bodies developed. A number of storms, including ones in 1881, 1889, 1905, 1913, and 1940, reached hurricane proportions.

Port Washington lost one of her own, the *Josephine Lawrence*, in the 1881 Alpena blow, and the storm of 1905 left the *D. C. Whitney* stranded at *Josephine*'s doorstep. The *D. C. Whitney* was steaming along the west shore of Lake Michigan when the captain decided that he, his 23-year-old ship, and the crew had had enough and came to anchor under the bluffs of Port Washington. A slight switch in the wind, nominal power, and dragging anchors pushed the ship closer to the beach and it grounded just south of Port Washington. The ship was lucky, as many vessels were lost during this storm. Following the *D. C. Whitney*'s grounding at Port Washington, it was towed off and rebuilt. In 1909, the ship was renamed the *Gargantua* and was used for short hauls and salvage work. It was idle after 1914, sold in 1920, and cut down to form a floating dry dock, eventually rotting and finally scrapped. So came the peaceful end of the *D.C. Whitney*, a small steamer that survived one of the worst storms to hit those freshwater "ponds" called the Great Lakes. The vessel is gone, but not forgotten.

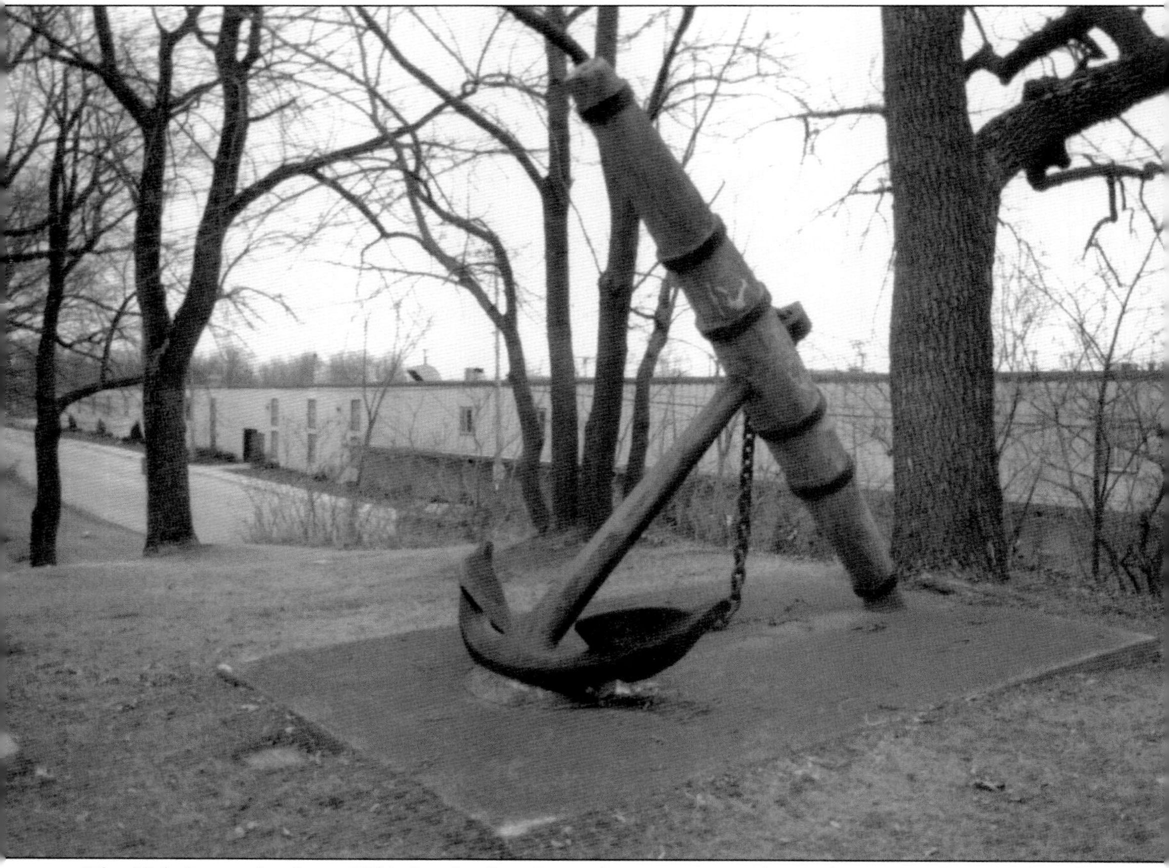

The *Toledo* was built in 1854 for the freight and passenger trade in the upper Great Lakes for Charles H. Lee and Associates by B. B. Jones of Buffalo, New York. It had a wooden hull and measured 178.58 feet long, 29.17 feet wide, and 11.83 feet deep and was powered by a direct-action steam engine produced by the Shepard Iron Works, also of Buffalo. In 1855, American Transportation Company was formed. The firm took over Lee's vessels along with the *Cataract*, *New England*, *Charter*, *F. W. Backus*, *Detroit*, *Scioto*, *Ohio*, *Forest Queen*, *Pocahontas*, *Niagara*, and *Chicago*. The first fleet was a combination of freight and passenger steamers that operated in all of the lakes west of Buffalo.

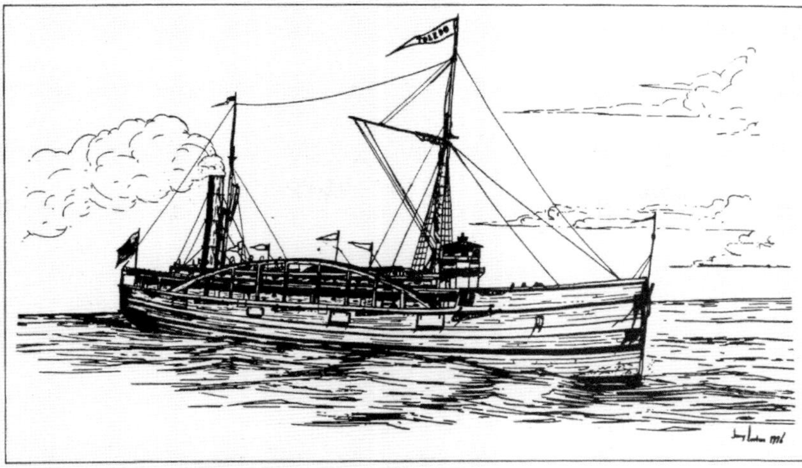

Out of the past

Gale drove Toledo to shore just off Port Washington

Marine historian Rick Smith of Port Washington, traces his interest in the past to his childhood in Upper Michigan. A member of the Port Washington Historical Society, Smith supplied the information on the steamship Toledo, which sank in an autumn gale just off Port Washington on Oct. 22, 1856.

The Toledo was built for the freight and passenger trade to the upper Great Lakes for Charles H. Lee and associates in 1854.

In 1855, American Transportation Co. was formed. The firm took over Lee's vessels along with the Cataract, New England, Charter, F. W. Backus, Detroit, Sciota, Ohio, Forest Queen, Pocahontas, Niagara and Chicago.

This fleet was a combination of freight and passenger steams operating over all of the lakes west of Buffalo. The fleet was patronized by many European immigrants making their trek to the farms of Wisconsin and Minnesota.

On Oct. 22, 1856, the Toledo docked at Port Washington on her way to Chicago.

Some passengers and freight left the ship in Port Washington, where a deck-load of cord wood was taken aboard to be used as fuel for the rest of the trip. Eighty-one passengers remained aboard. The ship was well off shore when it was struck by a terrific autumn gale that sprung up almost without warning.

The force of the wind drove the ship back toward shore, although every ounce of available power of her engine was used. An attempt to anchor failed as the anchor was fouled in the chains.

The Toledo struck sand bottom with tremendous force that broke her framing. She was quickly pounded to pieces by the huge rollers that broke over her.

Only three of the more than 80 people on board were saved.

The cargo was estimated to be worth $100,000. Much of the cargo was picked up along miles of shoreline in the Port Washington area after the storm blew itself out.

In 1900, a fishing tug recovered the anchor of the Toledo from the bottom of the lake and brought it into Port Washington. The anchor is found in Union Cemetery on Park St., Port Washington, where the bodies of the Toledo victims were buried. A replica of the anchor is in the Smith Bros. and Harborside Motor Inn parking lot at the Port Washington harbor.

Both the original anchor and the replica serve as a monument to the victims of the Toledo and Niagara disasters. The Niagara sank off Port Washington Sept. 24, 1856, after a fire broke out and rapidly spread throughout the steamer. Sixty lives were lost.

Steamship Toledo
Builders: B. B. Jones, Buffalo, N. Y.
Machinery: Shepard Iron Works, Buffalo, N. Y.
Hull: Wooden-178' 7 by 29'2 by 11'10.
Weight: 585 tons.
Engine: Direct-action engine.
Cylinder: 28'1 by 4' stroke.
Owners:
Charles H. Lee and Others 1854-55.
American Transportation Co. 1855-56

7

On October 22, 1856, the propeller *Toledo* docked at Port Washington on its way to Chicago. After dropping off several passengers and freight, the vessel took on a deck load of wood to be used as fuel for the rest of the trip. While well offshore, a strong autumn gale struck with little warning. Before the ship could load the wood, the *Toledo* left the exposed pier to weather the storm on the lake. The force of the wind drove the ship back to shore, despite the full effort of its engine. An attempt to anchor failed when the anchor became fouled up in the chains. The *Toledo* struck the sand bottom with tremendous force, breaking the framing. It was quickly pounded to pieces by the huge rollers that broke over top. Eighty-one passengers were on board when the steamer left, as well as a large cargo of household goods and hardware. Three of those on board survived the wreck. The bodies of the 50-some passengers lost that day were recovered and, if not claimed, buried in a common grave in Union Cemetery in Port Washington, where the ship's anchor serves as a monument.

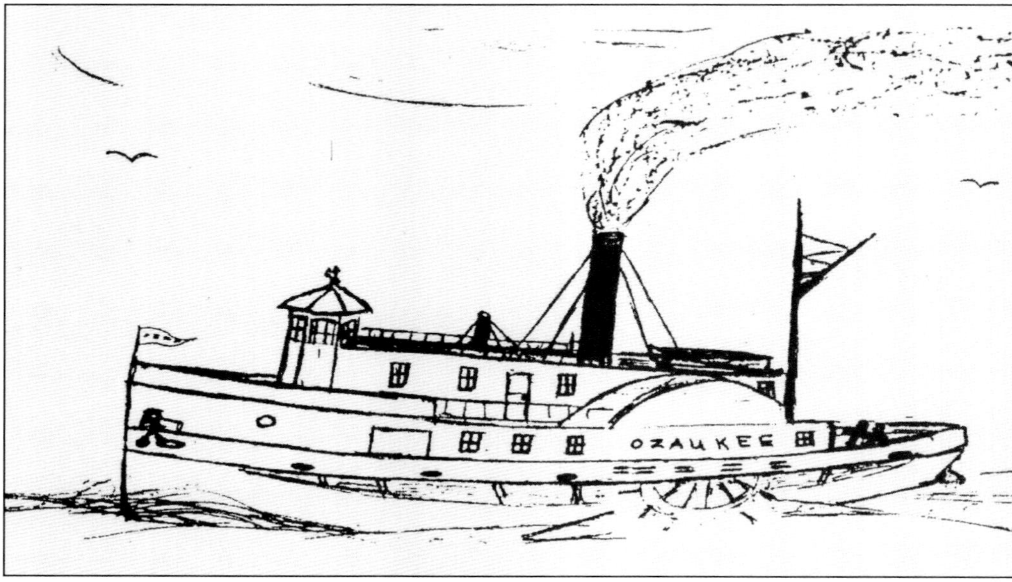

The side-wheel tugboat *Ozaukee* was built right on the shores of Lake Michigan in the growing community of Port Washington. It was launched in July 1857 and enrolled in Chicago on July 7 as a river-type tugboat. Alva Trowbridge was the managing owner of the vessel and L. L. Slyfield was the first master. Large for a river tugboat, the *Ozaukee* measured 94 feet in length, 17.5 feet in width, and 6.2 feet in depth, and had a listed tonnage of 66 gross tons (33 tons net). It was steam driven and considered powerful.

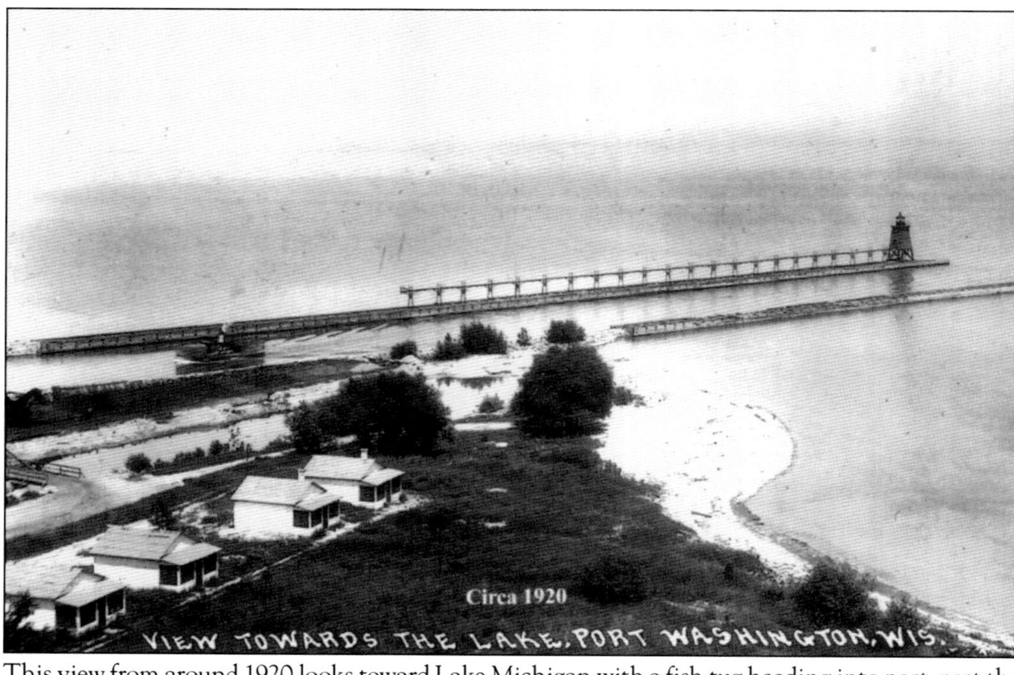

This view from around 1920 looks toward Lake Michigan with a fish tug heading into port, past the 1889 lighthouse and cottages built on the old Schramka brickyard. The remains of the schooners *Bohemian* and *J. B. Prime* were buried by the sand buildup behind the south pier.

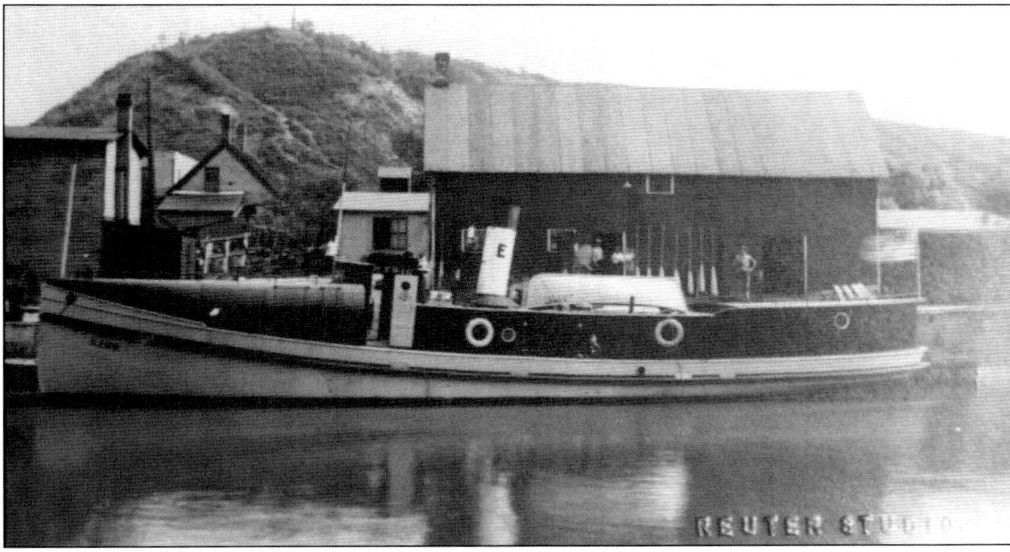

The Ewig brothers rebuilt the 1908 steam tugboat *Herbert* into the largest fish tug on the Great Lakes. Here the *H. Ewig* lies in the west slip at the net shed. The natural shape of the south bluff can be seen in the background. This bluff was one that gave Port Washington its nickname as "the little city of seven hills." This photograph was taken prior to the construction of the Wisconsin Electric Power Company's coal-fired power plant in that bluff area. The *H. Ewig* still sails as the bow tug *Roy R. Love*.

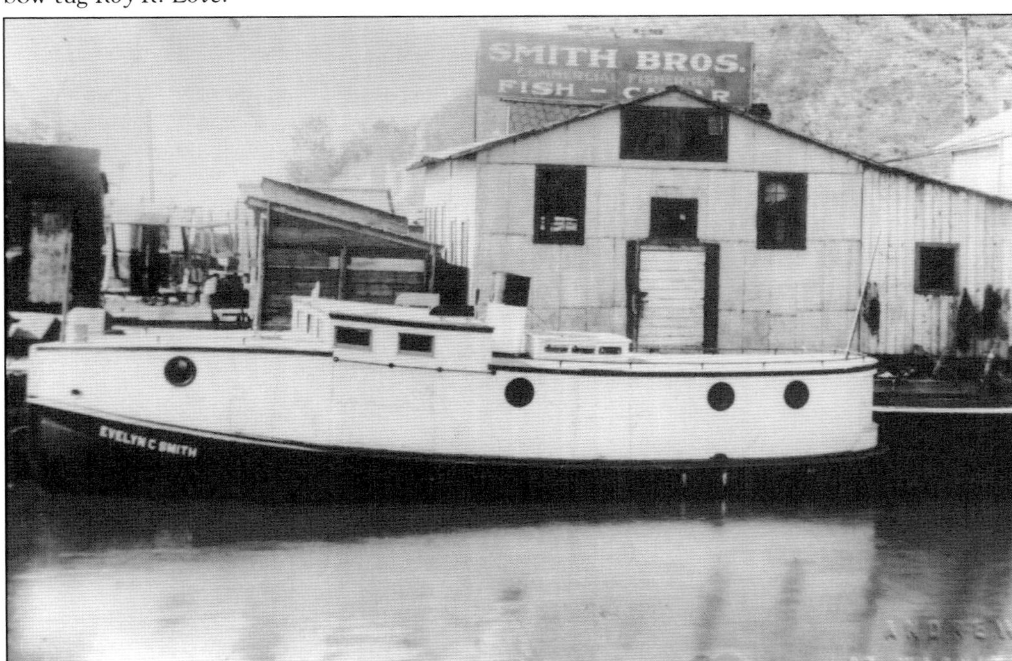

This photograph shows the Smith Brothers tugboat, the *Evelyn C. Smith* (named after the cofounder of the Smith Brothers restaurant), before it sunk in the west slip due to a seacock that was left open. The tugboat was raised and used as a pilot boat. It was later renamed *Stella* and again was used as a fish tug until the mid-1980s.

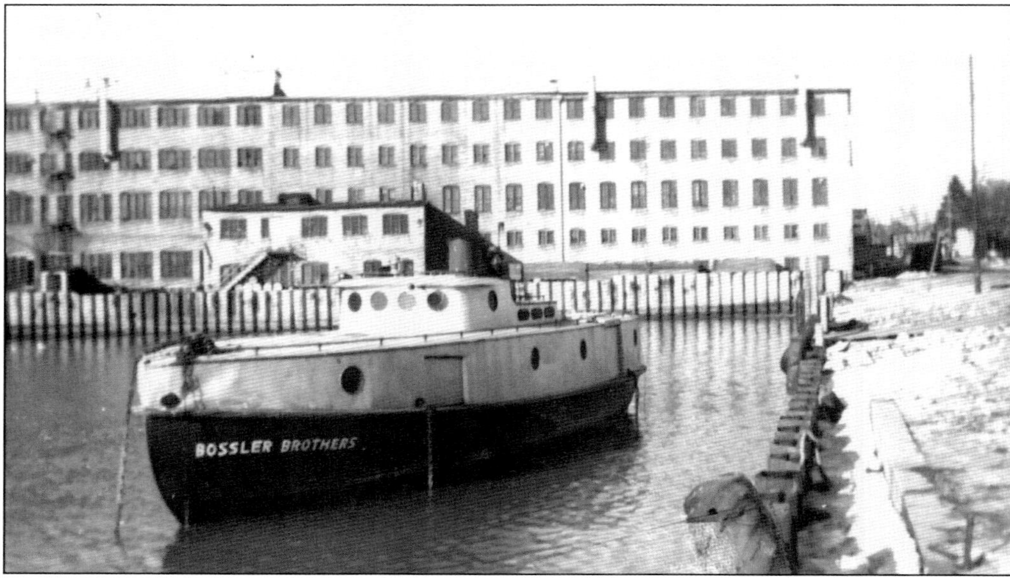

The diesel tug *Bossler Brothers* was built to replace the *J. T. Bossler* due to its age and obsolescence. Note the dent in the port-side bow from a collision with a much larger steamship. Fish tugs were built tough. This tug is still fishing out of Two Rivers for the Kulpa Fish Company. The Wisconsin Chair Factory is in the background.

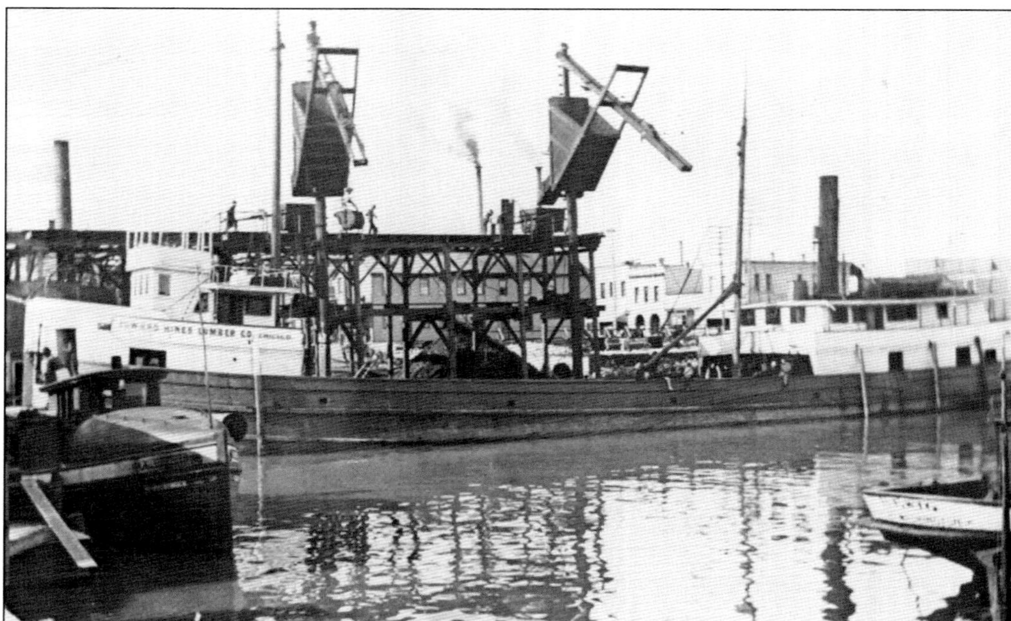

Prior to construction of the Wisconsin Electric Power Plant in 1934, coal for domestic and industrial use was delivered by small steamers and earlier by schooners to the Ubbink and Sons Coal Company, located on the north side of the west slip. Here the Edward Hines steamer *Louis Pahlow* is seen unloading a cargo of coal in the west slip. Normally vessels of this size carried lumber but would occasionally carry cargo where bigger vessels could not go. Also visible are the fish tugs *P. Reckinger*, owned by the Van Ells family, and the Ewig brothers' *H. Ewig*.

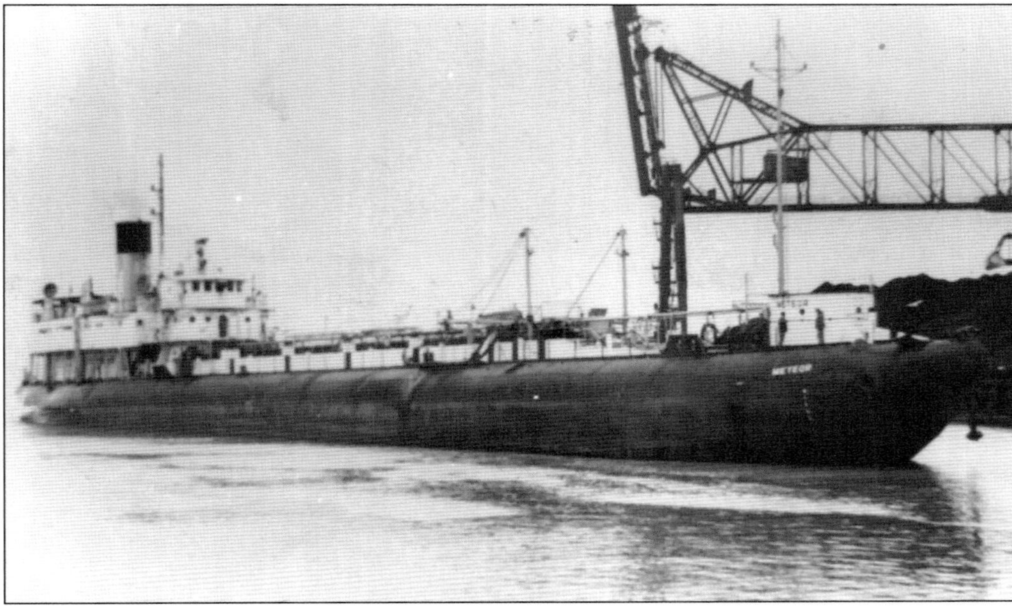

The north slip, which is now part of Port Washington's modern marina, not only provided dockage for the Wisconsin Chair Factory, fish tugs, and pleasure craft, but it also had tankers dock on its north side. Shipments of gasoline and fuel oil were brought in and piped to Murphy Oil Company's tank farm on the south side of the city. Here the last of the historic whaleback fleet, the *Meteor*, is about to drop its starboard anchor to assist in making the sharp turn into the west slip.

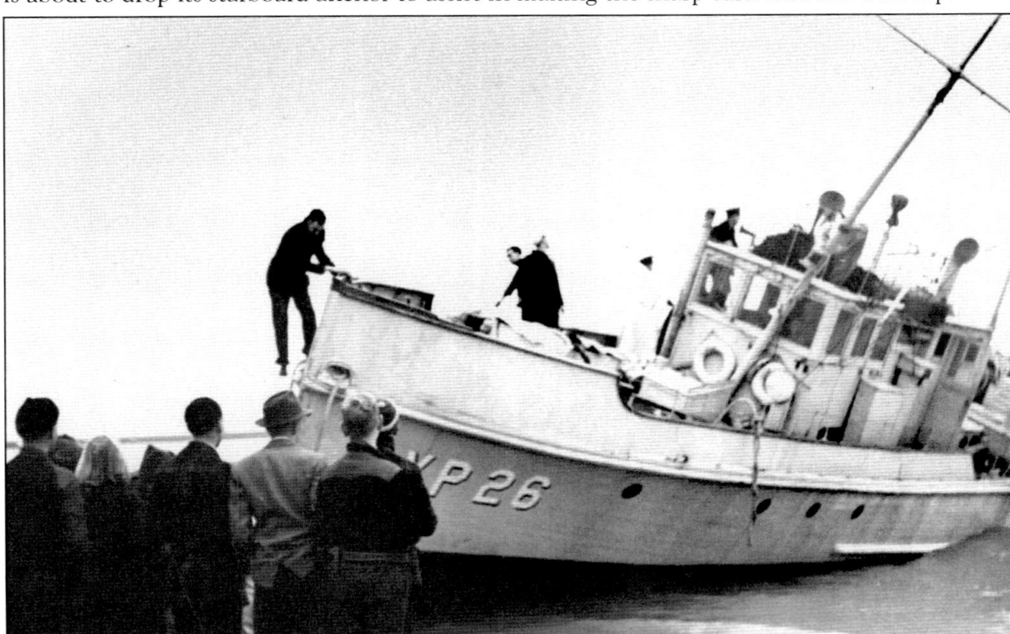

Even the military occasionally fell victim to Port Washington's once notorious harbor. Here the U.S. Navy training vessel *YP26* is seen after it was blown onto the beach in the harbor. It was later pulled off the sand by local fish tugs and the lighthouse tender *Hollyhock* and the cutter *Antietam*.

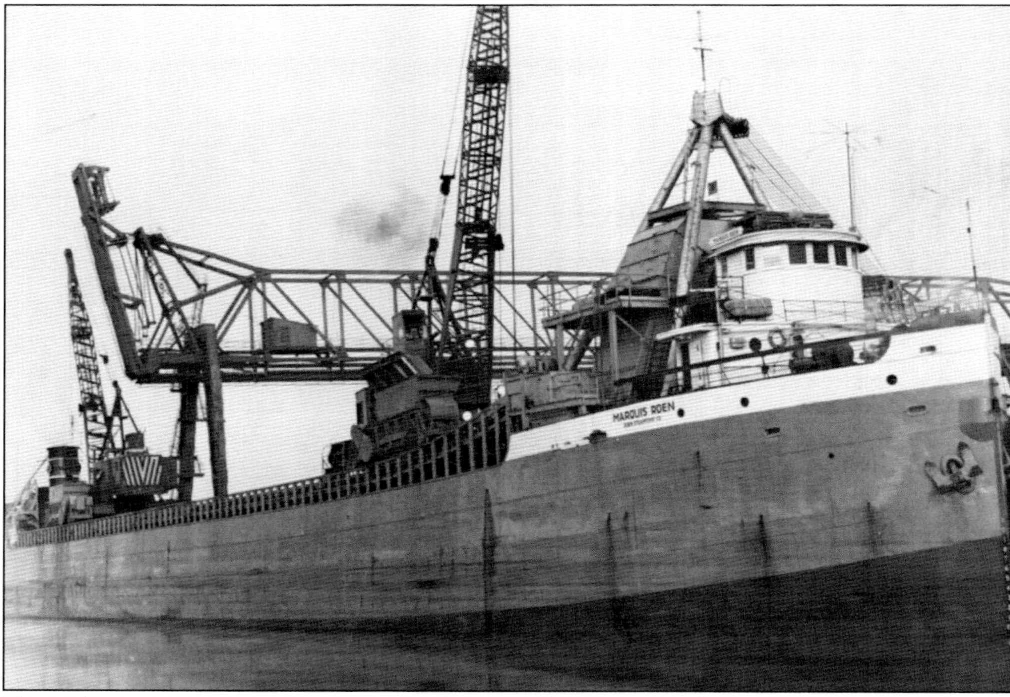

Ships of many types once visited Port Washington's harbor. Here the barge *Marquis Roen* unloads at the Wisconsin Electric Power Plant's coal dock. This is an example of an older steamer that was converted into a self-unloading barge, thereby extending its useful life.

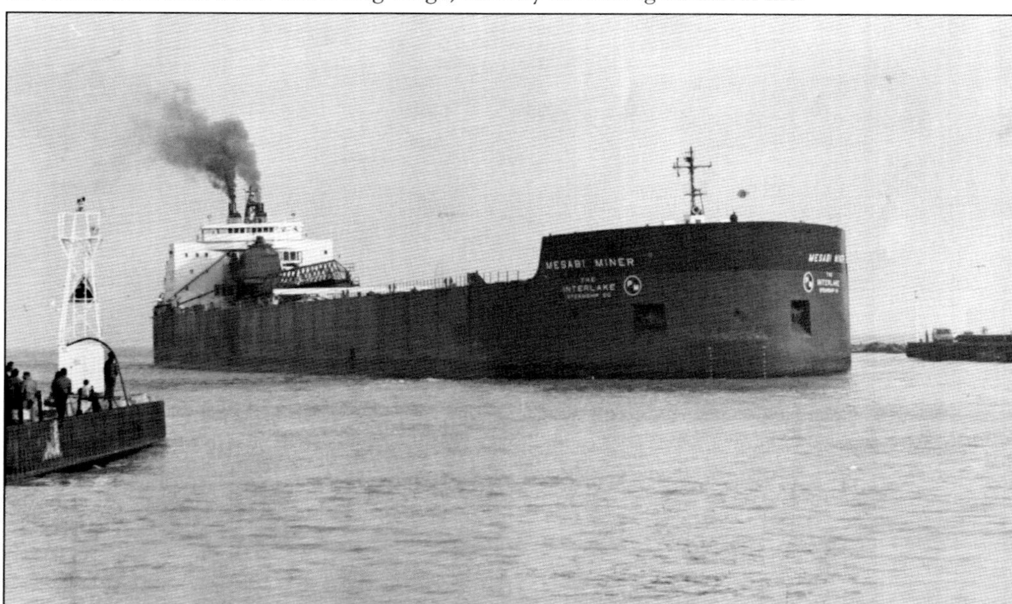

At one time, ships as large as 1,013 feet could dock at Port Washington and bring in coal cargoes as large as 35,000 tons. Here the 1,005-foot *Mesabi Miner* maneuvers to dock at the Wisconsin Electric Power Company coal dock. The public enjoyed watching these large ships. Today ships no longer dock in Port Washington because the power plant has been converted to natural gas.

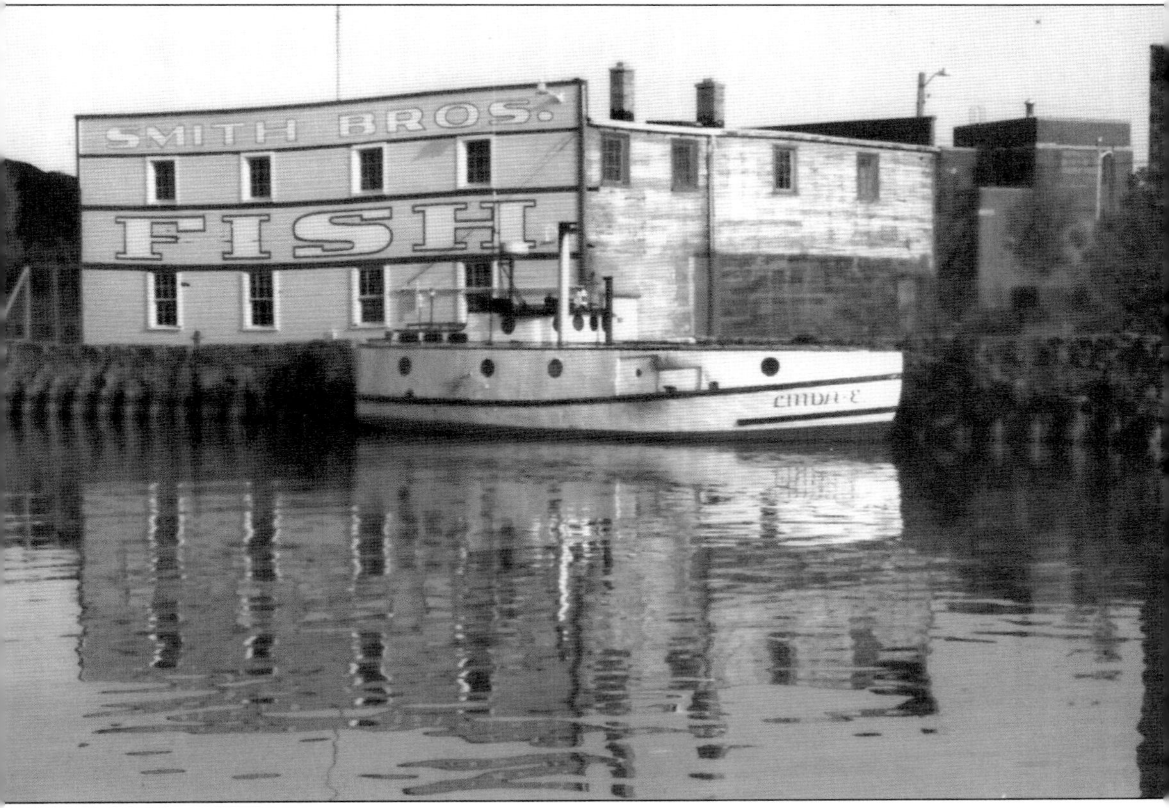

During the early morning of Friday, December 11, 1998, Leif Weborg, Warren Olson, and Scott Matta left Port Washington on a calm, clear, sunny day. Around 10 a.m. they contacted Smith Brothers Food Service, relaying that they had 1,000 pounds of chubs and were just finishing setting back and heading in. That was their last communication. They never made it into Port Washington. There was no sign of the tug or its crew and a lengthy search proved fruitless. Speculation as to what had happened to the *Linda E* and its crew ensued. Months later, the U.S. Navy was employed and while using sonar devices it discovered the *Linda E* on June 18, 2000, in Lake Michigan. It was later determined that the vessel was run down by a southbound 500-foot-long barge. The *Linda E* was the last commercial fishing vessel to leave Port Washington.

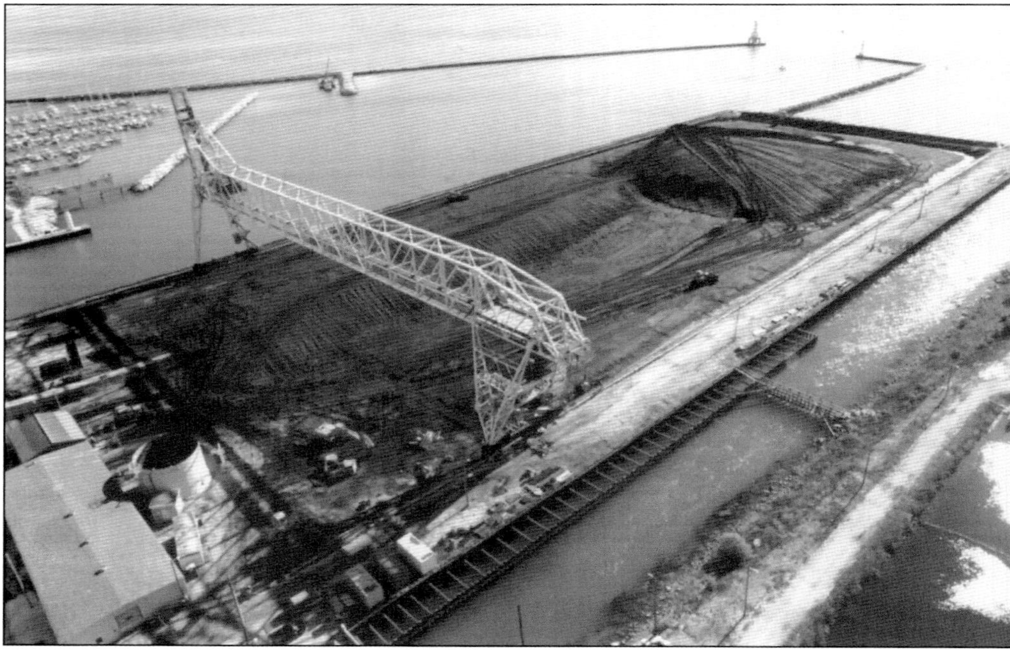

Port Washington once had the second largest coal-unloading bridge on the Great Lakes. It was demolished when most coal boats were converted to self-unloaders. At one time it was painted light blue and was known as the "Blue Dinosaur."

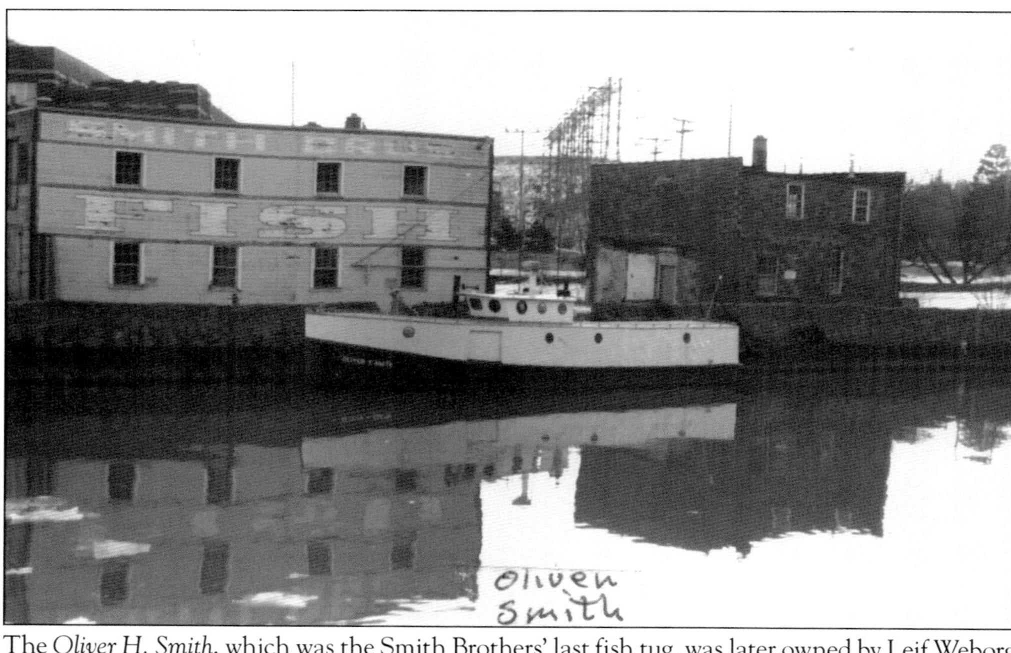

The *Oliver H. Smith*, which was the Smith Brothers' last fish tug, was later owned by Leif Weborg. At the time of the loss of the *Linda E*, the *Oliver H. Smith* was laid up in Milwaukee. Leif used the *Linda E* in the winter because it was easier to heat and he considered it a better sea boat.

Six

A Thriving City

Since its founding, Port Washington has been a very industrious little city with businesses based on agriculture, manufacturing, the lake, and service. This chapter illustrates just a very few examples of the early ways of life in this little city. It is not in the scope of this work to cover everything, but to give a taste of the variety of what Port Washington was in its early years.

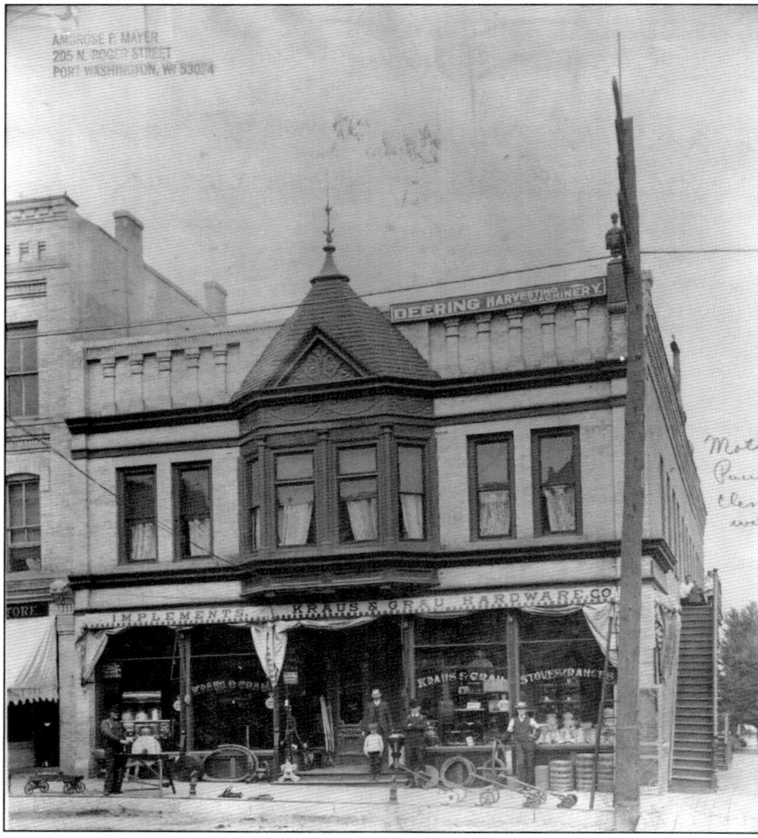

Kraus and Grau Hardware Company, pictured here in 1905, was on the corner of Franklin and Pier Streets. Grandpa Kraus stands at the stone wheel at the left. The interior photograph below shows the stoves for sale at the store. John Kraus is at left, Peter Kraus in back, and Adam Grau is seated.

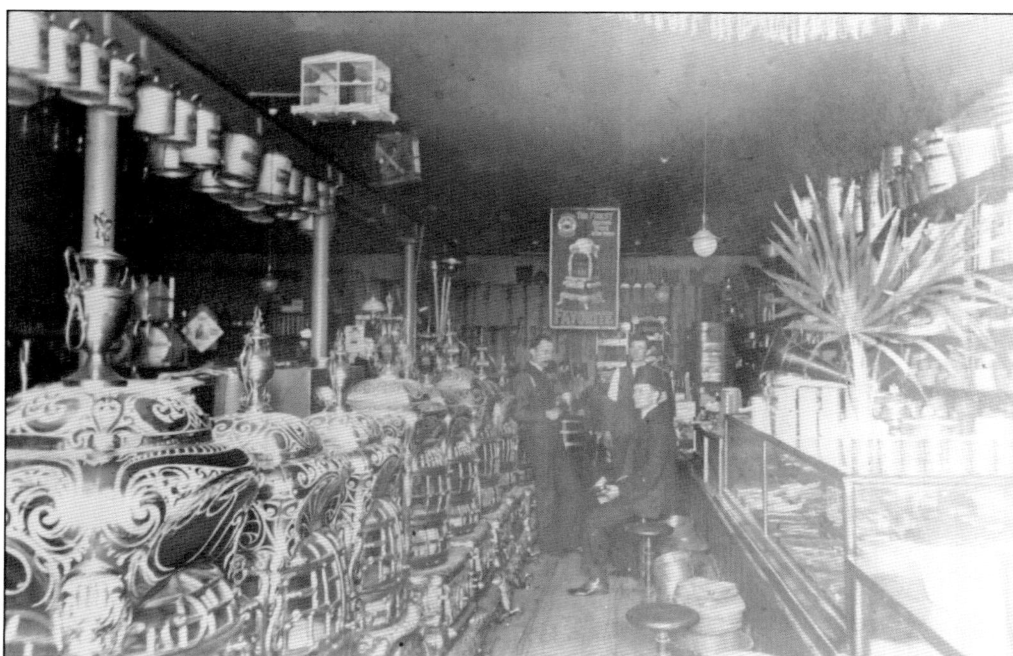

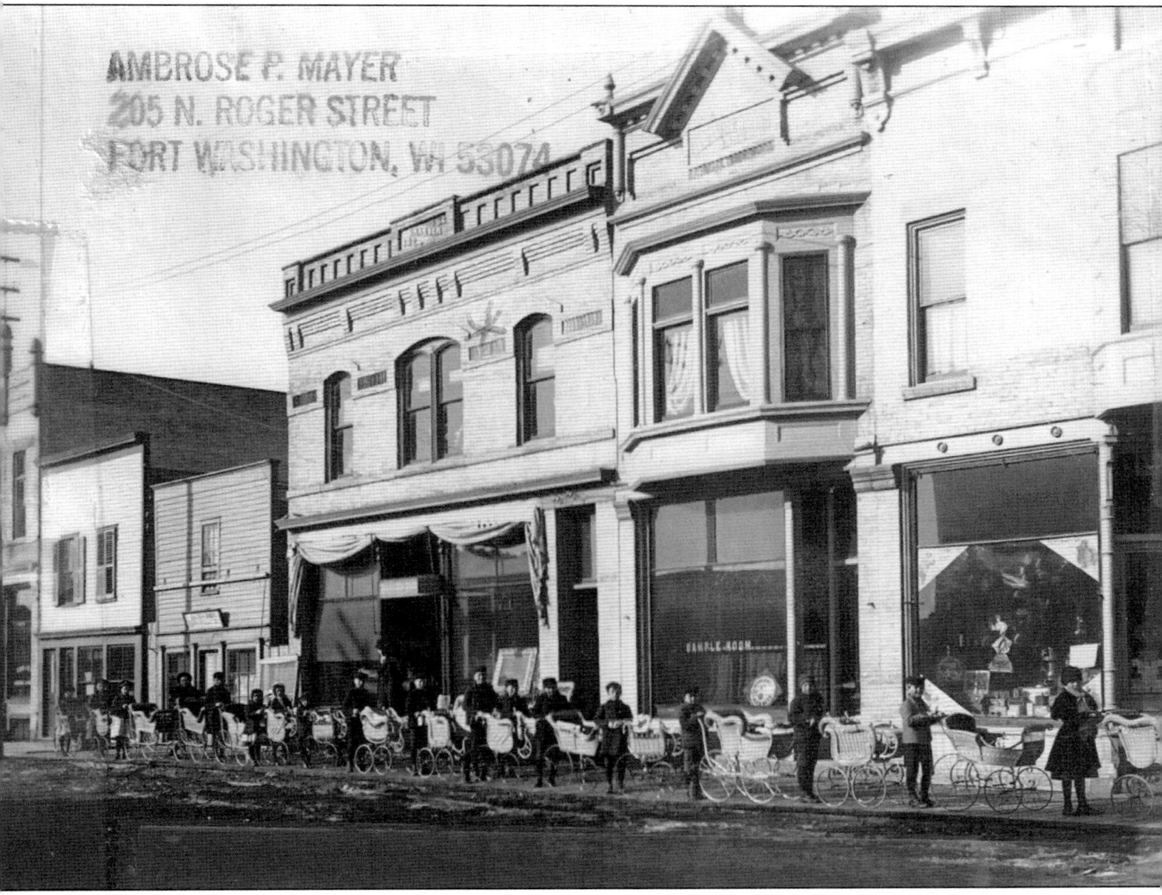

Here is a unique picture of a baby carriage parade in turn of the century Port Washington. Note the wicker carriages, dirt streets, and wooden boardwalk.

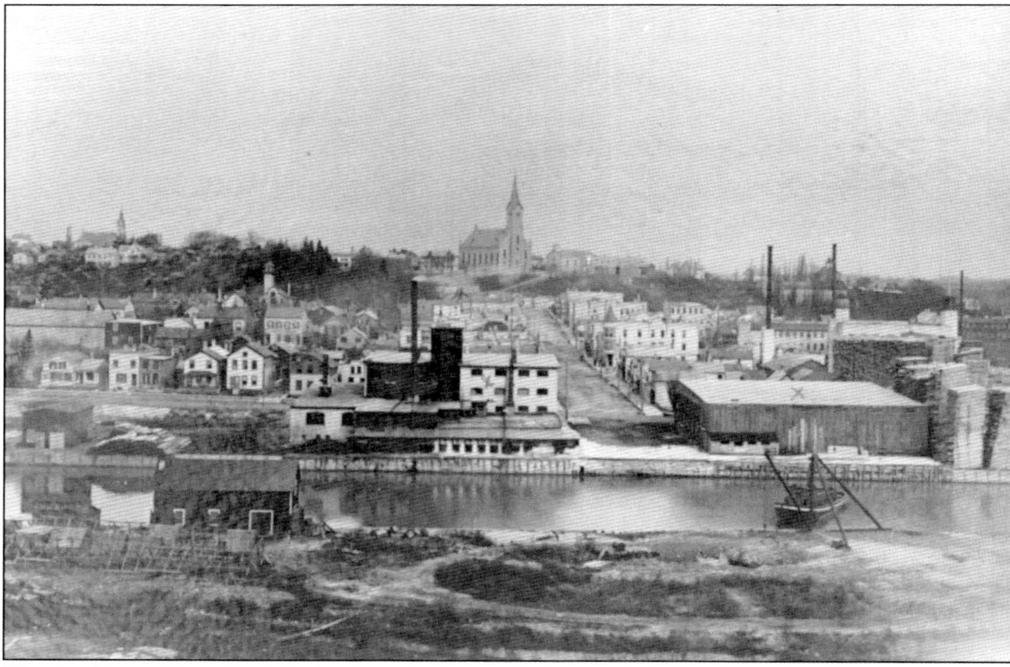

This mid-1890s view up Franklin Street shows the booming harbor town that Port Washington had become. St. Mary's Catholic Church dominates the horizon. C. A. Mueller Tannery and Bark Shed is in the foreground.

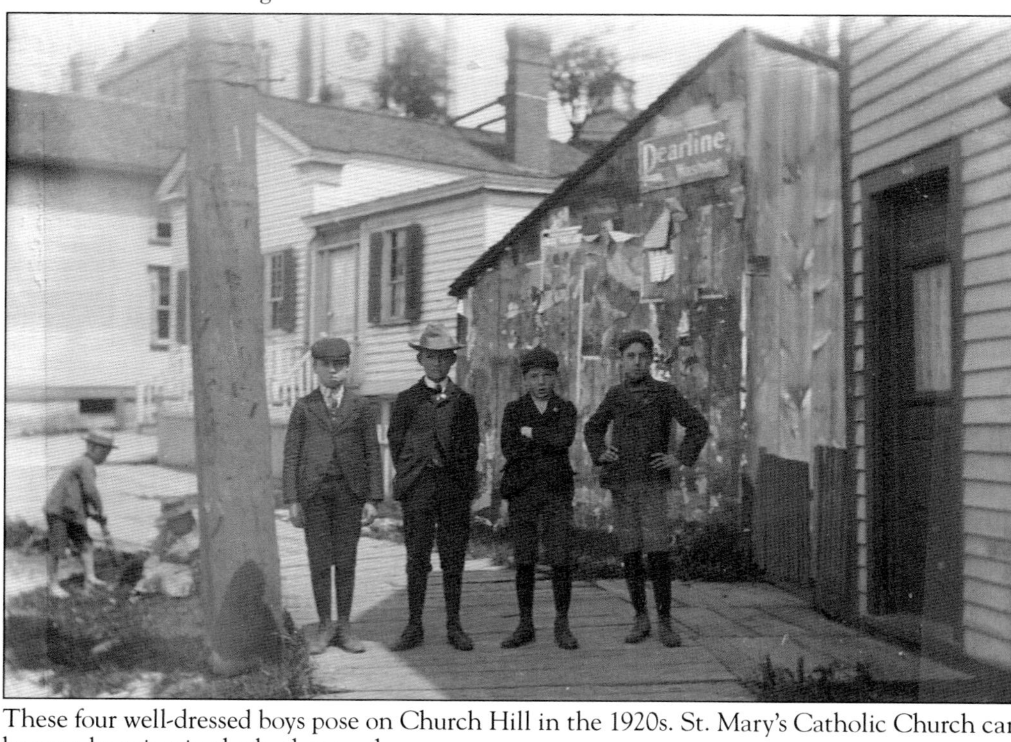

These four well-dressed boys pose on Church Hill in the 1920s. St. Mary's Catholic Church can be seen looming in the background.

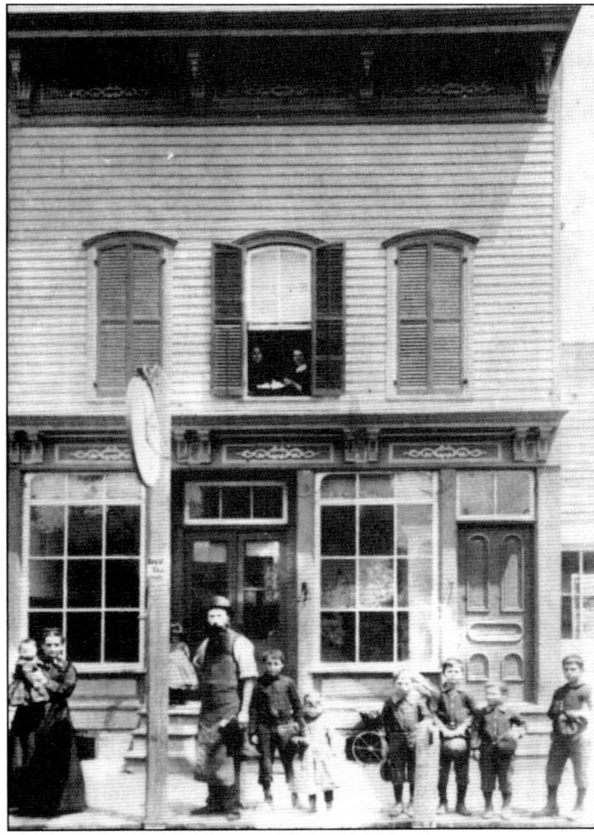

The Sturm family, posing some time prior to 1899, is in front of the Sturm Cobbler Shop, which was located on Franklin Street just north of Smith Brothers corner. The family consisted of 16 children, one of whom (Matt) built the Light House Restaurant (pictured below) in 1928. It was located on Grand Avenue, in the space now occupied by the Pebble House.

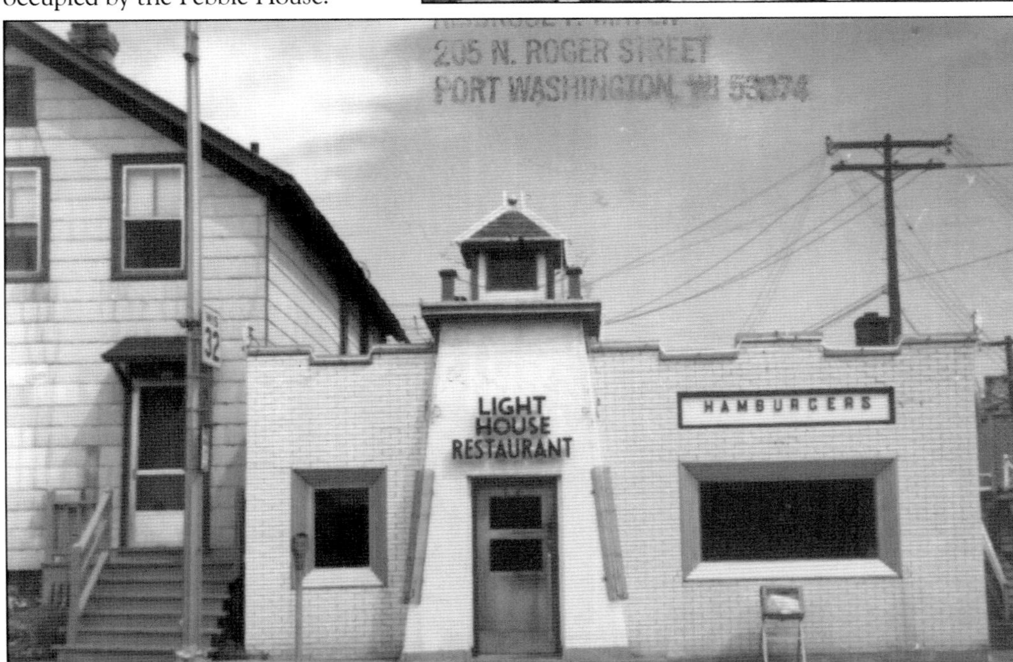

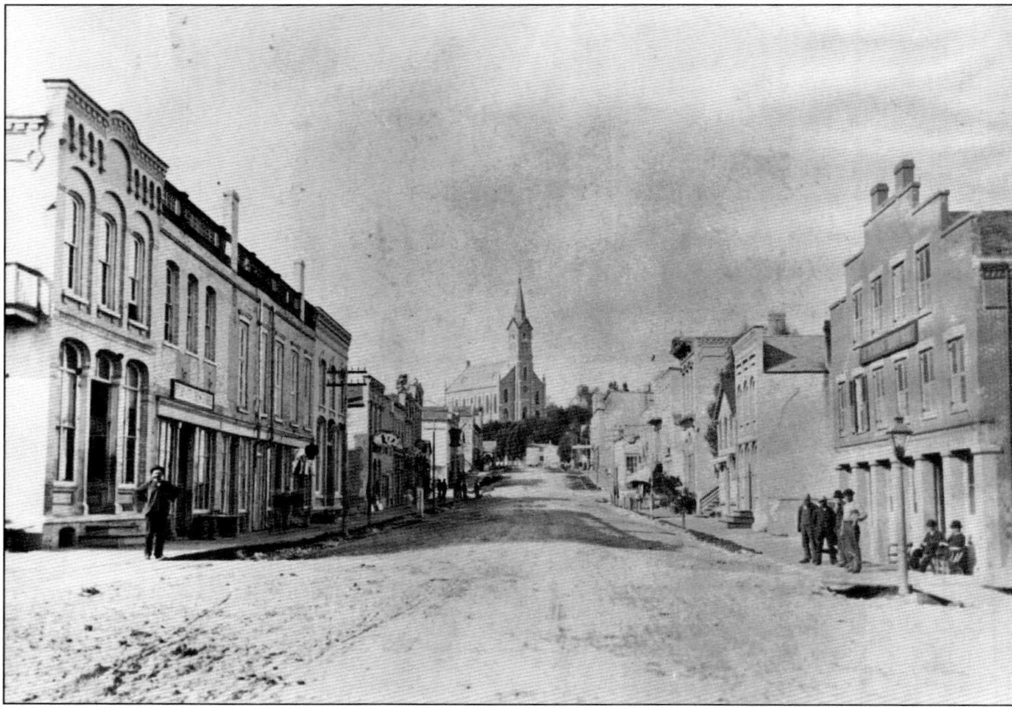

In the beginning days of the busy little city, Port Washington's Franklin Street is pictured looking north around 1884.

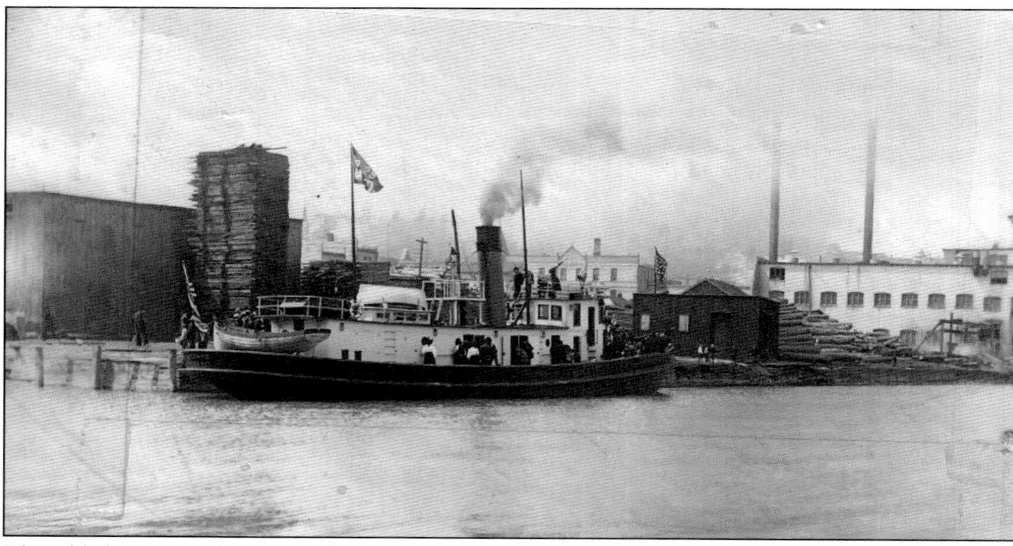

This old photograph shows a tugboat with the Wisconsin Chair Company factory in the background. The Wisconsin Chair Company was founded in 1888 when John M. Bostwick offered Fred A. Dennet of Sheboygan, Wisconsin, the large waterfront property that earlier had been occupied by the Port Washington Sash and Door Company. After a shaky start, the chair company soon became the largest employer in Port Washington. This photograph shows how extensive the manufacturing facilities in Port Washington were. The company also owned extensive lumber-producing sawmills, land, and a number of ships for hauling lumber.

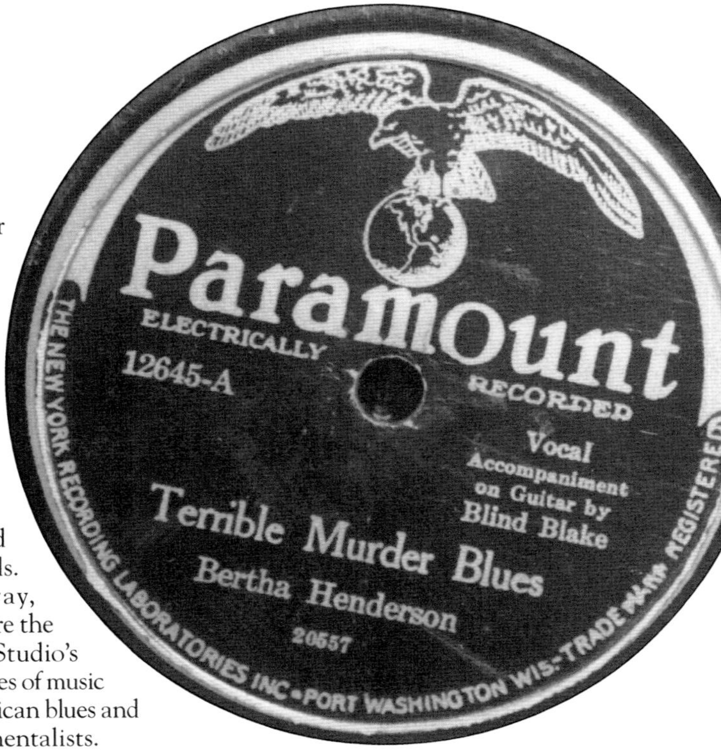

The Wisconsin Chair Company also bought the New York Recording Studio, which it moved to an unused furniture factory in Grafton, Wisconsin. Since the studio was making record cabinets for other recording companies, it decided to make its own records. Paramount, Broadway, Famous, and Puritan were the New York Recording Studio's labels. It recorded all styles of music including African American blues and jazz singers and instrumentalists.

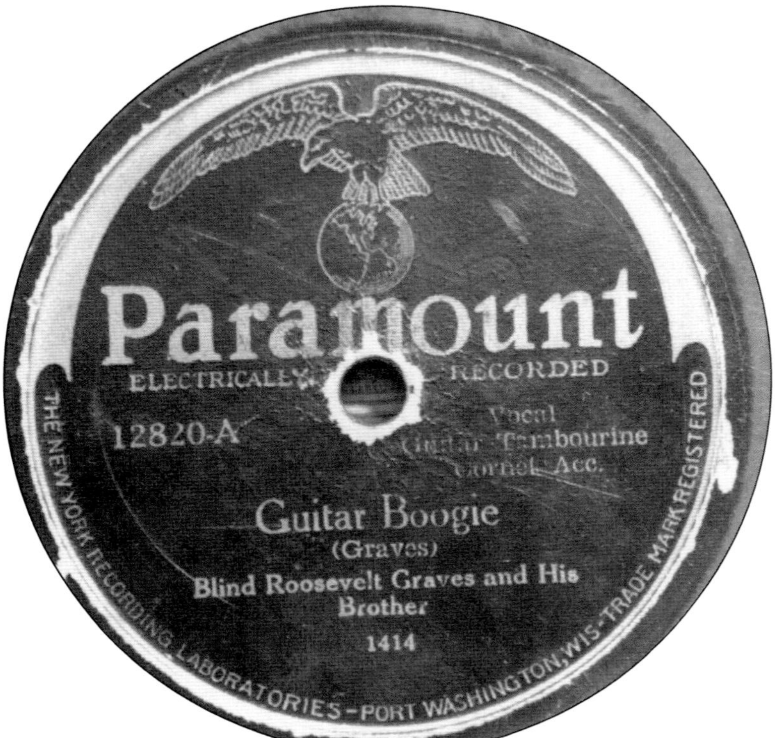

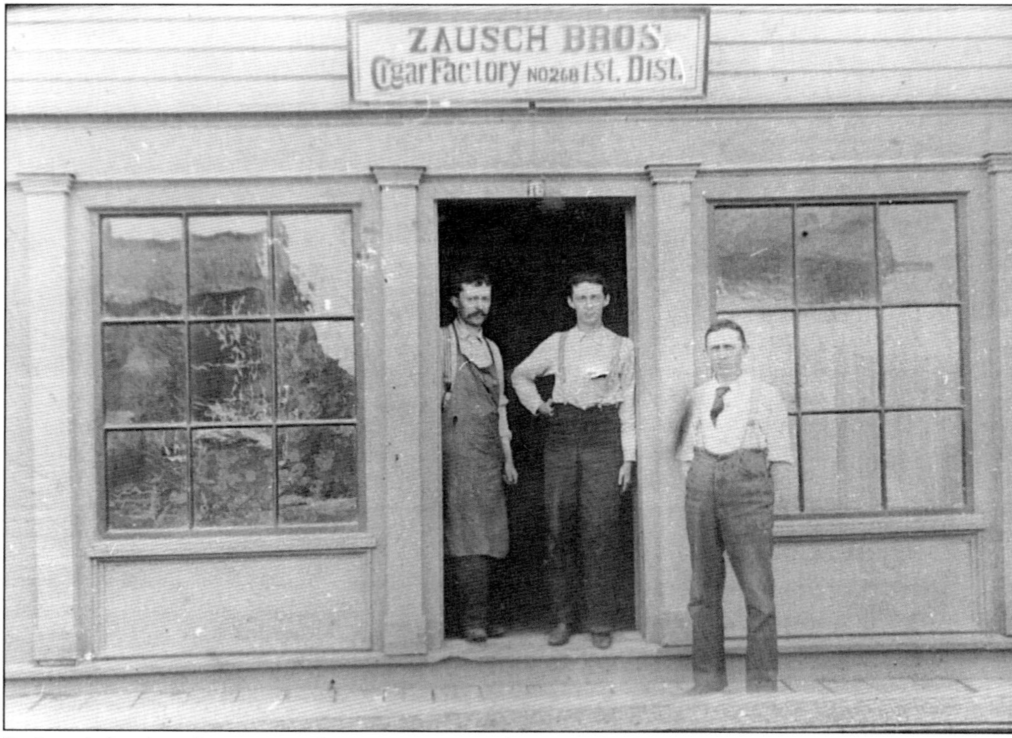

Before federal and state regulations, Port Washington had a number of cigar makers—Biever and Pastoret and Zausch Brothers. Here Carl and Herman Zausch stand in front of their cigar factory.

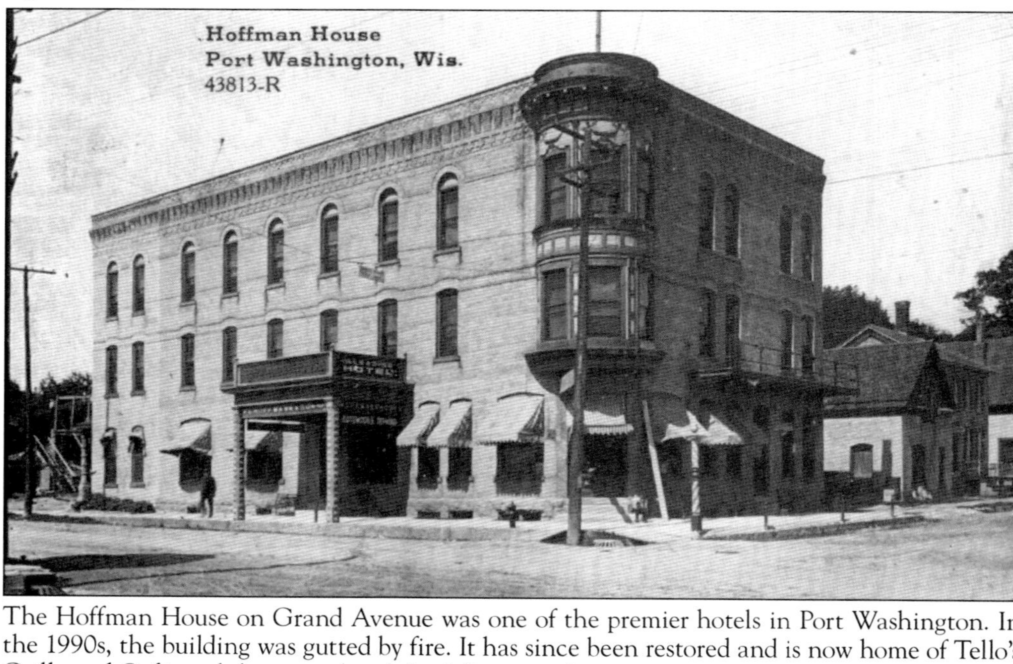

The Hoffman House on Grand Avenue was one of the premier hotels in Port Washington. In the 1990s, the building was gutted by fire. It has since been restored and is now home of Tello's Grille and Café; and the second and third floors are luxury apartments.

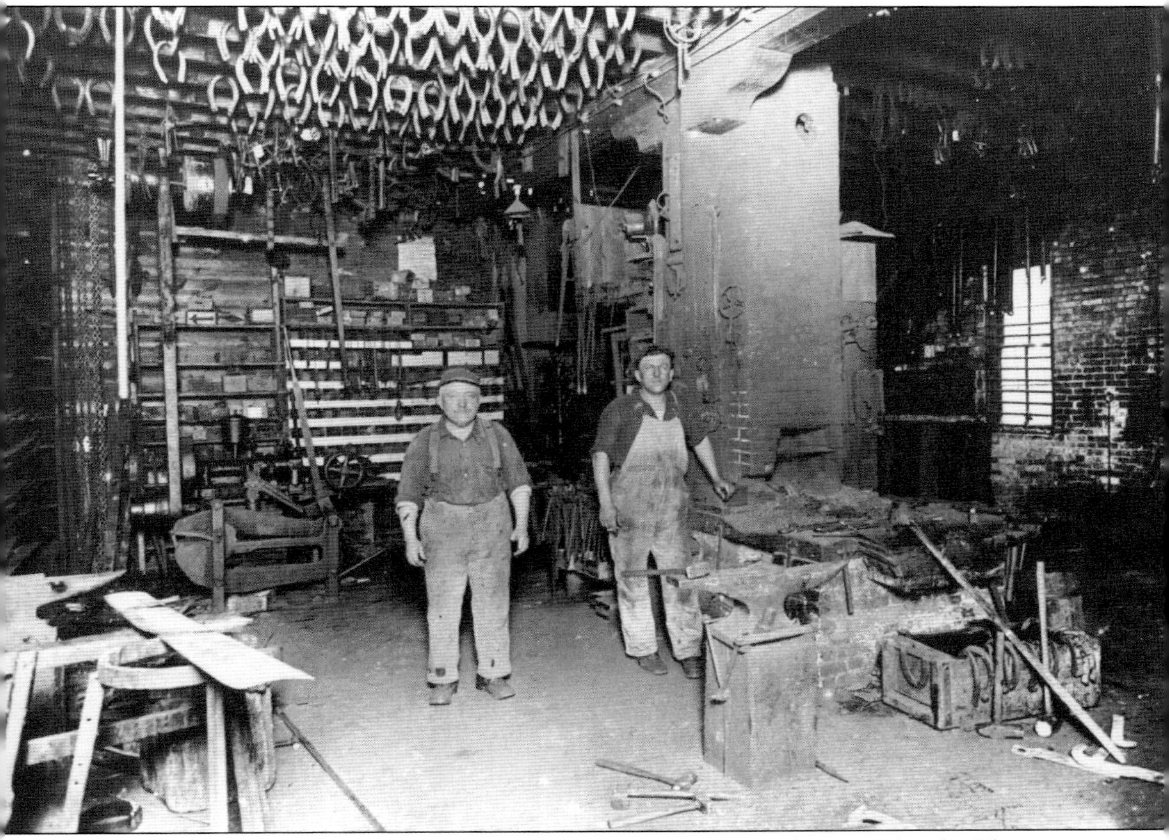

The Poull family—early settlers in Port Washington—was an industrious family. They were blacksmiths and wagon makers. The Nick Poull Blacksmith Shop and home was located at 311 Washington Street. The Poull family branched out to create a very successful hardware, plumbing, and heating business until the 1980s when descendants Jim and Dorothy Poull retired. Pictured in their blacksmith shop are Nick Poull Sr. (left) and Emil "Peter" Poull. In 1979, the shop and home were torn down and the area was turned into a parking lot.

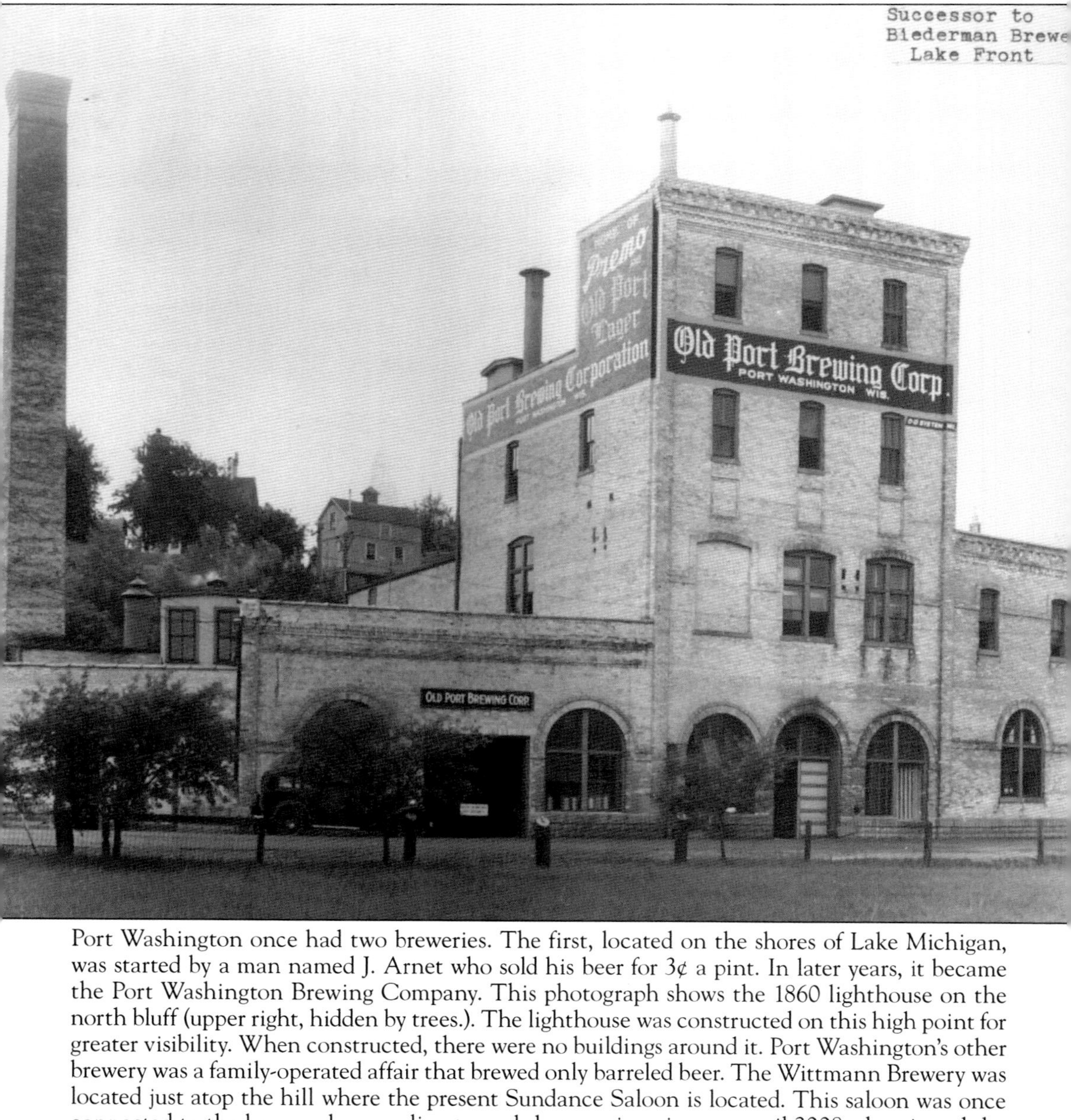

Port Washington once had two breweries. The first, located on the shores of Lake Michigan, was started by a man named J. Arnet who sold his beer for 3¢ a pint. In later years, it became the Port Washington Brewing Company. This photograph shows the 1860 lighthouse on the north bluff (upper right, hidden by trees.). The lighthouse was constructed on this high point for greater visibility. When constructed, there were no buildings around it. Port Washington's other brewery was a family-operated affair that brewed only barreled beer. The Wittmann Brewery was located just atop the hill where the present Sundance Saloon is located. This saloon was once connected to the brewery by a cooling tunnel that was in existence until 2008 when it and the brewery were destroyed for a housing project.

Premo—whose slogan was "the beer that made Milwaukee furious"—was brewed by the Port Washington Brewing Company. Pictured is an advertisement in a 1915 Port Washington publication.

Premo Beer, A Real Tonic.

There is no remedy oftener prescribed by competent physicians for persons in nced of a Tonic than well aged lager beer; not the kind that is aged by chemicals, but the kind that is aged by time, in clean cellars.

Our beer is a healthy drink, because it is made of pure barley malt and selected Bohemian hops, in one of the cleanest and best equipped little breweries in the world. From the time that the malt is mashed and boiled, until the finished product is placed in casks for aging, its manufacture is under guidance of a skilled brewmaster, whose attention to every detail has made PREMO a beer second to none.

IT IS A HOME PRODUCT MADE BY HOME LABOR.

Order by phone or postal card.

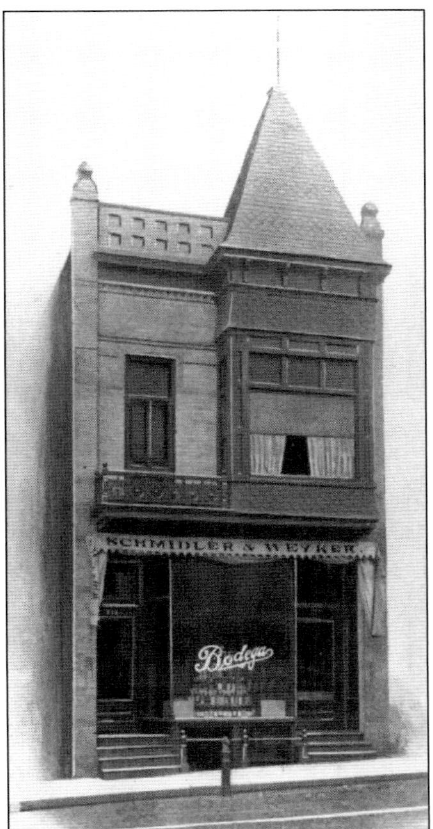

Not only a saloon but also a pool hall, restaurant, and social center, the Bodega is still recognizable downtown and although it has had many name changes, it is still often referred to by its original name.

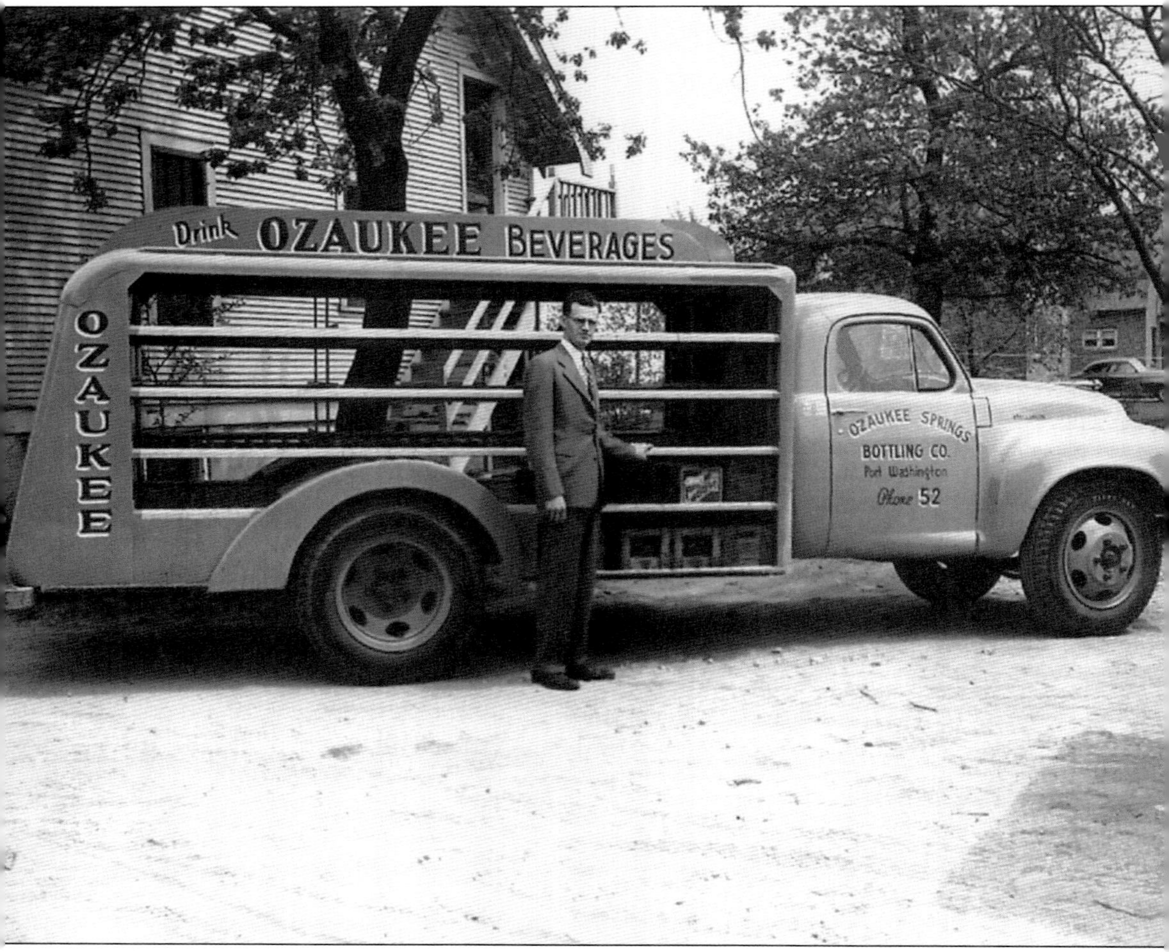

Besides the two breweries in the city, Port Washington also had the Ozaukee Springs Bottling Company that used water from the artesian spring called Ozaukee Springs. The first Ozaukee Springs bottler was James Cooney, who also bottled beer.

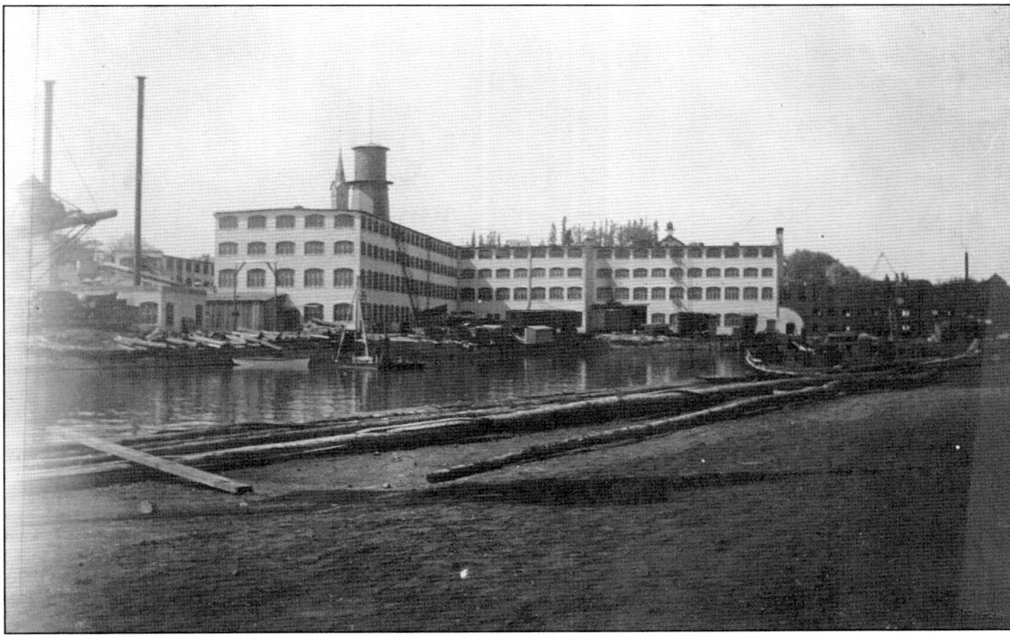

Port Washington's north slip was once lined with fishing vessels. The Wisconsin Chair Company factory is in the background. A small fish tug, a steam tug, and a motor launch are in the foreground. Notice the opening in the chair factory on the left for the interurban to pass through on its way to Belgium, Cedar Grove, and Sheboygan.

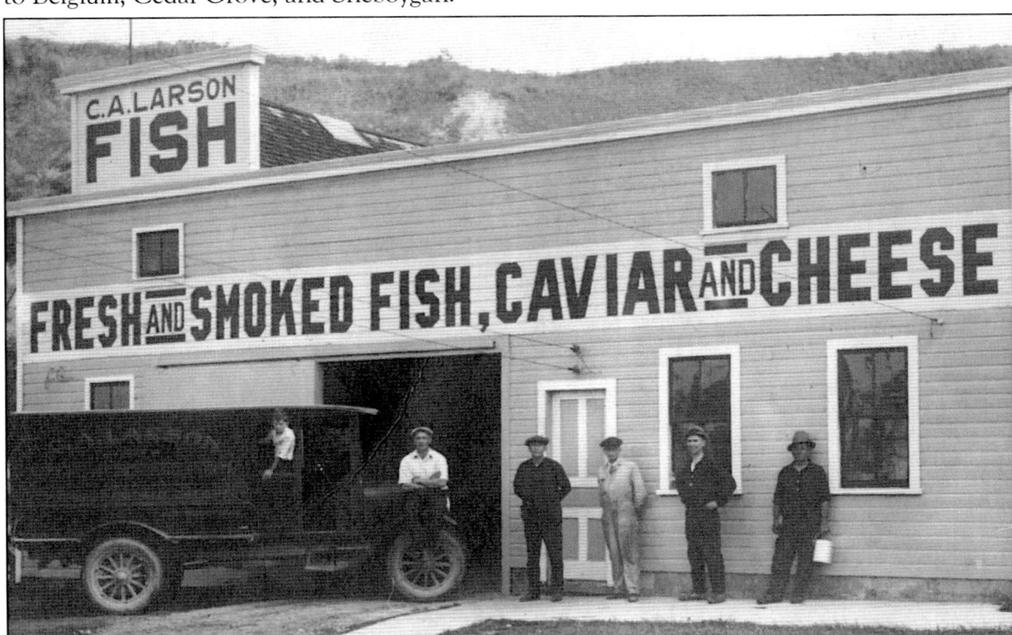

C. A. Larson sold and peddled smoked fish for many years in Port Washington and the surrounding cities. He bought the fish from local fishermen. His son Charles grew up to become a prominent citizen of Port Washington and served as a circuit court judge for many years. He lived to the age of 102.

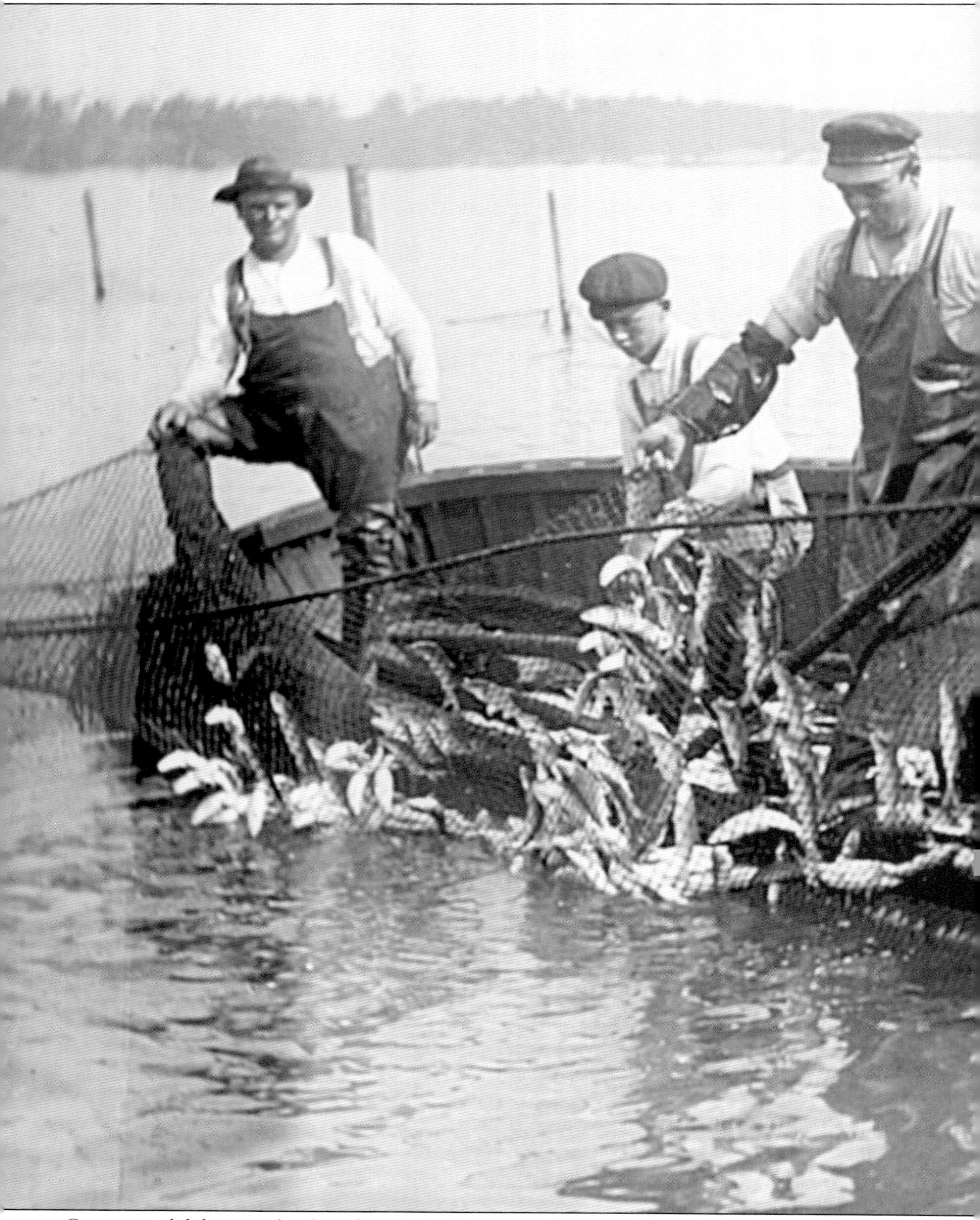

Commercial fishermen haul in their pound nets near shore on a calm day. Fishermen not only used gill nets and hooks but also used pound nets to entrap the fish. Spilings were sometimes set

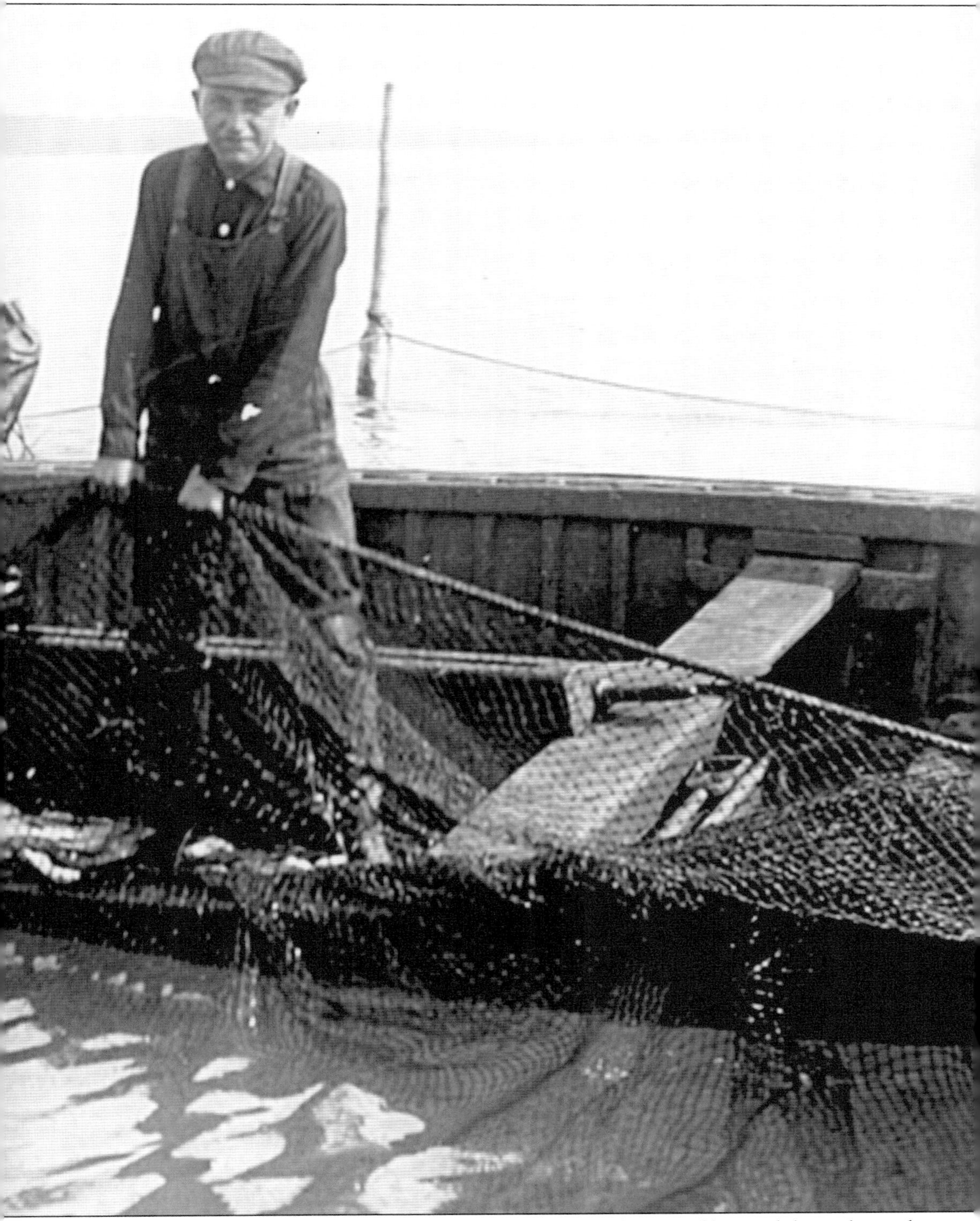

all the way down to 90 feet. It was heavy work, but the fish were harvested live and the undersized or unwanted could be released.

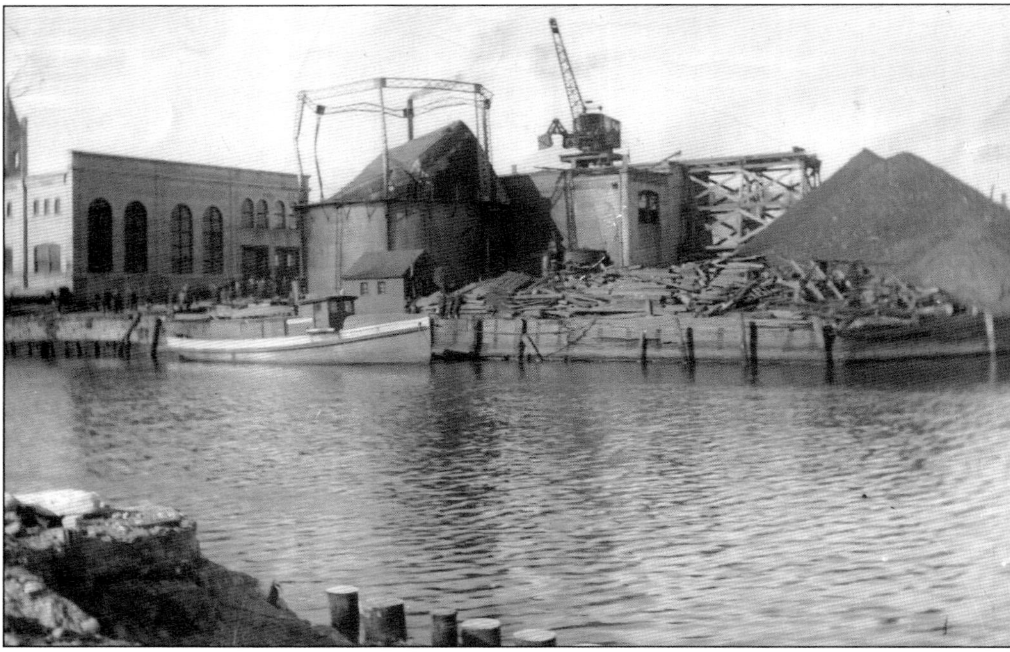

When the Ewig family began fishing out of Port Washington after 1894, they owned the steam tug *Hannah Sullivan*, which had been built in lower Michigan. This photograph shows the *Sullivan* tied up in the west slip sometime after 1908. The Ewigs fished the *Sullivan* until its hull became unsound and they bought the steel-hulled *Herbert*, which later became the *H. Ewig*. The Milwaukee Electric Railway and Light Company (TMER&L) gasification plant was used to produce electricity for the interurban electric railroad and provided gas lighting. It is seen in the background.

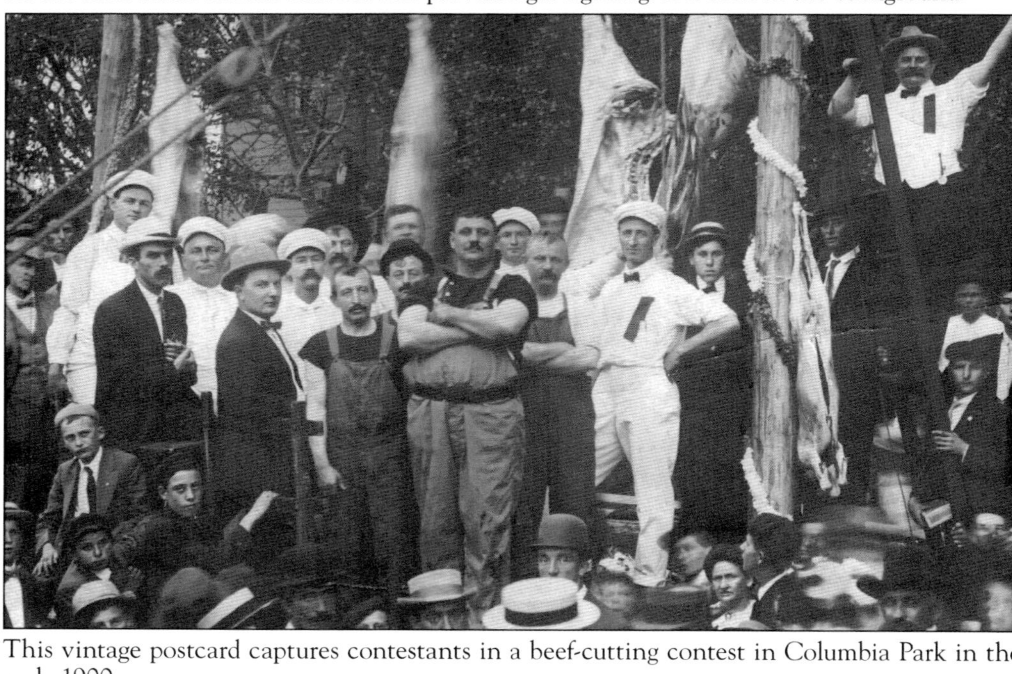

This vintage postcard captures contestants in a beef-cutting contest in Columbia Park in the early 1900s.

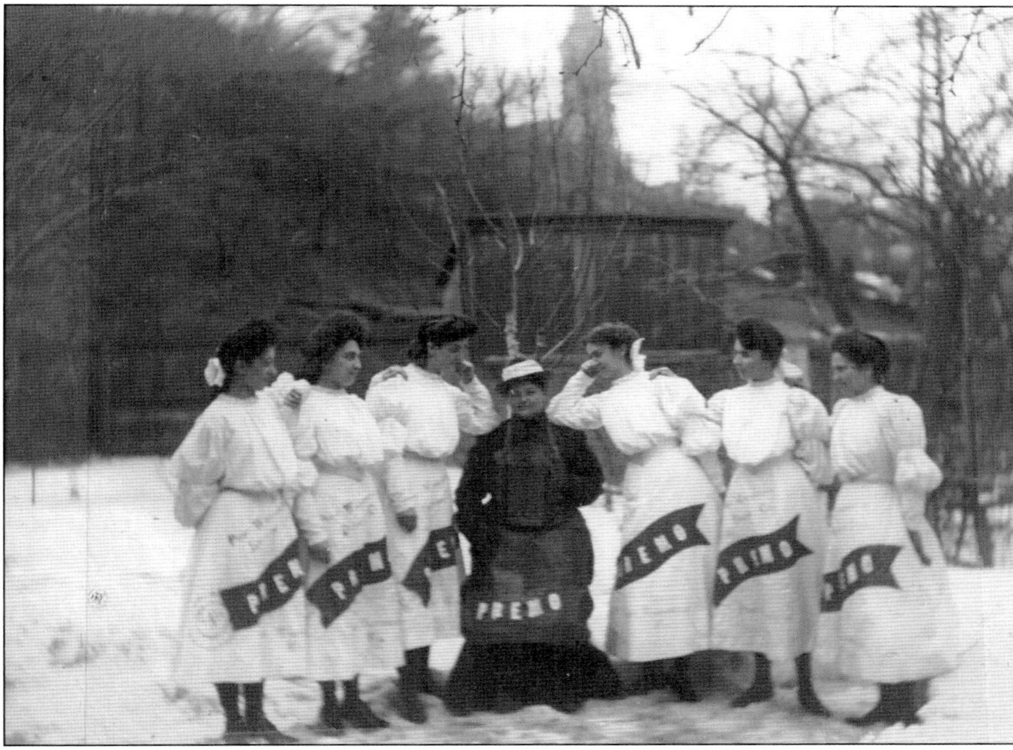

Even in midwinter, Port Washington's Premo cheerleaders show their pride in "the beer that made Milwaukee furious."

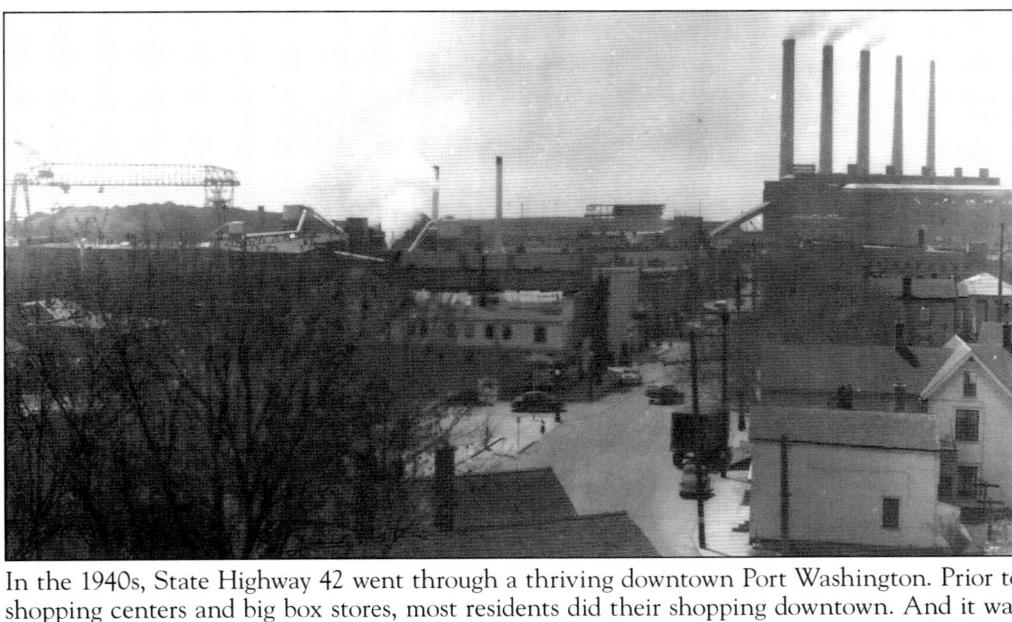

In the 1940s, State Highway 42 went through a thriving downtown Port Washington. Prior to shopping centers and big box stores, most residents did their shopping downtown. And it was literally "downtown," as at the time, most of Port Washington was nestled between the bluffs. In this photograph, the Wisconsin Electric Power Plant is seen. A coal-fired plant, it had five generating units. There were also many more residential homes in the downtown area during this era.

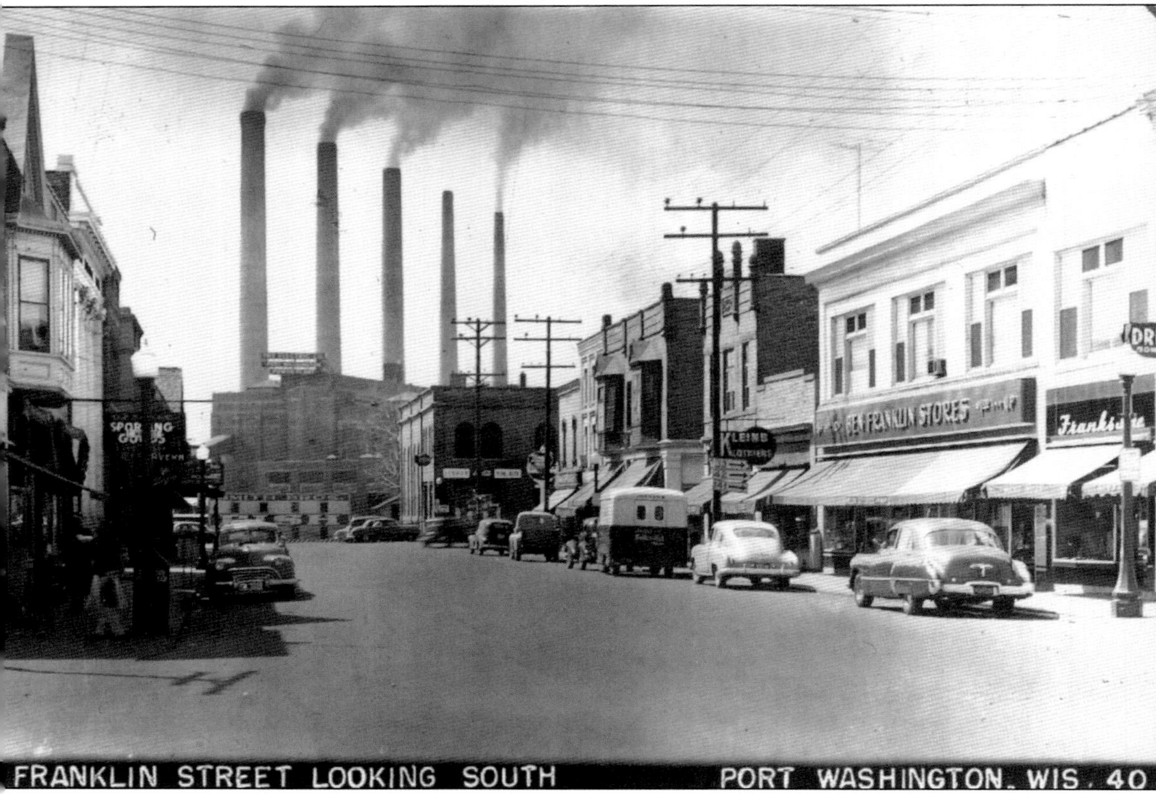

Every city's buildings have had multiple uses. This early-1950s photograph shows Franklin Street looking south, dominated by the Wisconsin Electric Power Company's power plant (note the five smokestacks pouring out smoke prior to pollution control). This one block had a pharmacy, jeweler, sporting goods, clothiers, fish and meat market, and liquor stores—all creating a vibrant downtown.

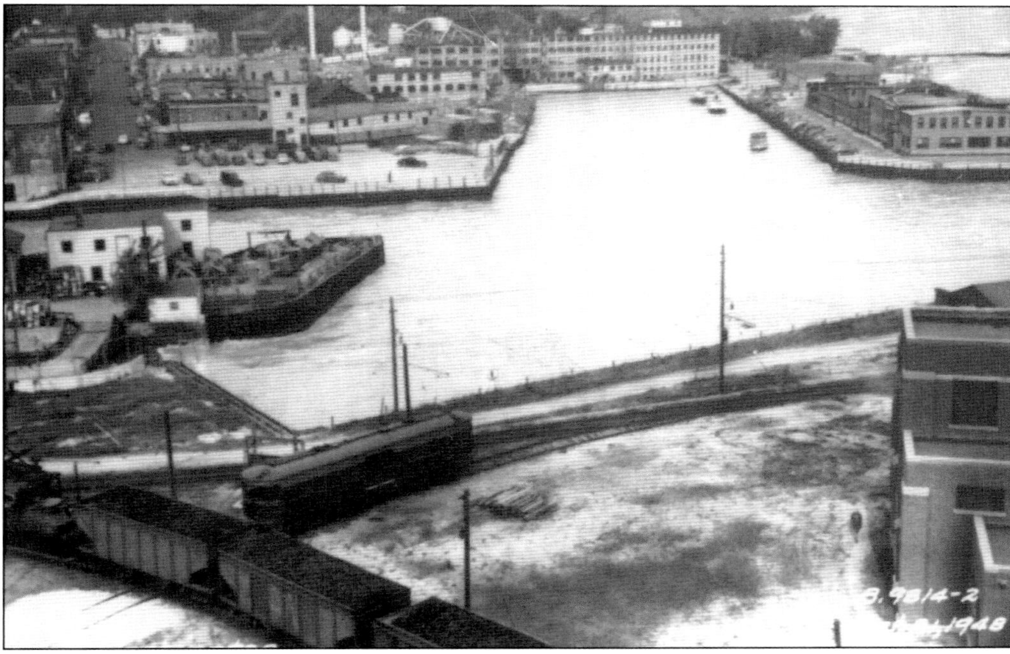

The Wisconsin Electric Power Company coal-fired power plant, which replaced the earlier TMER&L plant and city power plant, received coal not only from the lake steamers but by rail. The coal cars were brought from the Chicago and North Western Railway to the power plant by electric locomotives just visible on the left. Also in this picture is one of the interurban maintenance cars.

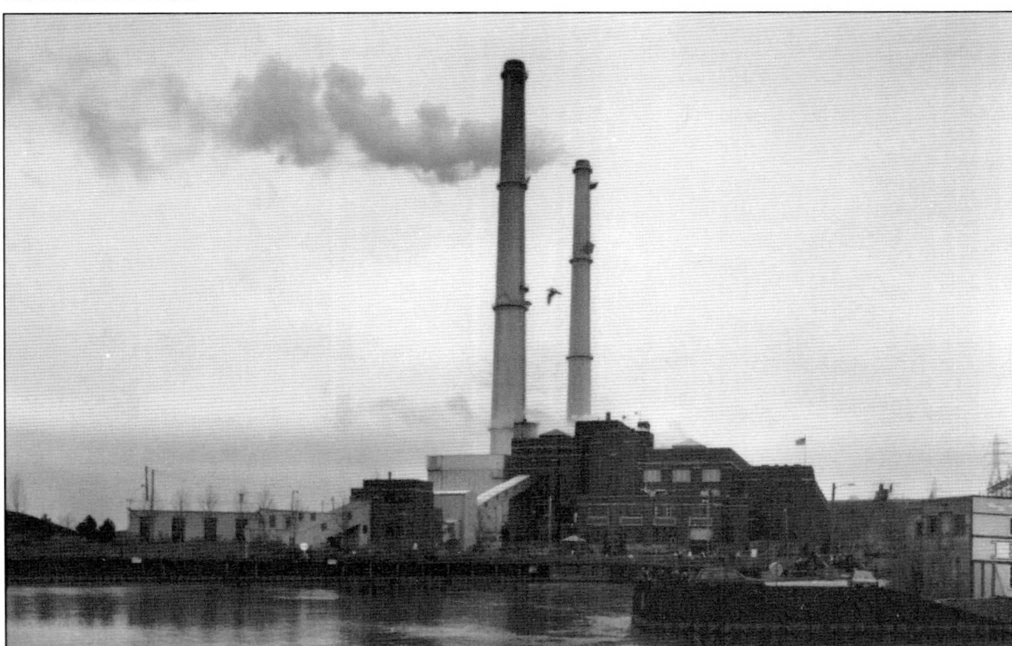

Although the number of smokestacks has changed over the years since the plant was opened in 1935, the power plant has remained a dominant feature in the downtown area.

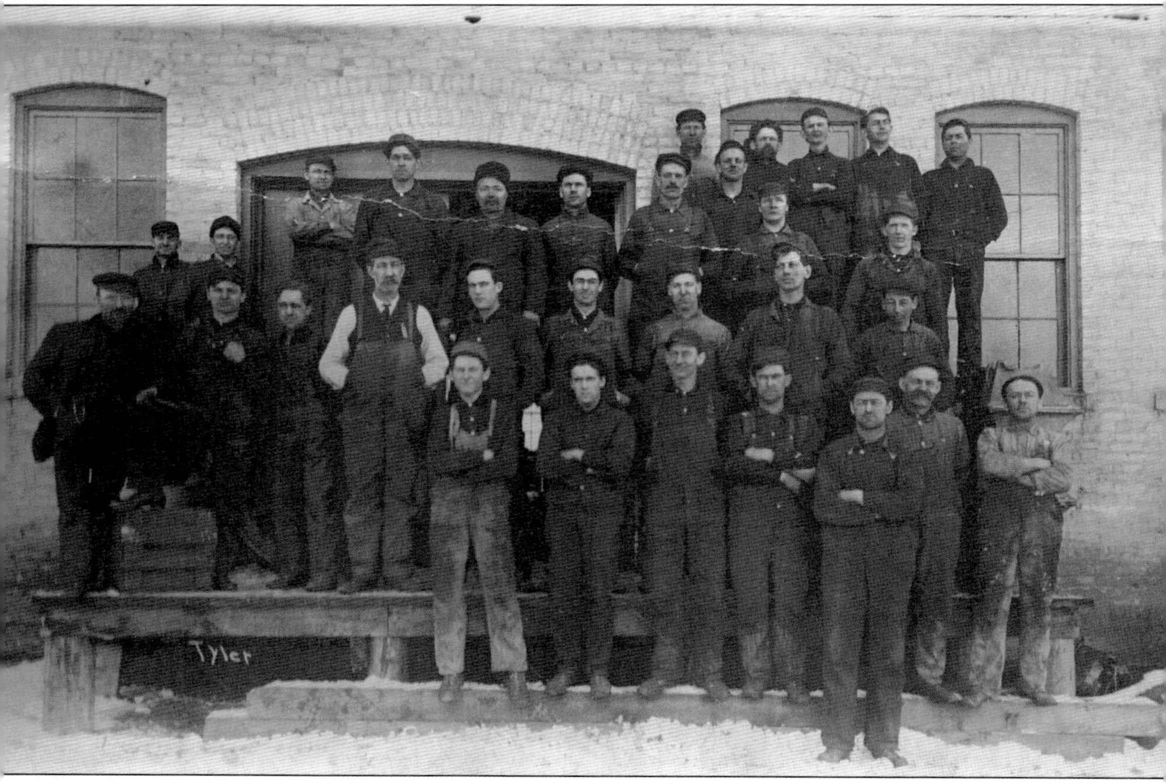

Workers pose in front of the grain mill in Port Washington. The building was later home to J&H Heating and Air Conditioning Company.

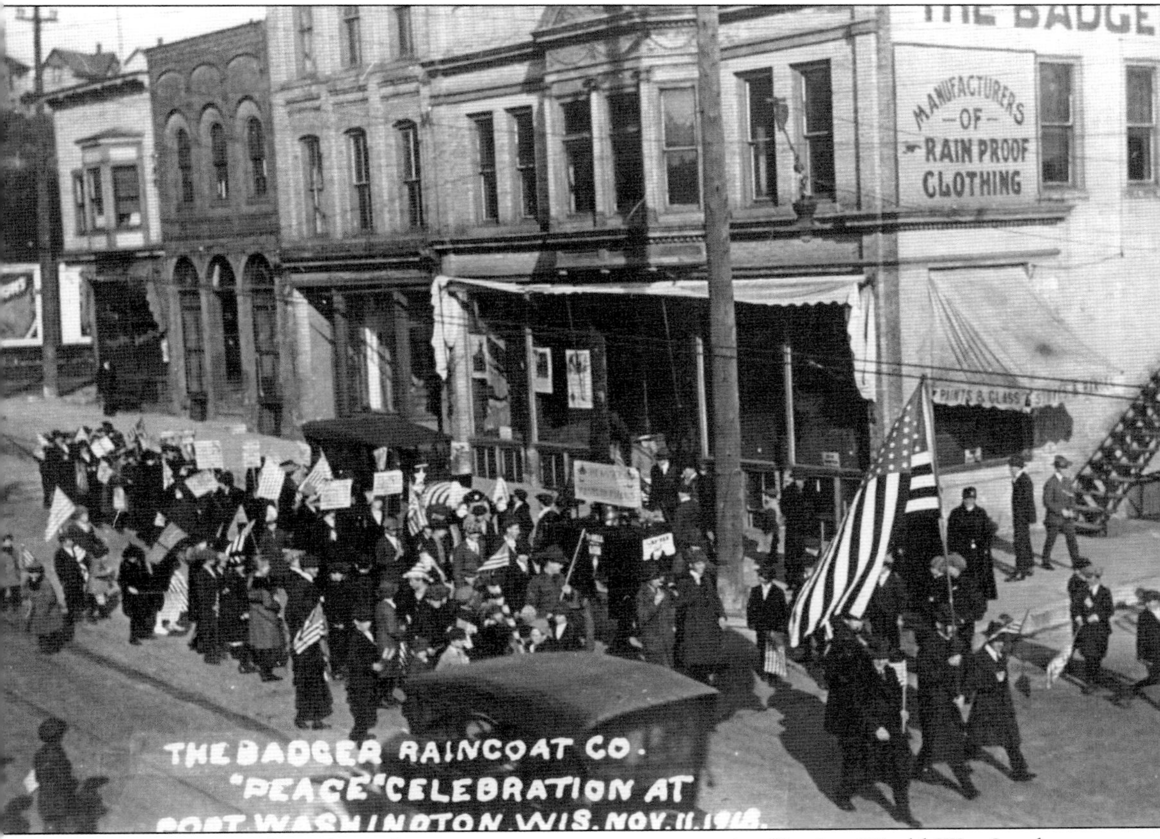

Port Washington has always been a very patriotic community. During World War I, a large contingency of volunteers served. One native son, Andrew Van Ells Jr., was wounded while serving in Paris, France, and later died of his wounds. Another hero, this time of World War II, was Lt. Robert L. Schanen, who lost his life while serving as navigator on a B17 that crashed in Wales after a bombing raid over Germany. The Van Ells-Schanen VFW Post, located along the shore of Lake Michigan in Port Washington, is named in their honor. This photograph is of a "peace celebration" that broke out in front of the Badger Raincoat Company in downtown Port Washington at the ending of World War I.

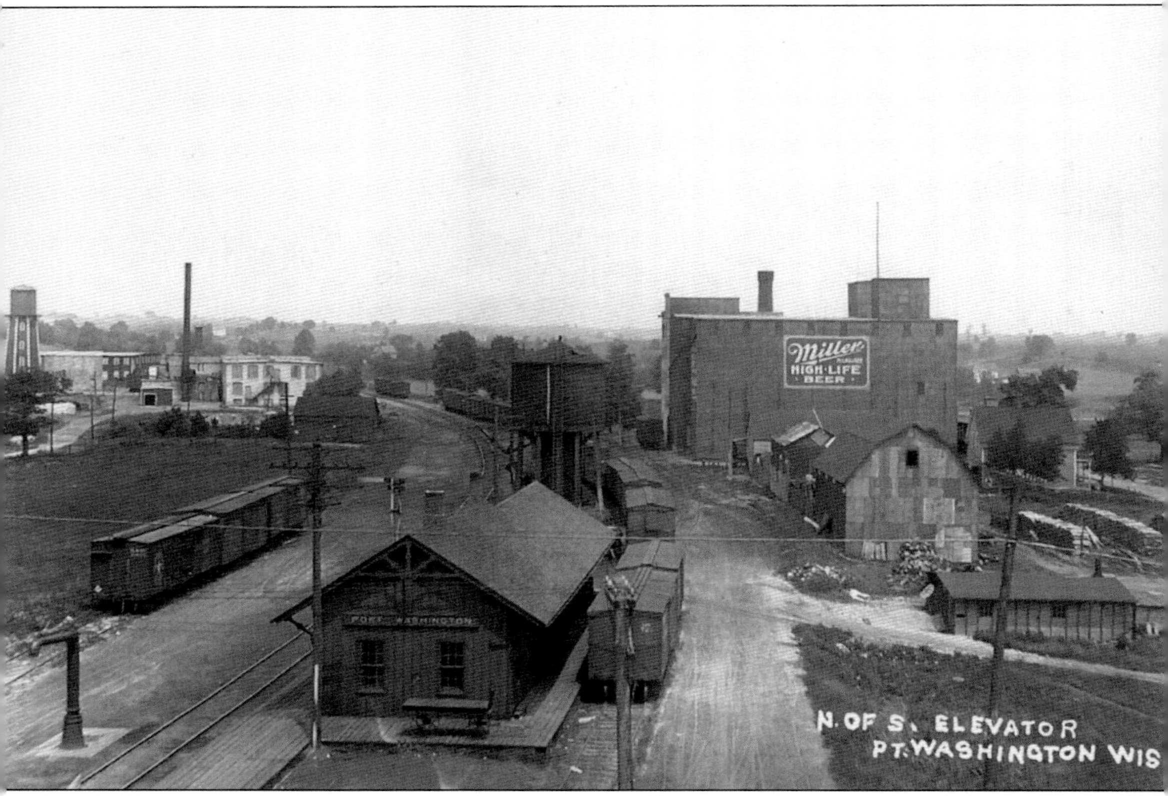

At one time, the railroad ran through the center of the town. The Milwaukee Northern, also known as The Milwaukee Northern Electric Railroad and Light, was the forerunner of the Wisconsin Electric and We Energies. It ran from Milwaukee to Sheboygan, passing through the center of Port Washington and many small towns along the way. The Chicago and North Western Railway ran along the west side and had spurs through town to the harbor. Today both are gone, but the Union Pacific still runs coal trains past Port Washington. As seen here, the Port Washington train depot and rail yard were once a very busy place. Note the number of rail sidings and the Port Washington Malt Company grain elevators in the background. All are gone except the brick buildings on the left. These were once the Milwaukee Glue Factory, Wisconsin Chair Company, and Simplicity Manufacturing. The little house at the left center is still standing.

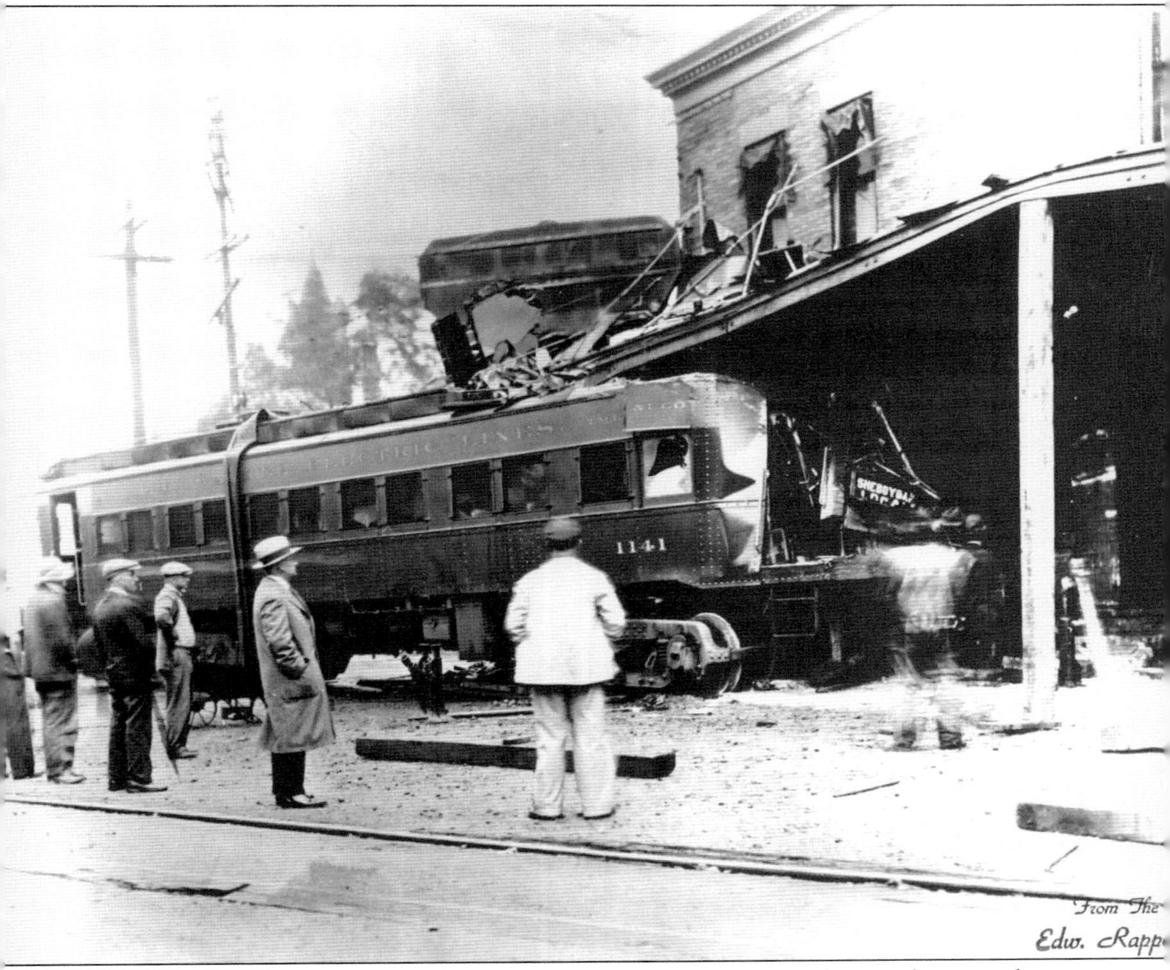

Sometimes days just do not go as planned. This 1930 postcard shows what can happen when an interurban motorman has a bad day. At one time, the tracks went right down the middle of the main street (now Franklin Street). Interurban car no. 1141, the "Sheboygan car" was going too fast and could not make the turn from Grand Avenue onto Franklin Street. It crashed into the Smith Brothers Fish Shanty Restaurant.

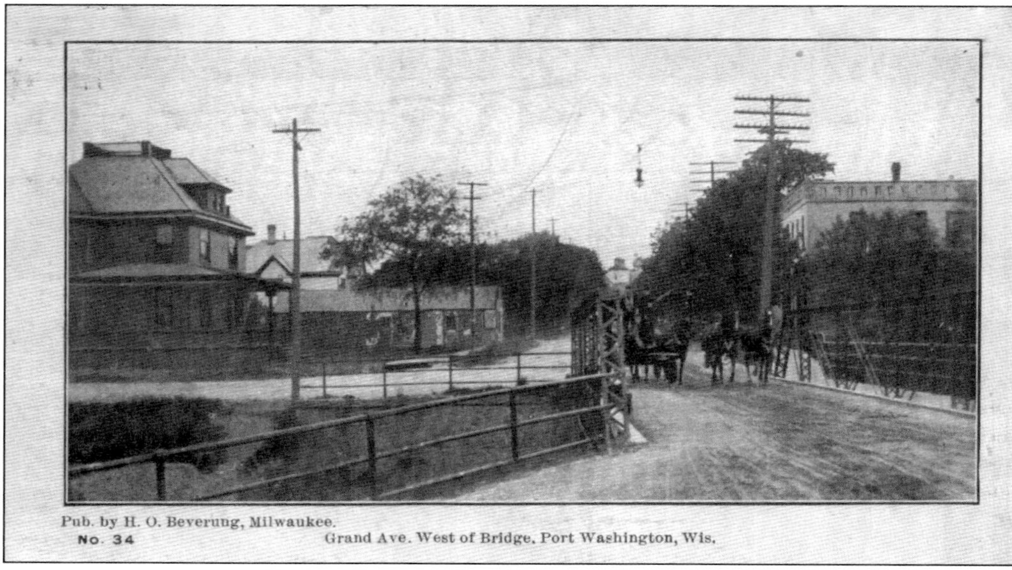

Before the advent of the automobile, horse-drawn buggies and carriages were a common sight crossing the Grand Avenue Bridge. Below, the same bridge is seen many years later with a young man waiting beneath the light post.

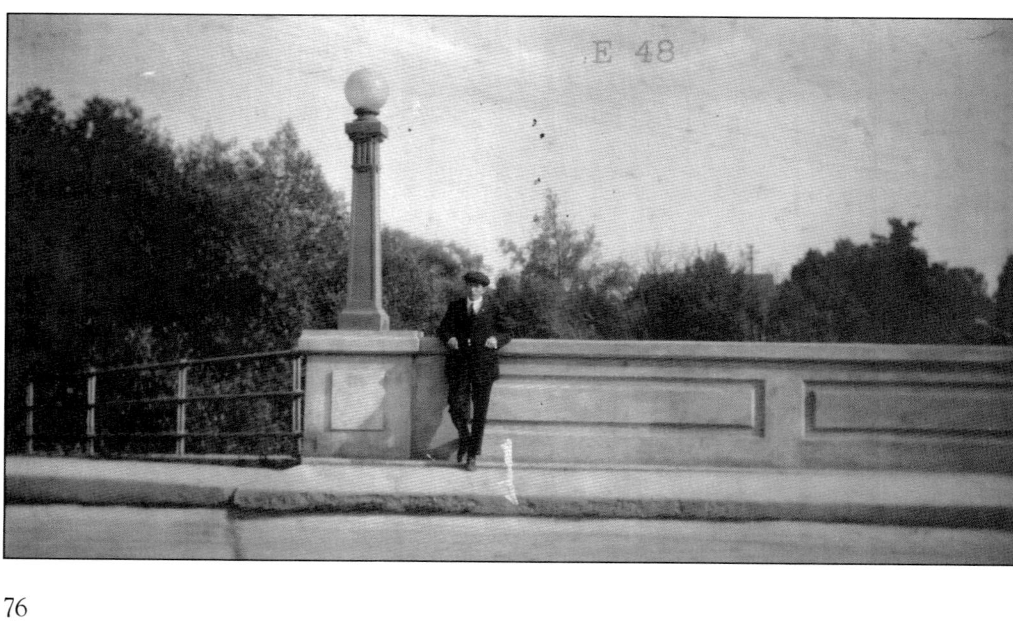

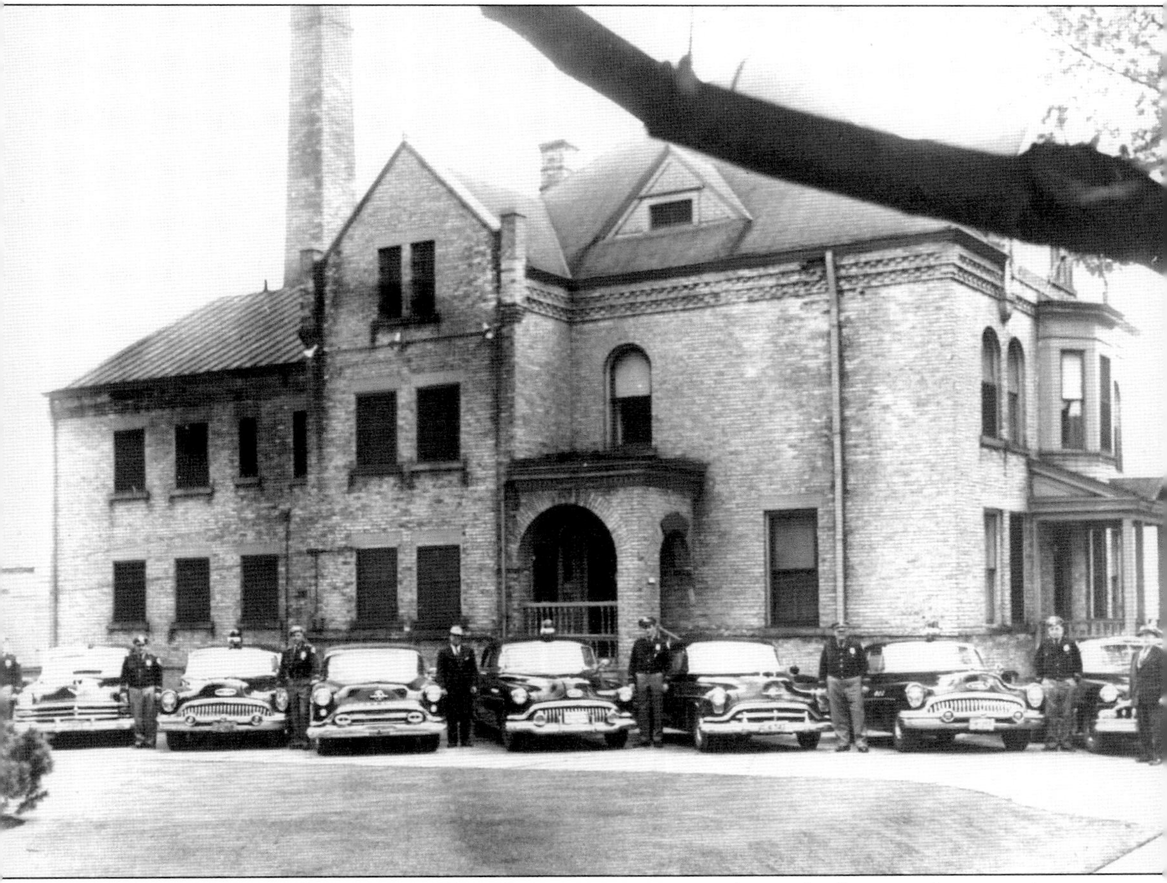

Members of the Ozaukee County Sheriff's Department pose alongside their spotless squad cars in front of the old jail on Main Street around 1950.

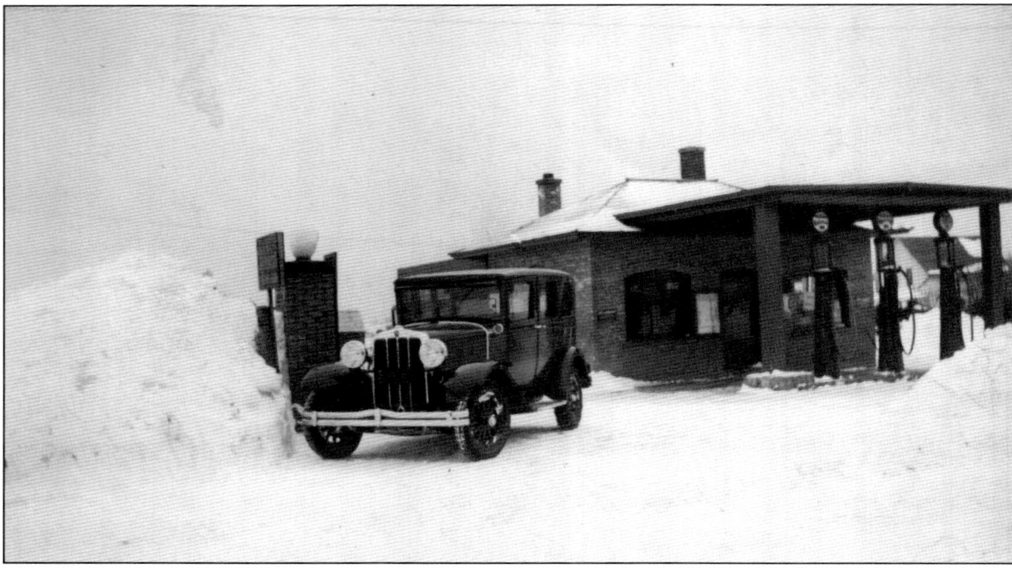

Here is Joseph Bruendl's DX Filling Station, open for business in the middle of winter. Joe rented it from his brother-in-law Otto Heiser.

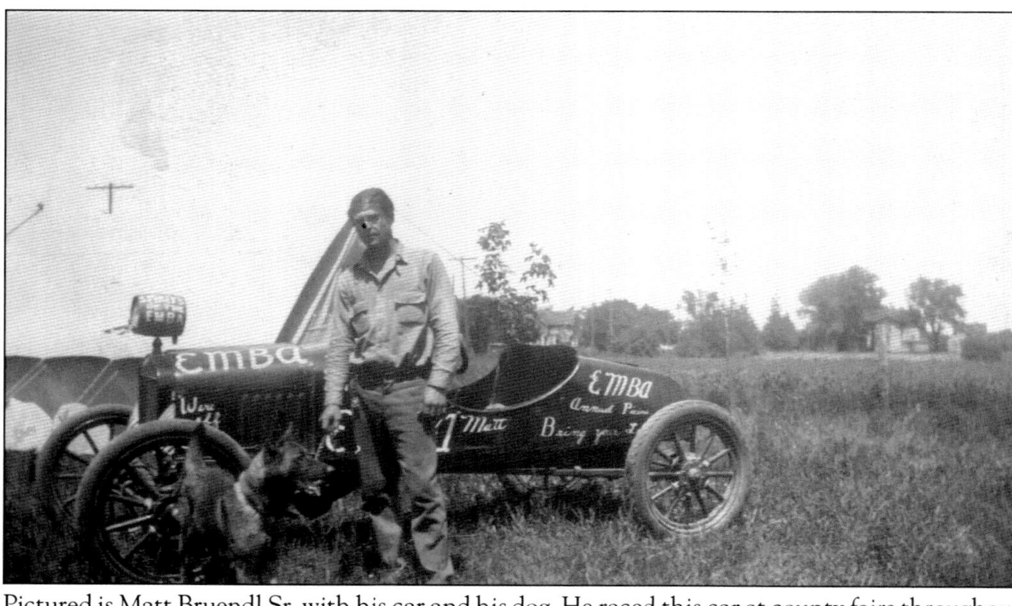

Pictured is Matt Bruendl Sr. with his car and his dog. He raced this car at county fairs throughout the state.

Seven

Schools, Churches, and Recreation

The core of any community is its schools, churches, and recreational activities. As times change, costs often dictate architecture and activities. In Port Washington, some have changed and some have remained the same.

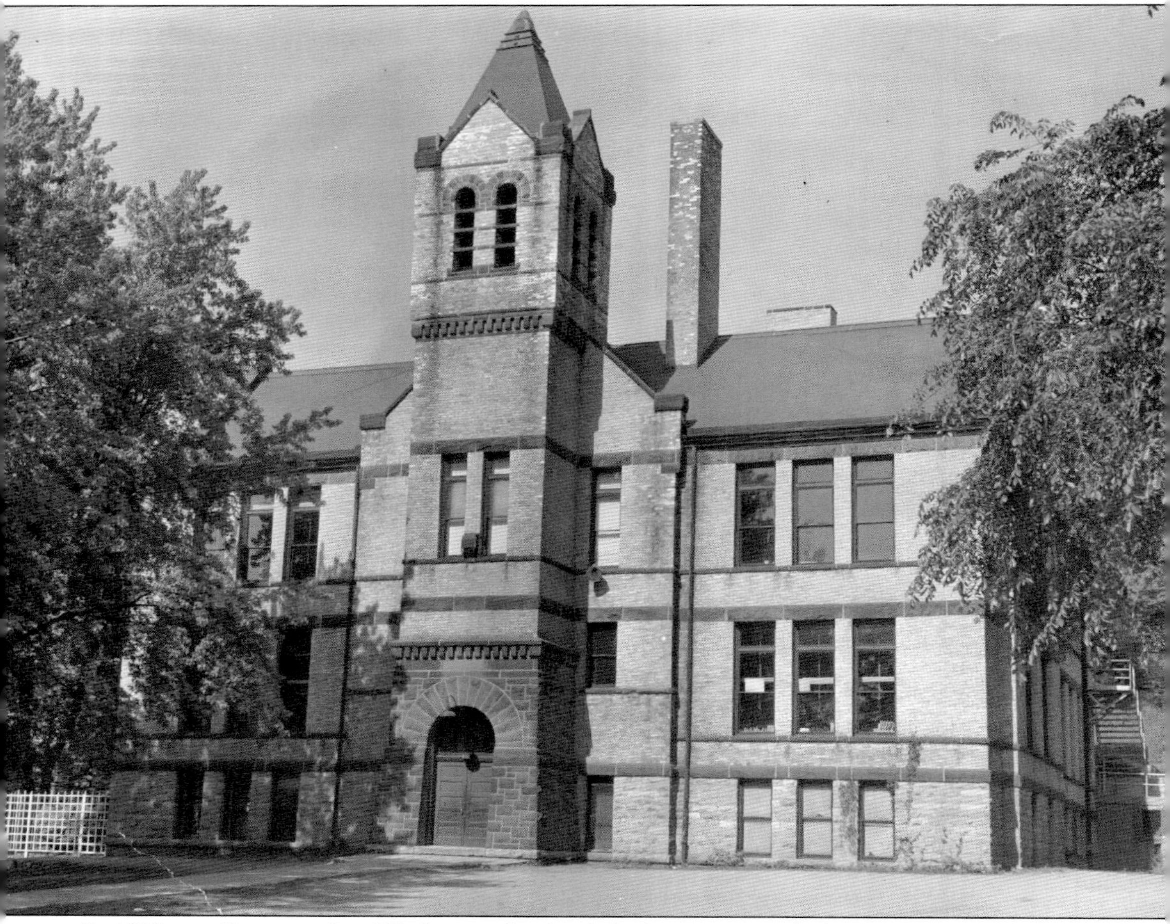

By 1893, enrollment in Port Washington's schools had grown enough that a new high school was needed. The previous 1881 school building across the street was used until the new structure was finished. In 1904, an addition was made. When the present high school was built in 1931, the old Wisconsin Street School was used as a vocational school. Sadly, like the Hill School, it also was destroyed in a fire in 1982. This site is the present location of the Port Washington police and fire departments. The Wisconsin Street School also served as the public library during the 1950s while the present public library on Grand Avenue was being constructed.

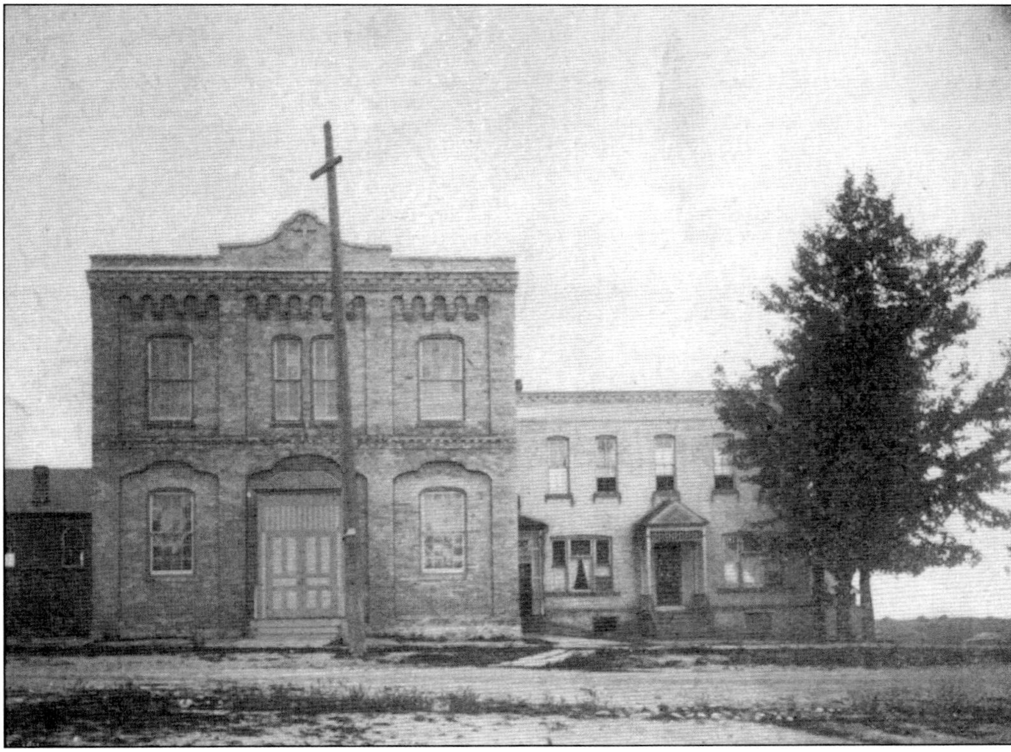

The first St. Mary's School was located on the site of the present-day school on what was then known as Lighthouse Hill.

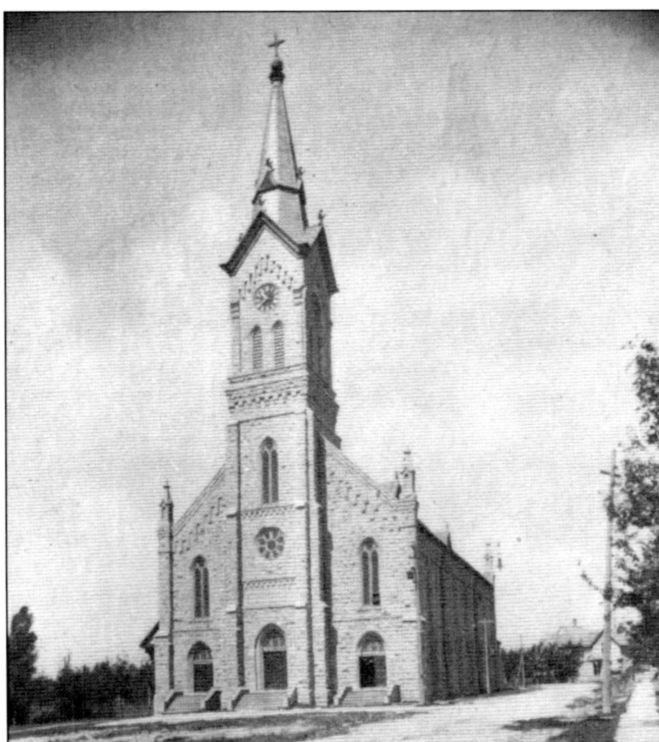

St. Mary's Catholic Church still dominates the view looking north up Franklin Street, but the parsonage has been replaced with a brick building.

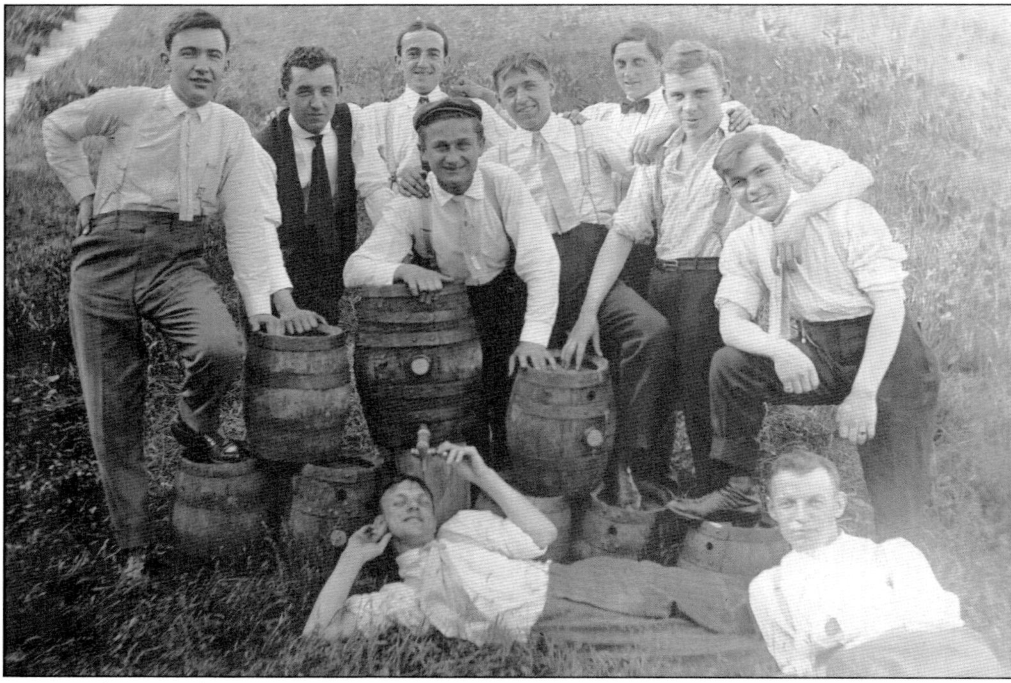

Port Washington breweries had many patrons. Here is a scene from a party at the foot of the bluff in the early 1900s.

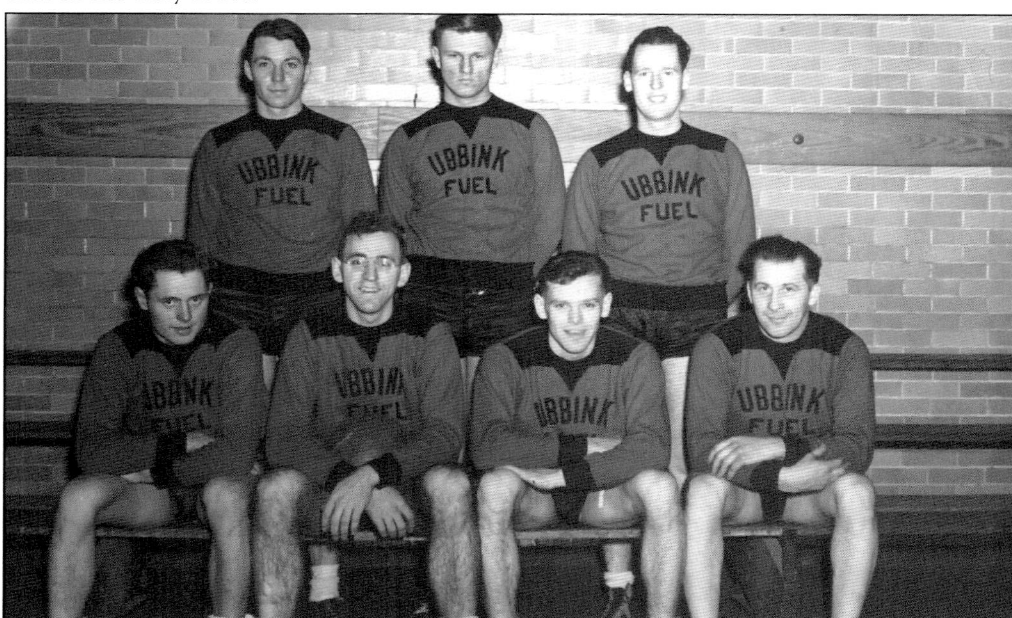

Port Washington once had a city basketball league. They originally played in the basement of the old opera house and shared the area with the police department and the U.S. Army Reserve. Pictured is the team, sponsored by Ubbink Fuel, that took second place. Players include, from left to right, (first row) Ray Schulz, Herb Bartelt, Herb Arendt, and Bert Liesch; (second row) Charles Wolf Jr., Art Miller, and Gene Merrill.

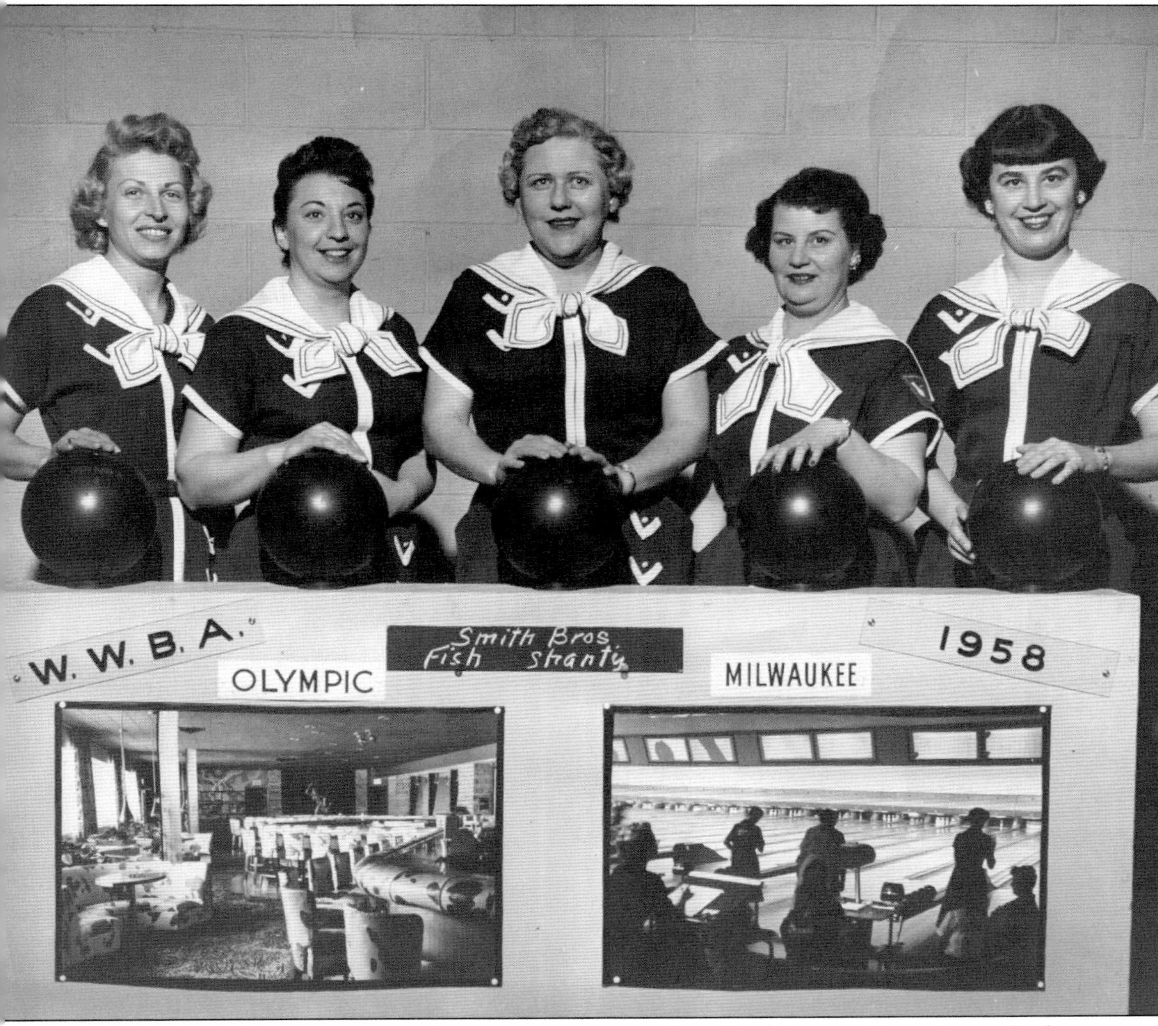

Bowling was a favorite sponsored sporting activity in Port Washington. From the early days, the gentlemen's club and a number of saloons had 10-pin alleys. By the 1940s and up through the 1960s, Port had two bowling alleys. This photograph is of a team sponsored by the Smith Brothers restaurant. Pictured are, from left to right, Lois Grunewald Swatek, unidentified, Esther Segermeister, Tillie Skruby Segermeister, and Dorothy Watry.

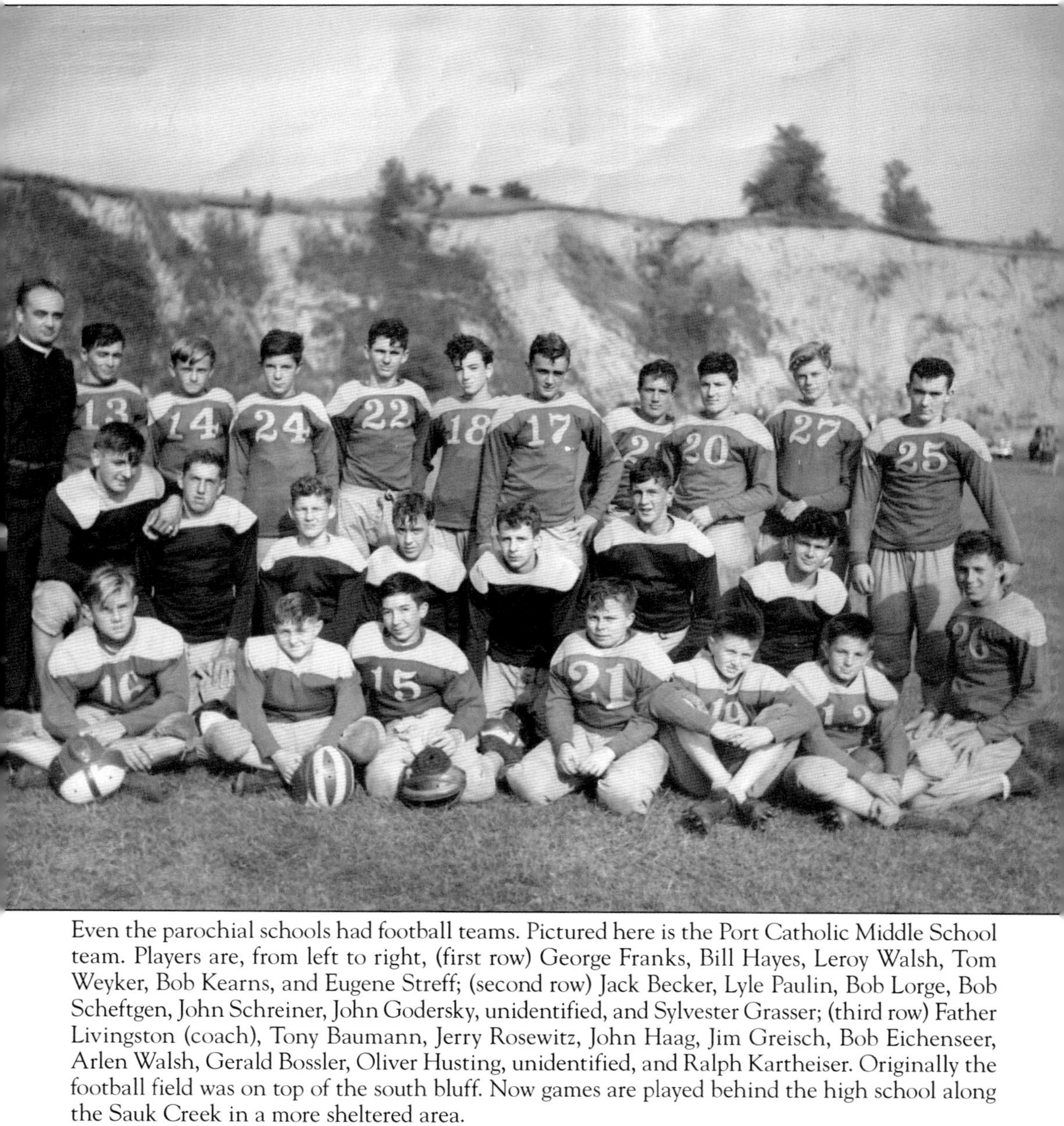

Even the parochial schools had football teams. Pictured here is the Port Catholic Middle School team. Players are, from left to right, (first row) George Franks, Bill Hayes, Leroy Walsh, Tom Weyker, Bob Kearns, and Eugene Streff; (second row) Jack Becker, Lyle Paulin, Bob Lorge, Bob Scheftgen, John Schreiner, John Godersky, unidentified, and Sylvester Grasser; (third row) Father Livingston (coach), Tony Baumann, Jerry Rosewitz, John Haag, Jim Greisch, Bob Eichenseer, Arlen Walsh, Gerald Bossler, Oliver Husting, unidentified, and Ralph Kartheiser. Originally the football field was on top of the south bluff. Now games are played behind the high school along the Sauk Creek in a more sheltered area.

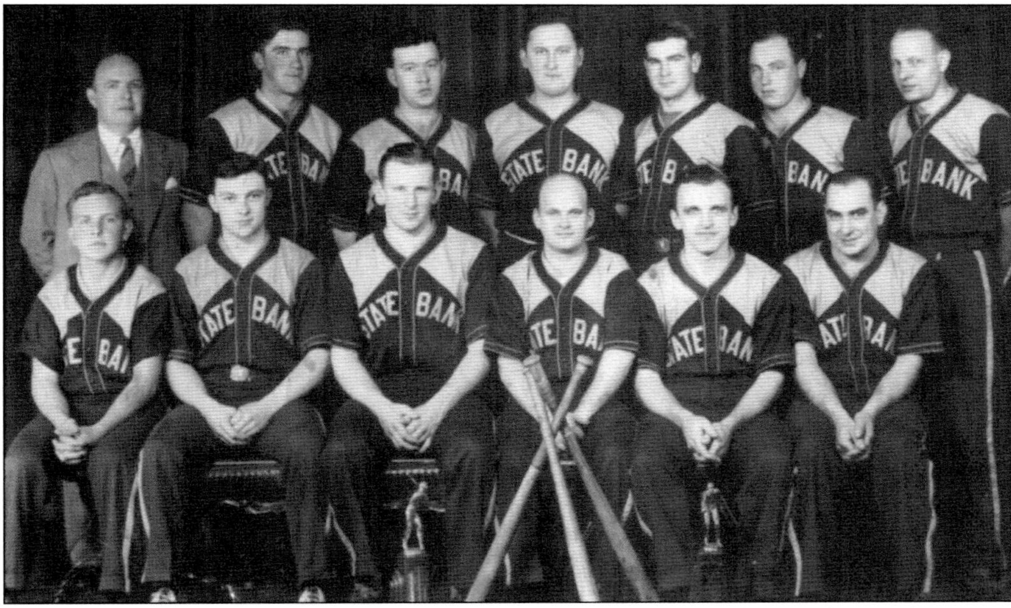

The Port Washington State Bank softball team of 1940 was not only the city champs, but it went on to win the second place trophy in the Wisconsin class B tournament. Shown in this photograph are, from left to right, (first row) bat boy Joe Tomazitis, Carl E. Gall, Orville Bathke, Jim Fowler, Frank Quader, and Fary Sauer; (second row) team sponsor C. Donald Hill, Oscar Dommer, Fritz Mangel, Joe Grotelueschen, Pete Yankunas, Ed "Wimpy" Rinn, and "Chibby" Lecher.

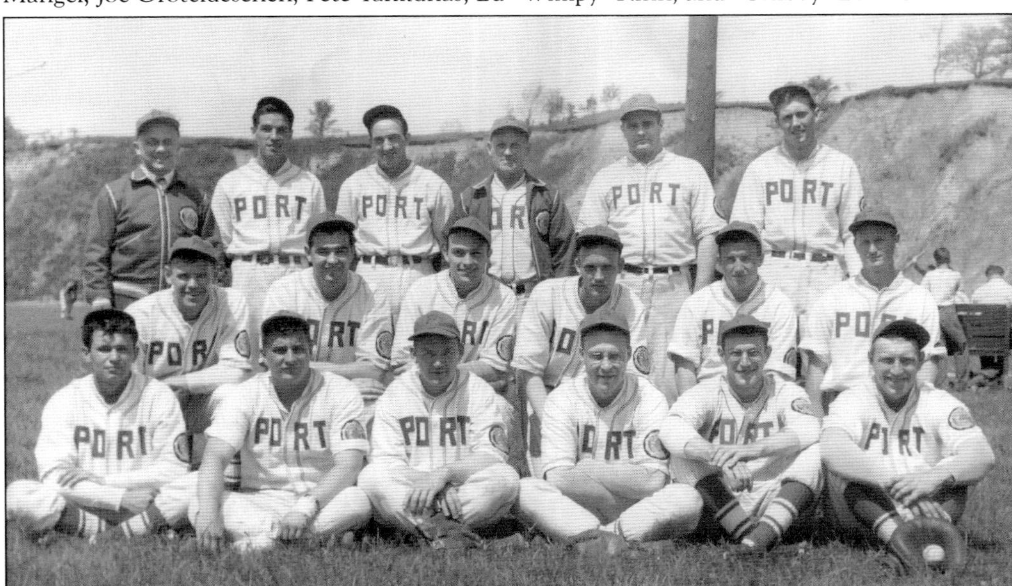

Port Washington has had baseball teams since the 1880s. This photograph is of the Port Lakers in the late 1940s. Pictured are, from left to right, (first row) Bill Weinrich, Jerry Graves, Nick Decker ?, Jerry Norman, Paul Godersky, and Elmer Godersky; (second row) Charlie Wolf, Wally Sauer, Carl Gall, Harold "Skinny" May, unidentified, and Rex Foster; (third row) coach Fred "Prof" Altendorf, Warren Haseley, unidentified, Matt Biever, Paul Schmit, and Ken Beer.

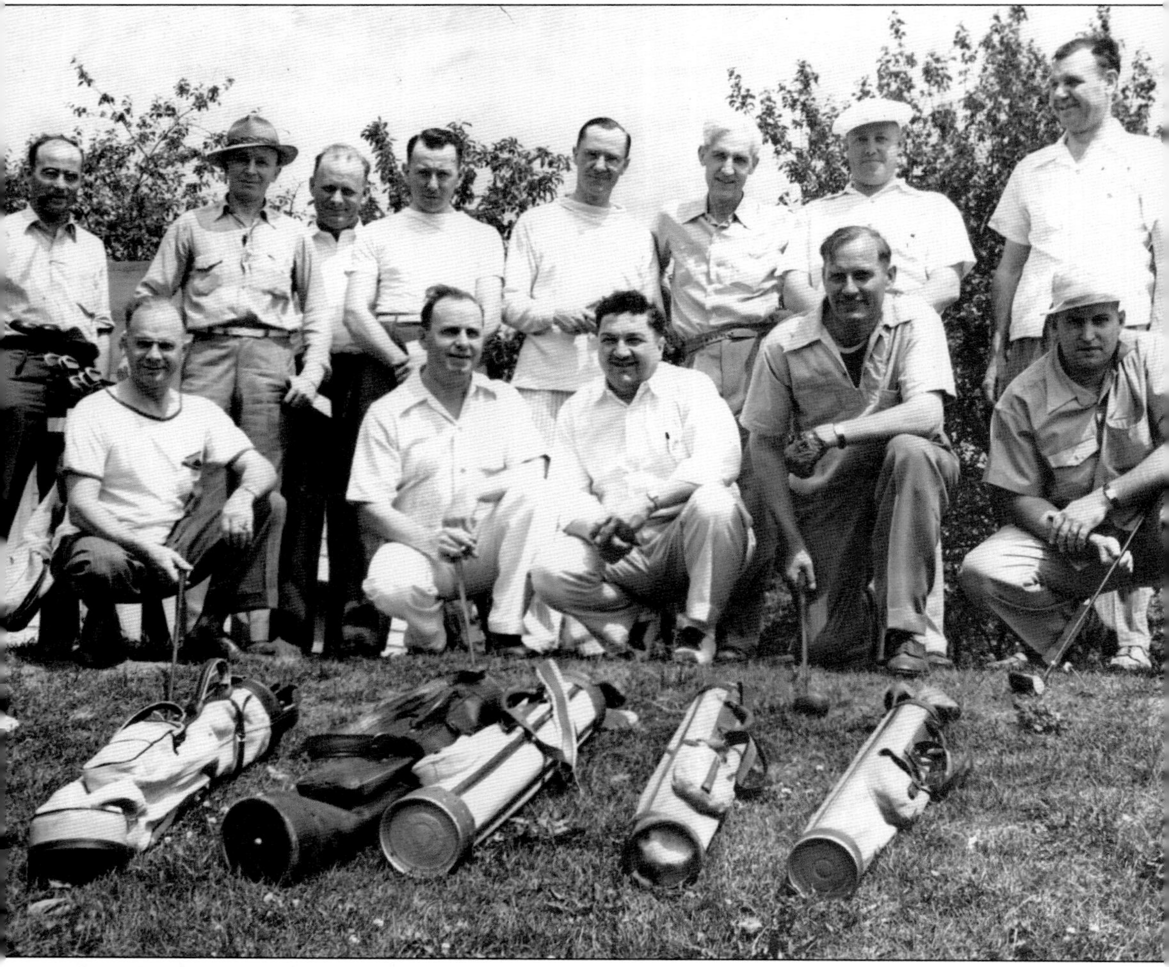

Port Washington also had a golf team in the 1940s and 1950s. Only two gentlemen in this photograph have been identified: standing, third from right, is Dr. Earl Huwatchek; and kneeling, center, is Vince Biever.

Eight

Living in Port Washington

Port Washington, one of the oldest cities in the state of Wisconsin, has a mix of architectural styles to its buildings. Many of the buildings in downtown were constructed prior to the Civil War. Other buildings were constructed over the remains of the original 1830–1840 structures, around the harbor area, and show a distinctive German-Luxembourg influence. The houses vary from a Japanese craftsman-style to East Coast Cape Cods, ranches, Greek Revival, Queen Anne, and Victorian. It is this array that gives the city part of its charm. The town has gone through many changes. Businesses have come and gone and so have people, but the town remains. This chapter gives a view of residential living in Port Washington.

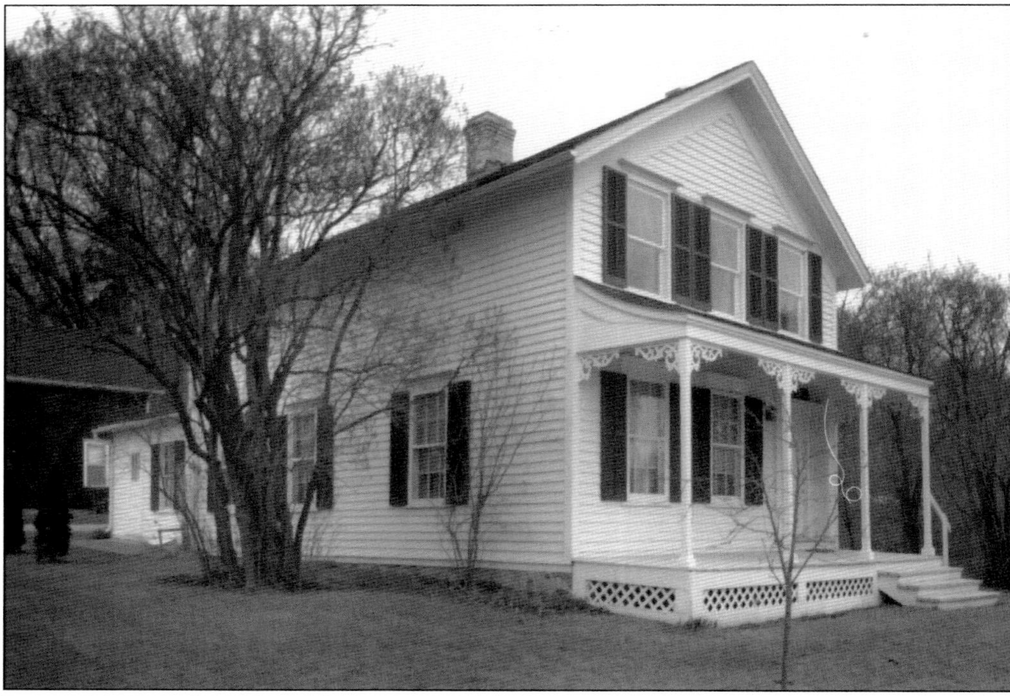

Pictured here is the Judge Eghart House located at 302 West Grand Avenue. This Victorian cottage was designed and built by Louis Teed for his brother Byron in 1872. Purchased in 1881 by Judge Leopold Eghart, it was continuously owned and occupied by his family until the death of his daughter Elisa in 1969. Restored through a donation by William J. Niederkorn, the cottage is furnished with Victorian antiques provided by local families and is maintained by a group of citizens who hold it open for tour on Sundays from mid-May to October.

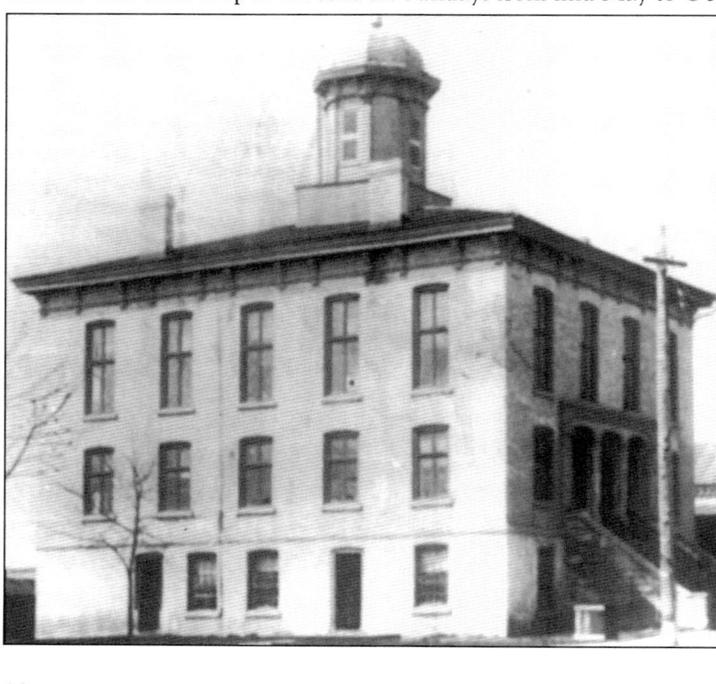

Port Washington County Courthouse is seen here around 1895. The first courthouse was built in 1854 on the southeast corner of Wisconsin and Main Streets. It was replaced with the present, grander Ozaukee County Courthouse in 1902. The jail, stable, and sheriff's home are to the right in the background. When it was no longer of sufficient size and in need of major repair, the building was demolished and a larger, more modern structure was erected.

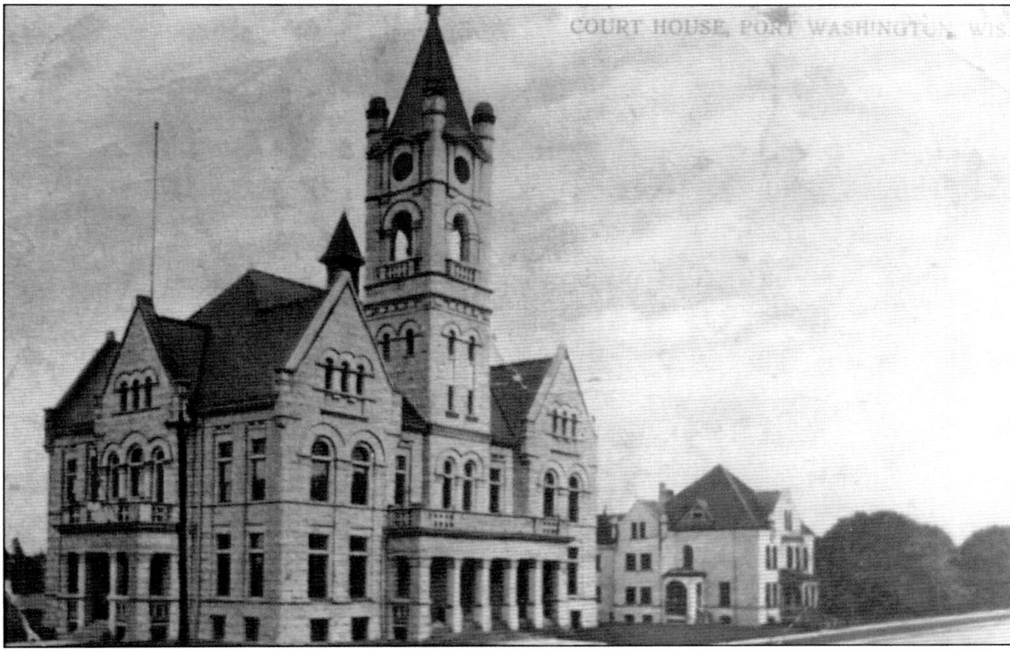

Shown here is the Ozaukee County Courthouse in the early 1900s. Located at 109 West Main Street, it was constructed in 1901 of rock-faced limestone from the Cedarburg Quarry. The clock tower is topped by a gold-leaved eagle that reflects the sun, providing a landmark to sailors approaching Port Washington's harbor. The older portion is on the National Register of Historic Places. Over the past five years, the courtroom has been restored through major fund-raising to its original art nouveau and art deco appearance.

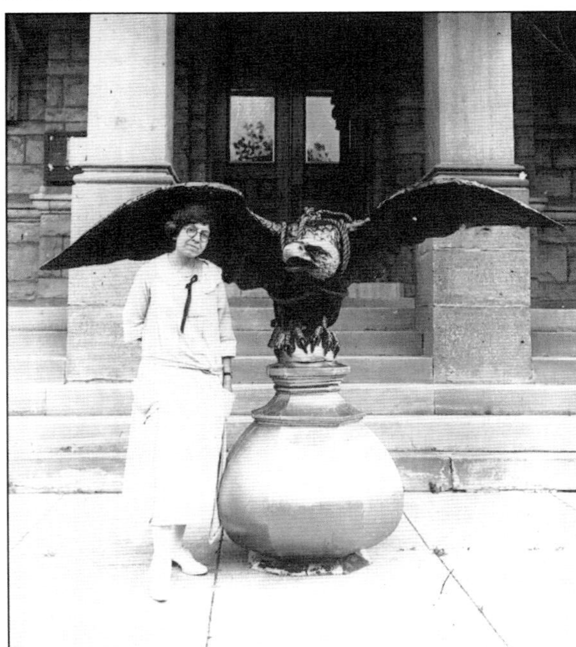

Lightning struck and damaged the courthouse eagle in the 1950s. It fell off, but was repaired, realigned, and replaced on the bell tower.

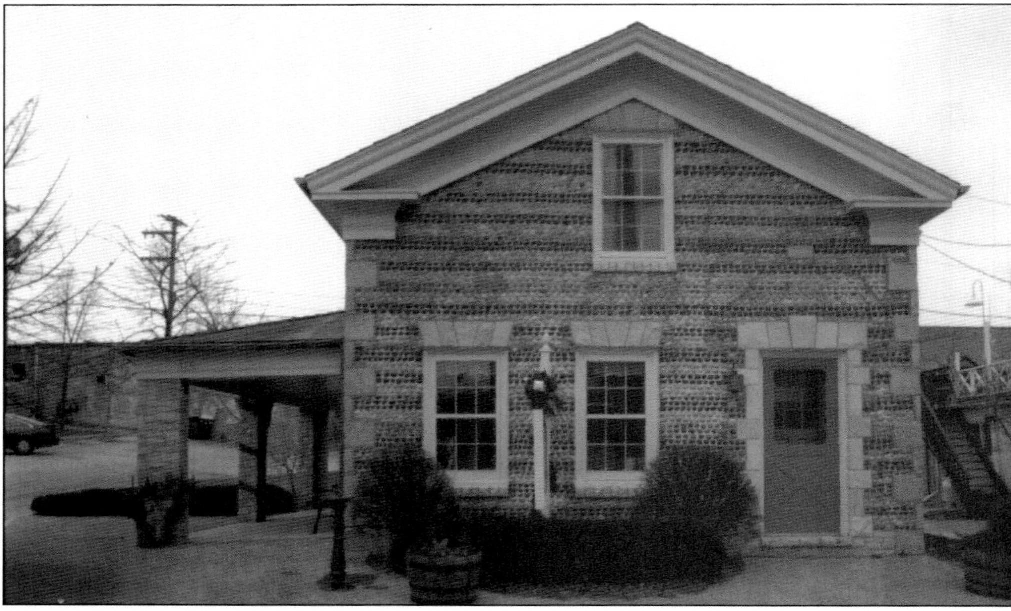

Photographed here is Dodge House (now called Pebble House) at 126 East Grand Avenue; it is one of the oldest, if not the oldest, residences in Port Washington. It was built in 1848 on the south bank of Sauk Creek by a blacksmith named Edward Dodge. He and his wife collected stones from the Lake Michigan beach to make up this unique exterior. The house was moved to its present site in 1985 where it serves as the visitor information center and the chamber of commerce office.

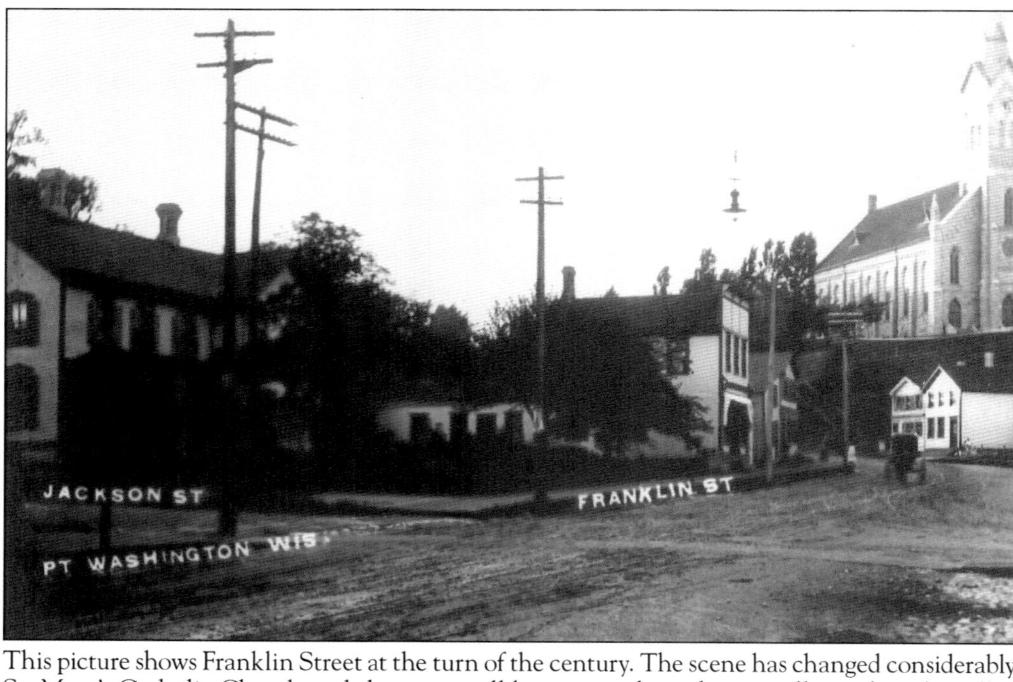

This picture shows Franklin Street at the turn of the century. The scene has changed considerably. St. Mary's Catholic Church and the two small houses on the right are still standing, but all of the houses on the left are gone, as is the horse and buggy and dirt road.

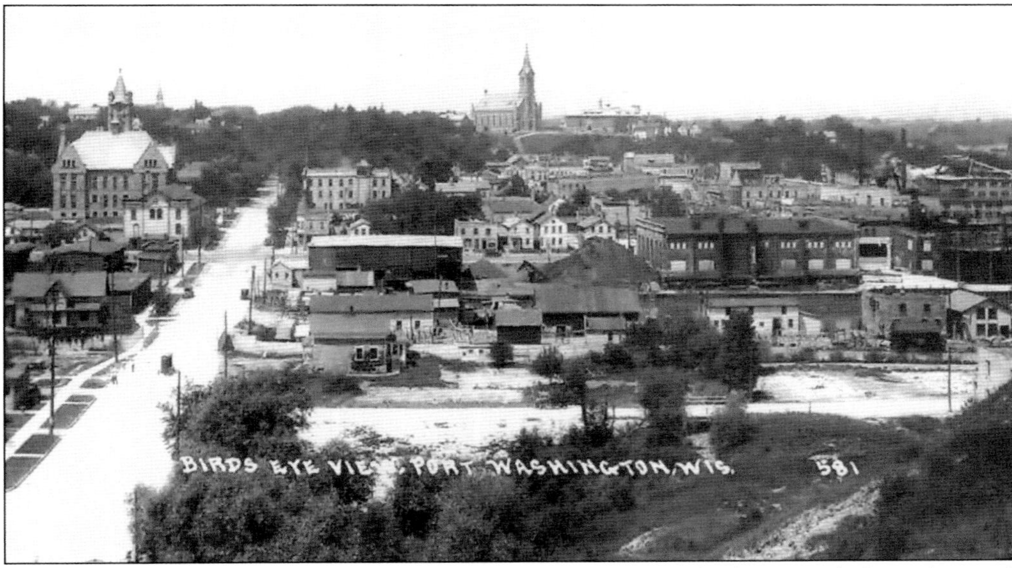

This photograph from the early 1900s shows Port Washington looking north from the south bluff. On the left can be seen the opera house just in front of the newly built courthouse. At the upper center is St. Mary's Catholic Church and School. Ubbink Coal and Dock, the interurban car barn, and the power plant can be seen in the center forefront. This site is now occupied by the Holiday Inn Harborview.

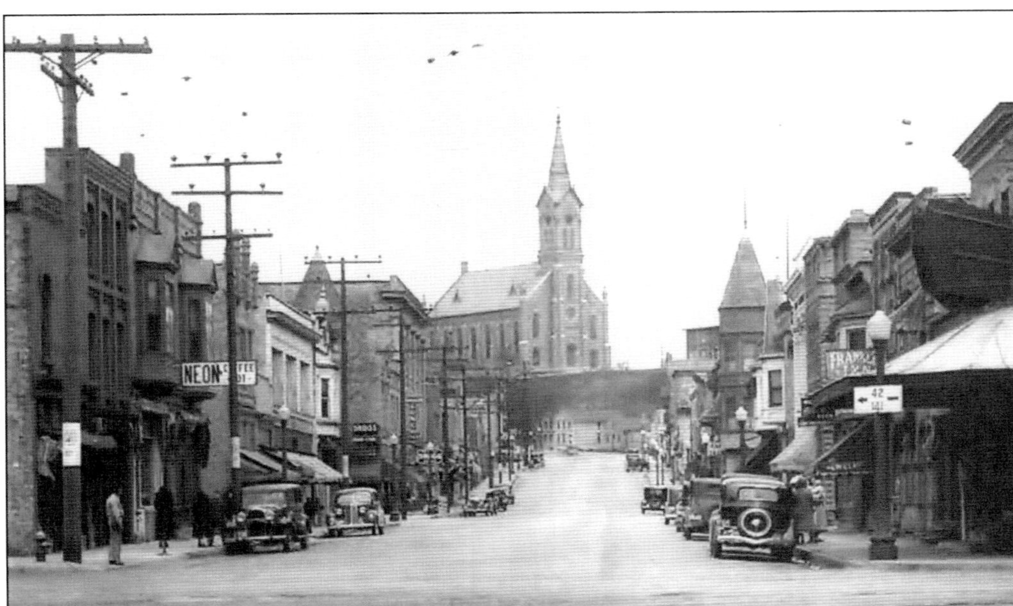

This is a view of Port Washington's other main road, Franklin Street, facing north. Franklin Street becomes Wisconsin Street when going north up the hill past St. Mary's Catholic Church. The church, constructed in 1882, was dedicated in 1884. Note the variety of architecture. At one time, Port Washington had more antebellum buildings than any other city in the state.

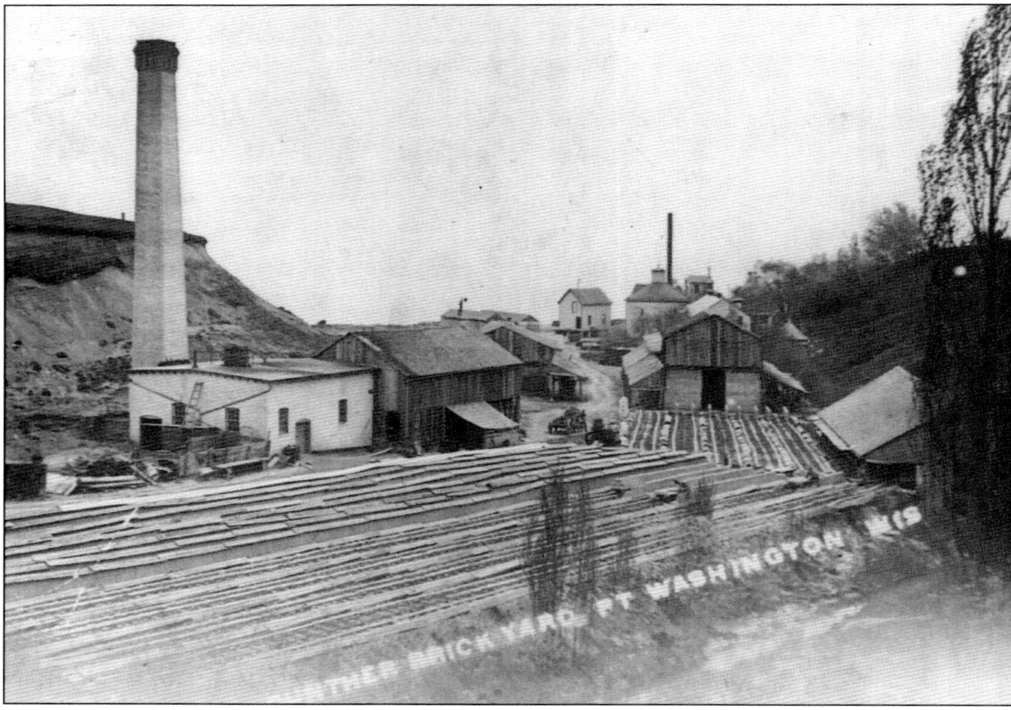

This northeast side of Port Washington was the site of the Guenther brickyard, where much of the cream city brick used in building homes in the area was produced.

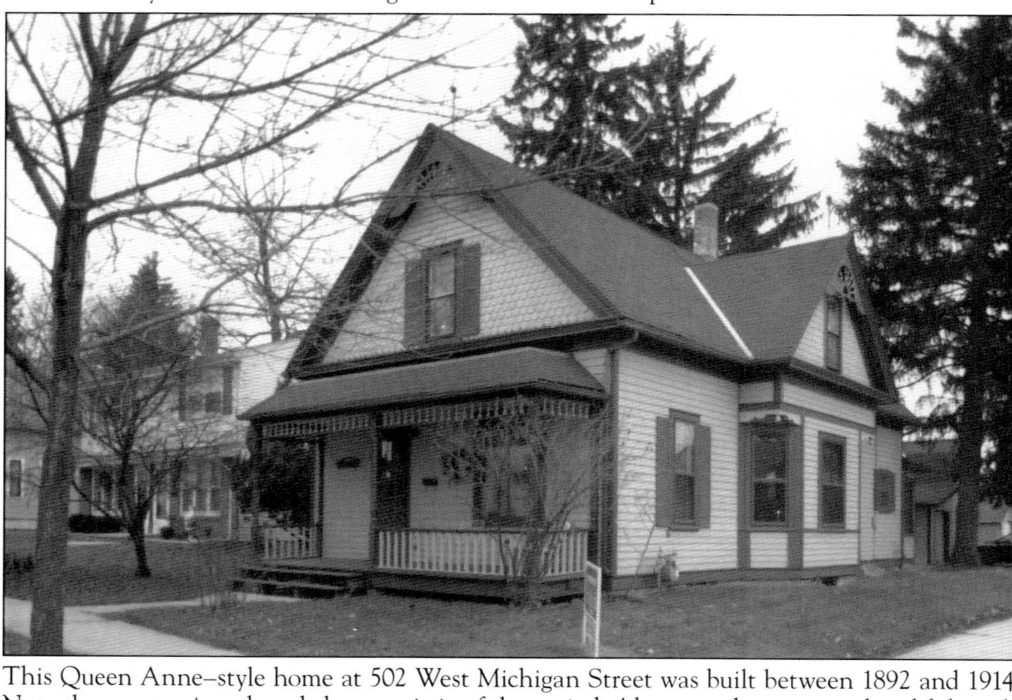

This Queen Anne–style home at 502 West Michigan Street was built between 1892 and 1914. Note the ornate gingerbread characteristic of the period. Also note the octagonal and fish scale shingles on the gables.

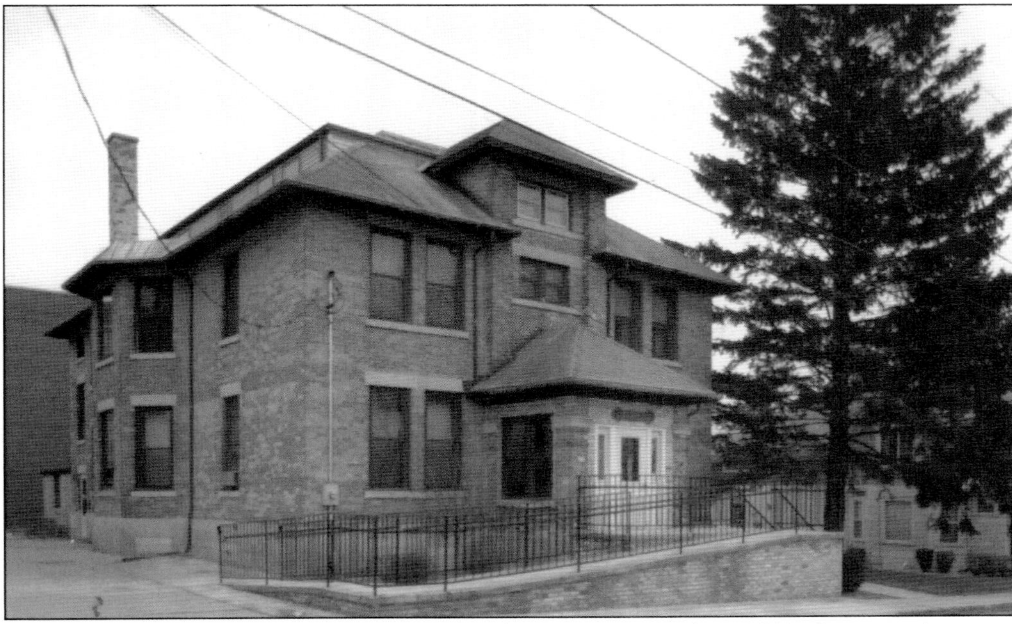

St. Mary's Convent is located at 430 North Johnson Street. Built in 1911, this is an American Foursquare–style building constructed with cream city brick. Now the St. Mary's Catholic Church Parish Center, it served as the convent for the School Sisters of Notre Dame, who taught at St. Mary's School.

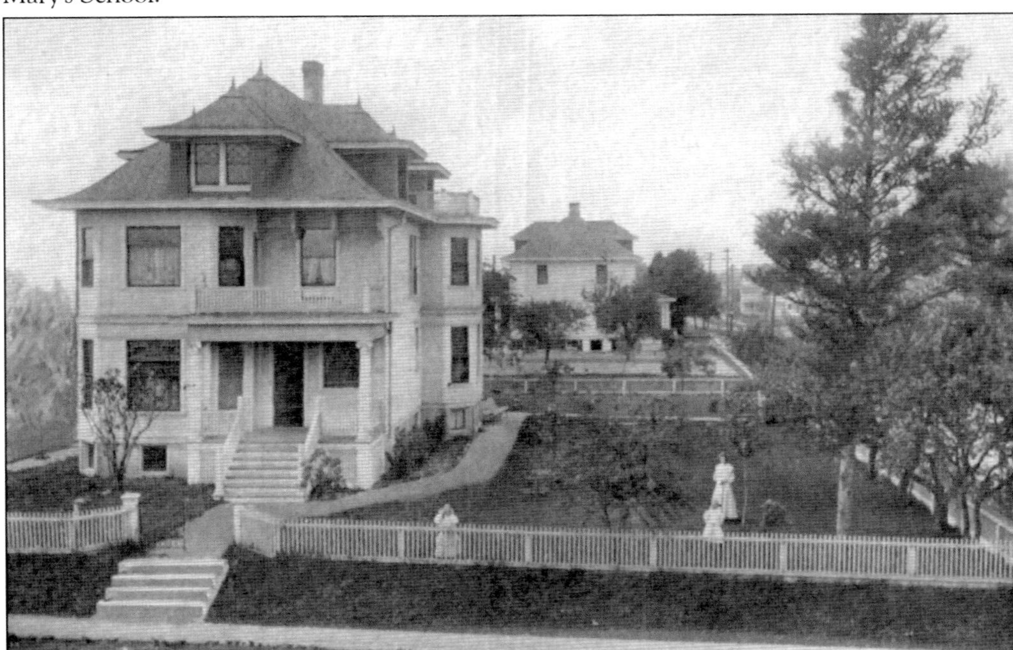

The George Blessing home at 308 West Washington Street and the home in the background still exist. Note the long dresses. Either it was a Sunday when this picture was taken, or the family members dressed up in their Victorian finery for this 1901 picture. The home is now the Port Washington Inn Bed and Breakfast.

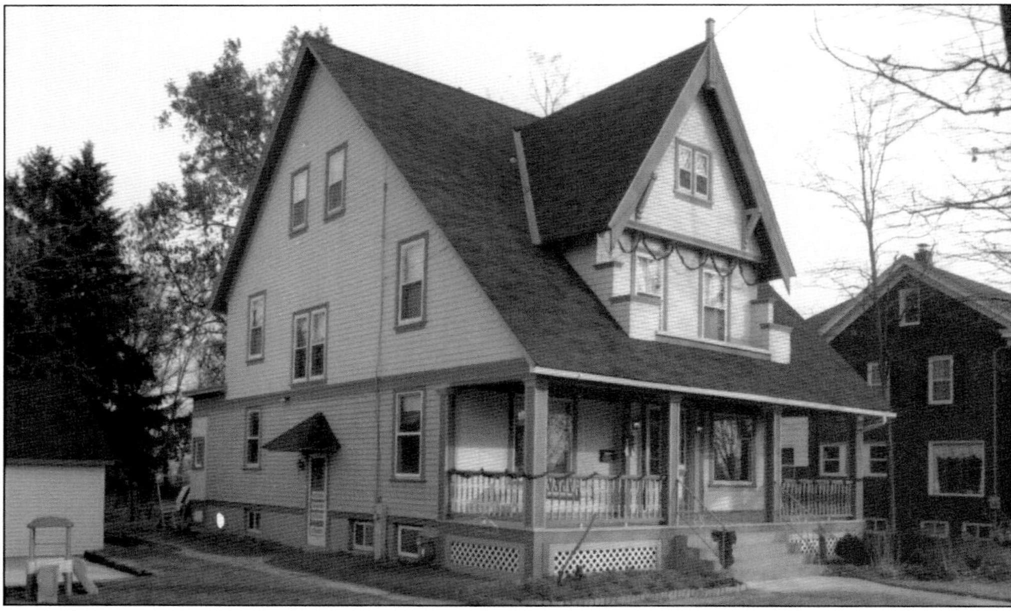

Grand Avenue was a quiet, tree-lined street, considered the elite place for a residence in the late 1800s and into the mid-1900s. This neighborhood was once "the neighborhood" in which to reside and was known as the "400 Club." It was fashionable to sit on your front porch and converse with passersby. Though still a beautiful neighborhood with the same stately homes, the advent of automobiles and semi-trucks changed this street, which is State Highway 33, and it is no longer the quiet thoroughfare of long ago. The above photograph is of the home that was built for Henry C. Boerner, whose family owned department stores in Port Washington, Cedarburg, and Milwaukee. This Queen Anne–style home located at 916 West Grand Avenue was built in 1901. It has a classic high-peaked roof, which sheds snow quite nicely.

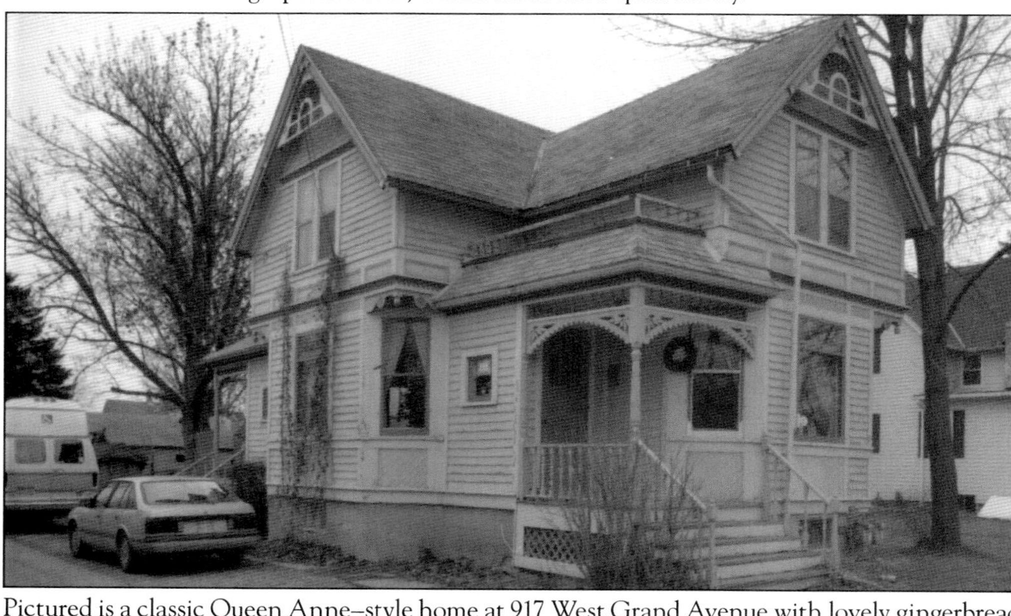

Pictured is a classic Queen Anne–style home at 917 West Grand Avenue with lovely gingerbread accents. Built prior to 1914, it has recently been restored.

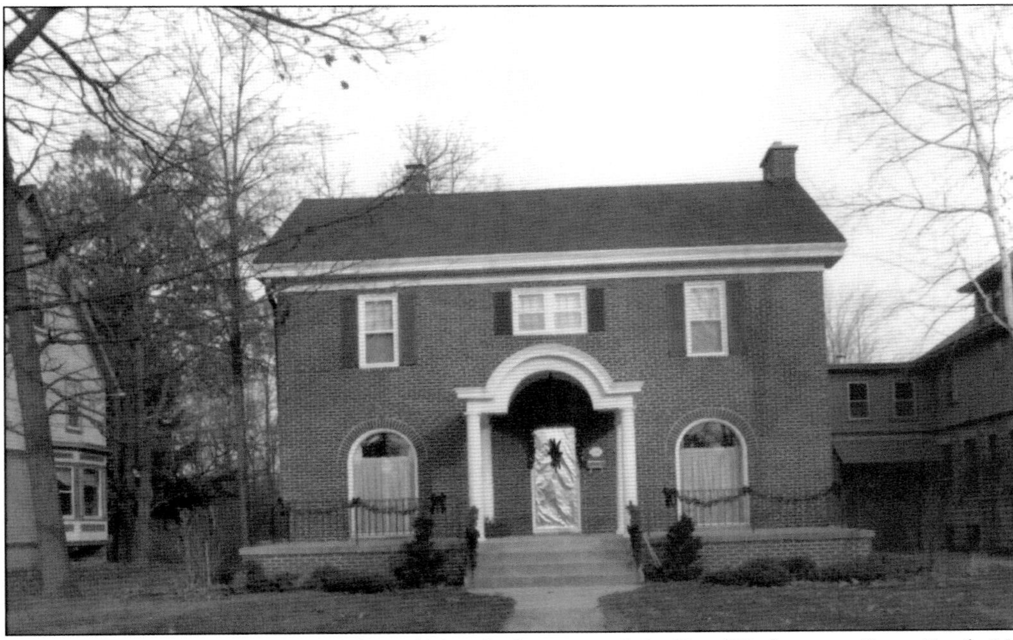

C. Donald Hill was a member of the Hill family that started the Port Washington State Bank. He owned this Georgian Revival home built at 908 West Grand Avenue in 1924, next to Clarence Hill's home. At one time, their residences actually shared water and heating oil. Judge Warren Grady later lived in this home.

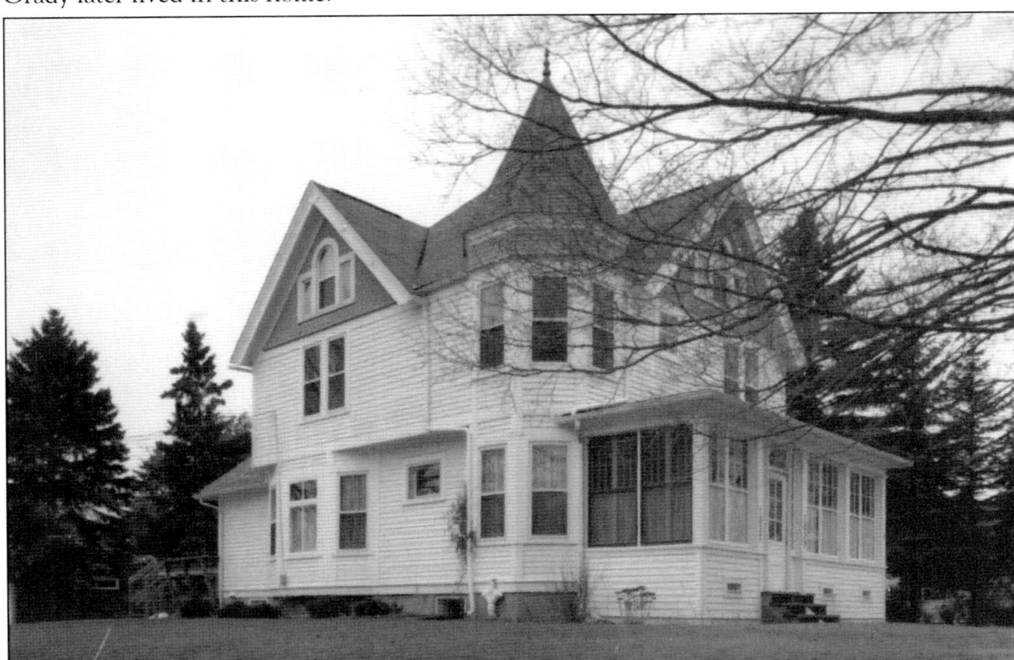

The address of another stately Queen Anne–style home is 1037 West Grand Avenue. It has stucco-clad foundation and wood shingle siding in gable ends. It was built before 1922, according to historic maps.

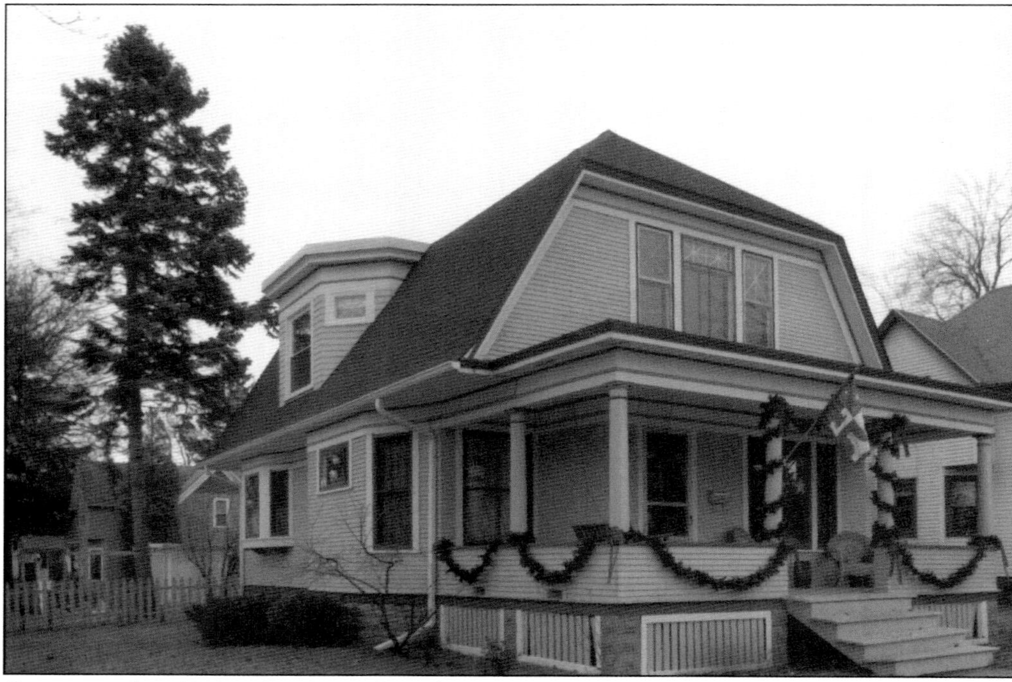

Constructed in 1893 at 741 West Grand Avenue, this modified Queen Anne–style house is a good example of a truncated turret.

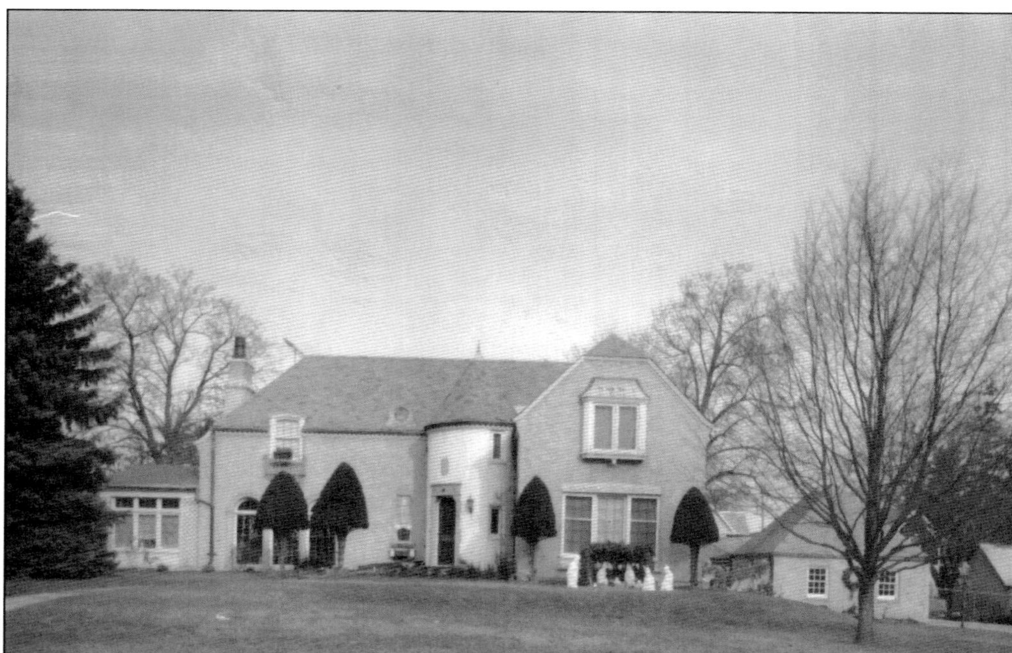

This elegant French Provincial–style structure at 746 West Grand Avenue was built in 1928 for lawyer William F. Schanen, founder of the *Ozaukee Press*, which is still owned and published by his descendants. It is the only example of the French Provincial style in Port Washington.

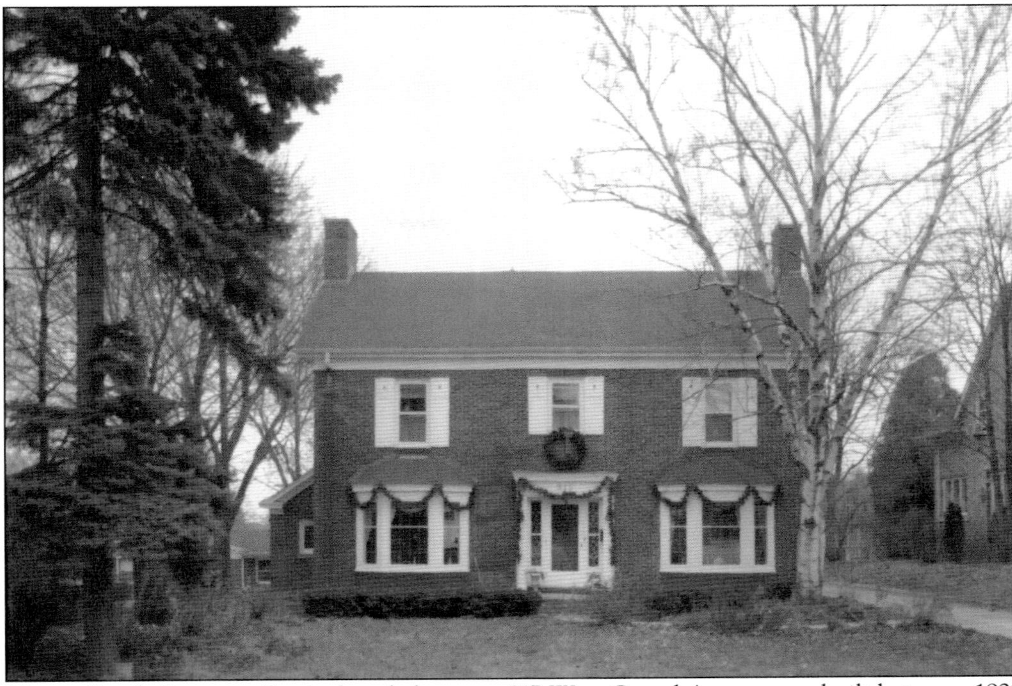

This redbrick Georgian Revival–style home at 817 West Grand Avenue was built between 1922 and 1938.

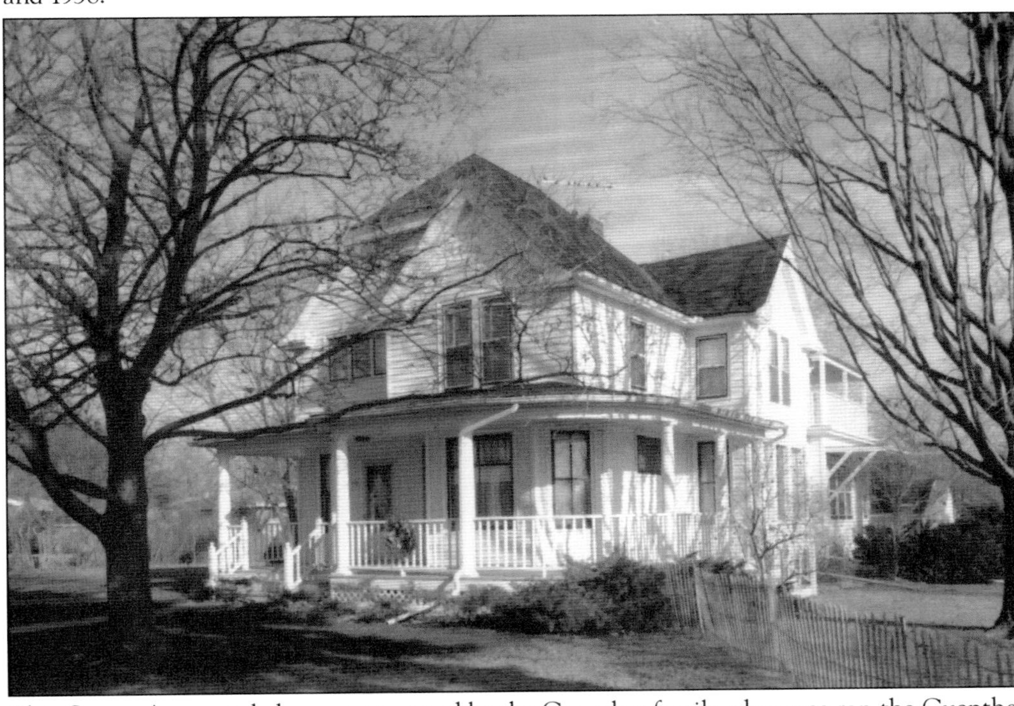

This Queen Anne–style house was owned by the Guenther family who once ran the Guenther brickyard. It was moved to 502 North Holden Street when its previous location was planned for new construction.

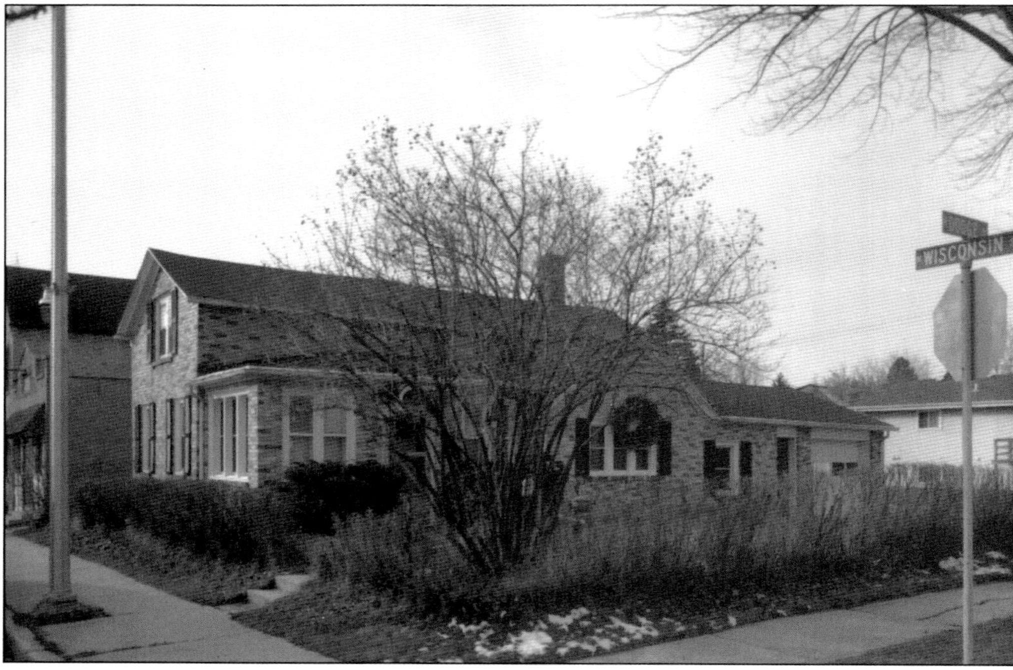

Originally built prior to 1883, this gabled, all-cream city brick home is just at the crest of the hill next to what was once a small grocery store run by ex-harbor master John "Jumbo" Freese. He not only aided the ships that came and went, but provided supplies to their crews.

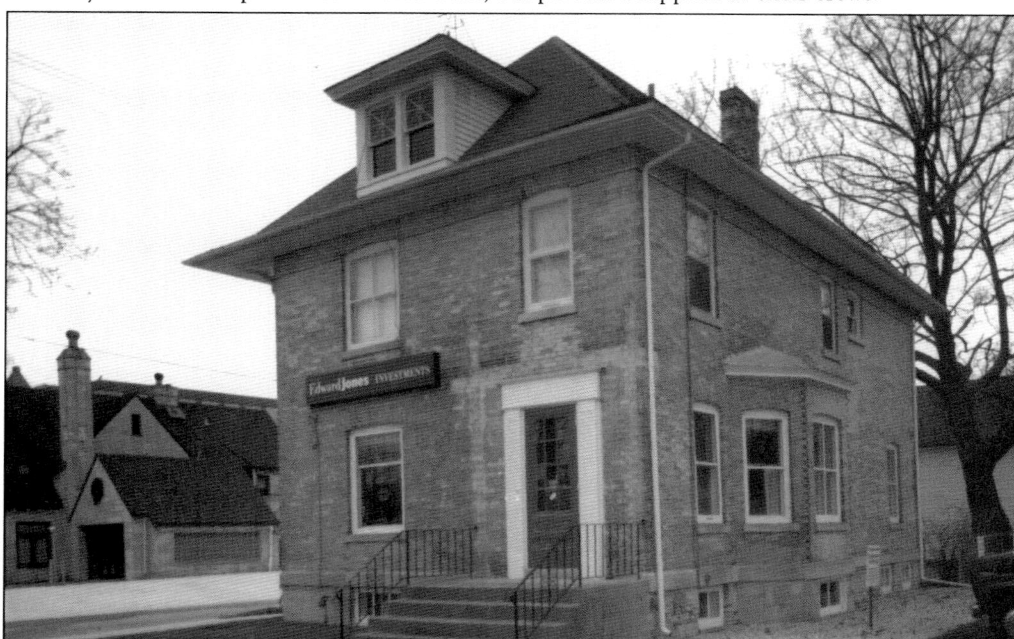

At the turn of the century, it was fashionable to live downtown next to a person's own place of business. This was once the home of the Runkel family of lawyers. Today it is an investment office located at 213 North Wisconsin Street.

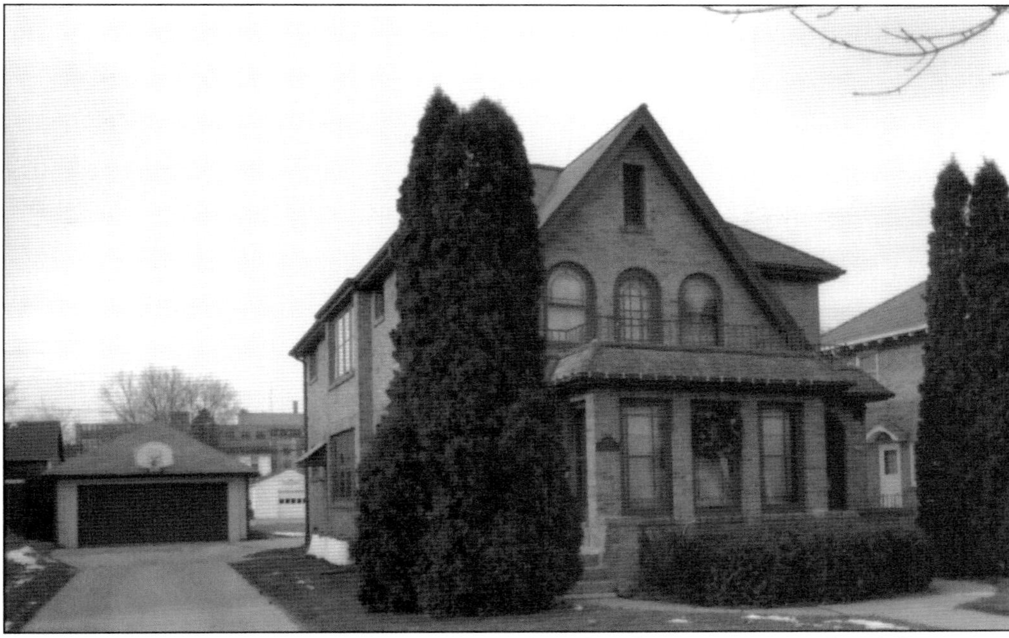

During the 1930s and the Great Depression, a number of Mediterranean Revival–style homes were built in Port Washington. Many were constructed as duplexes to either provide extra income or house extended family. This craftsman-influenced, Mediterranean-style duplex at 733–735 North Wisconsin Street was built in 1931.

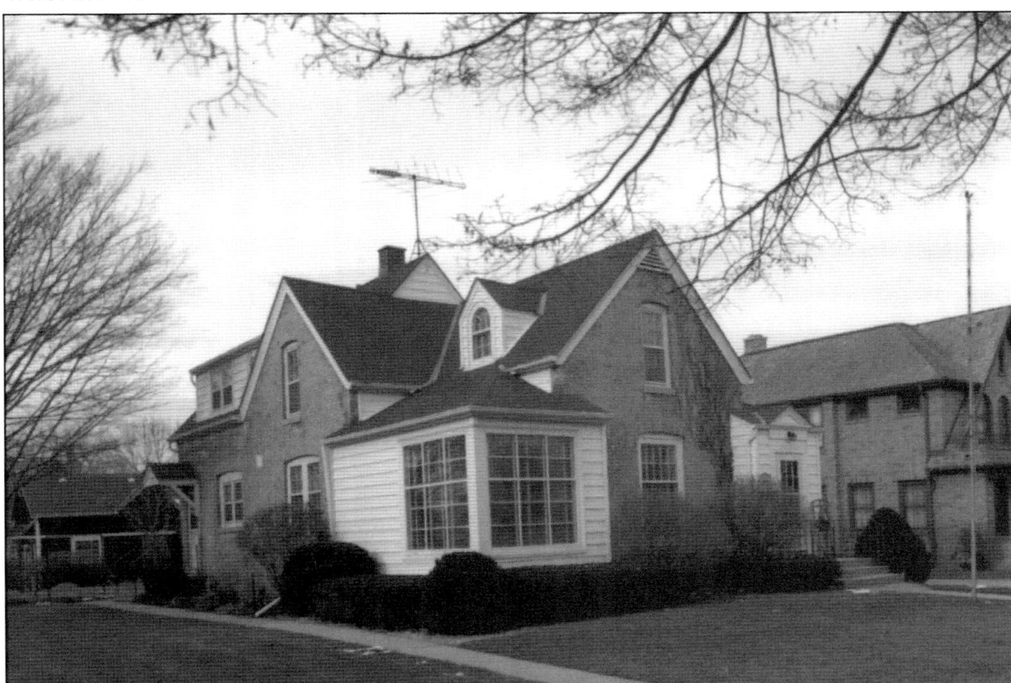

This lovely, cream city brick home at 727 North Milwaukee Street was built prior to 1914 and later modernized with Colonial Revival–style additions.

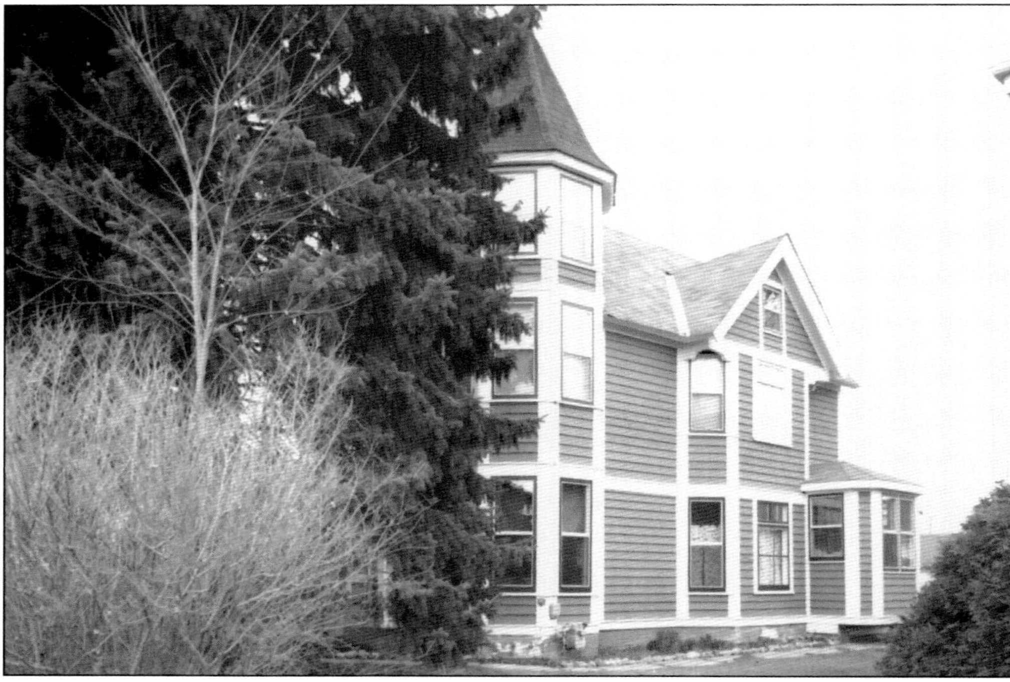

This Queen Anne–style home at 910 North Wisconsin Street was built prior to 1914. The turrets are characteristic of the era and add charm to the structure.

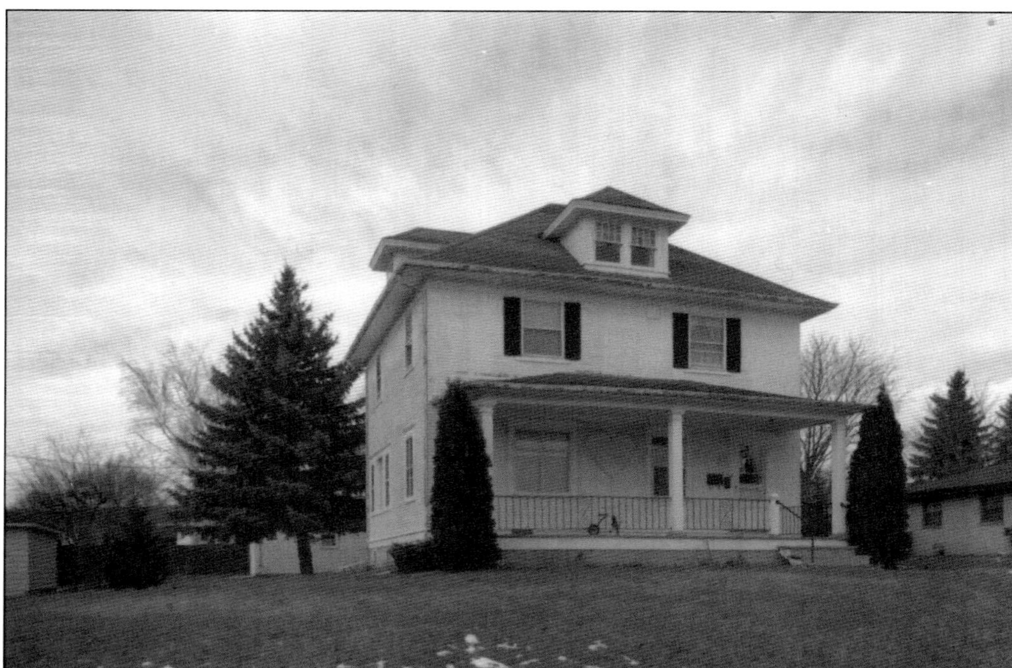

This American Foursquare at 913–915 North Wisconsin Street was built between 1914 and 1938. Its more modest design is typical of the then middle class family.

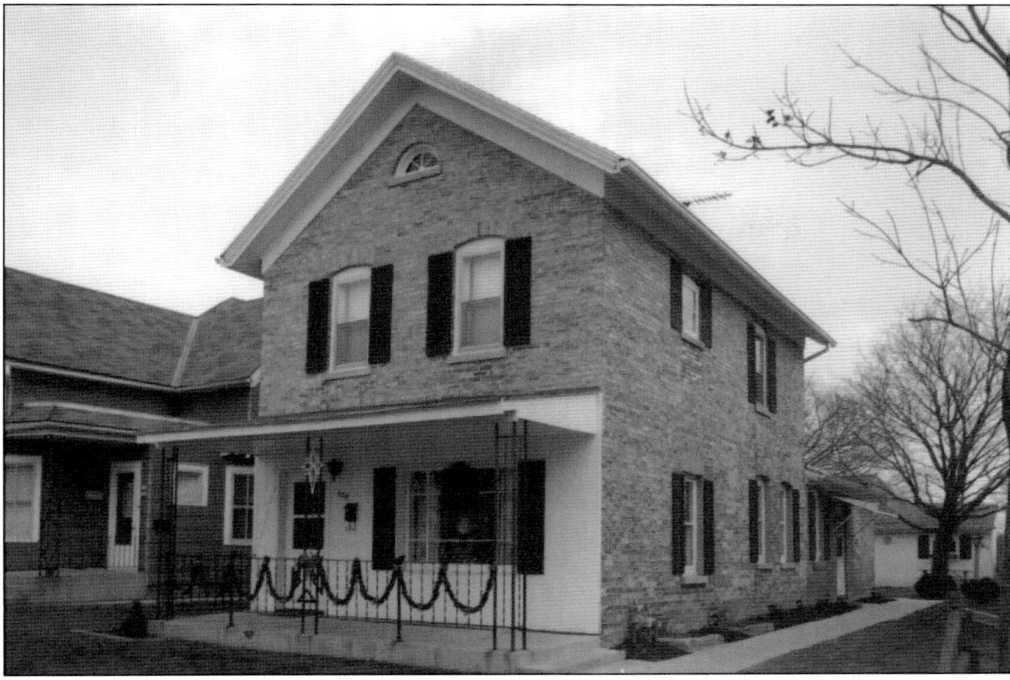

This front-gabled, cream city brick home at 604 North Wisconsin Street was built prior to 1893.

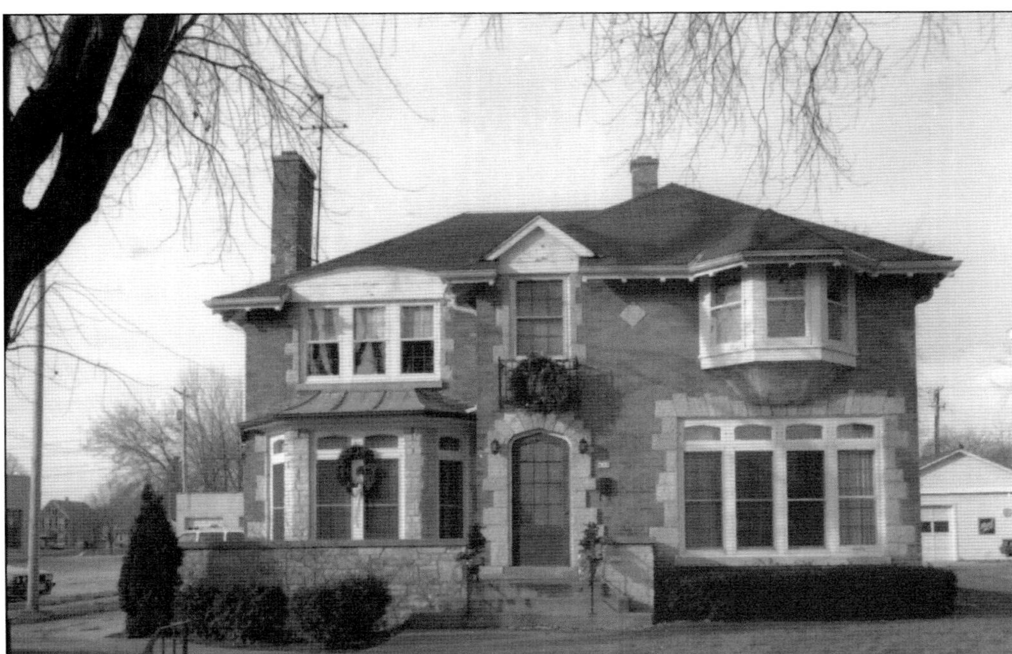

This lovely Tudor at 633 North Wisconsin Street was built between 1922 and 1938.

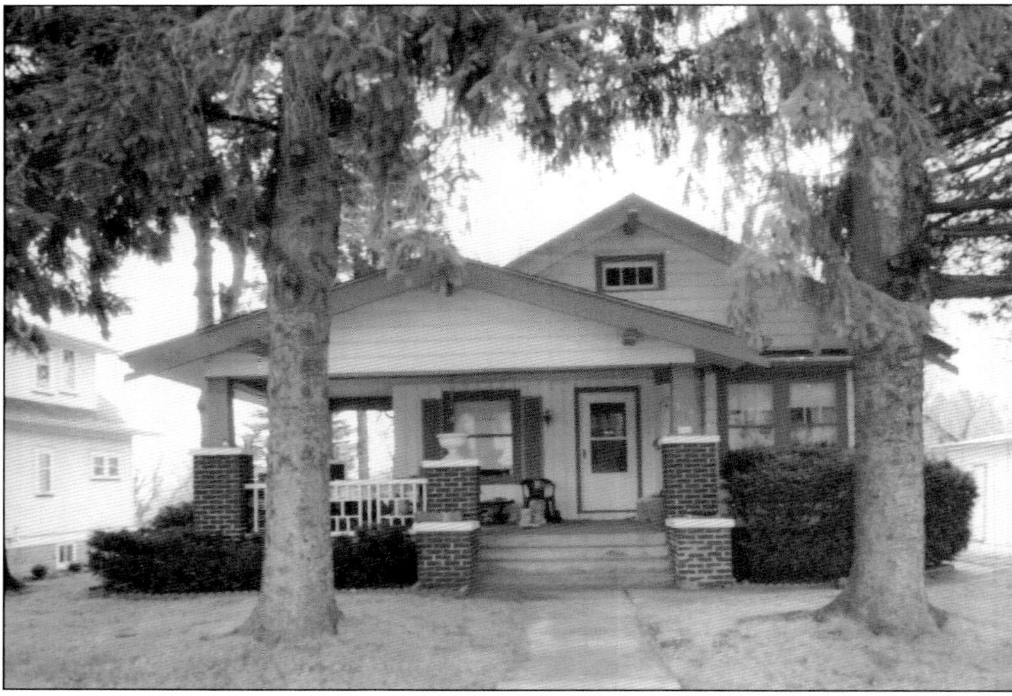

Located at 304 South Webster Street, this distinctive bungalow with Japanese/craftsman-style influence was built between 1914 and 1938.

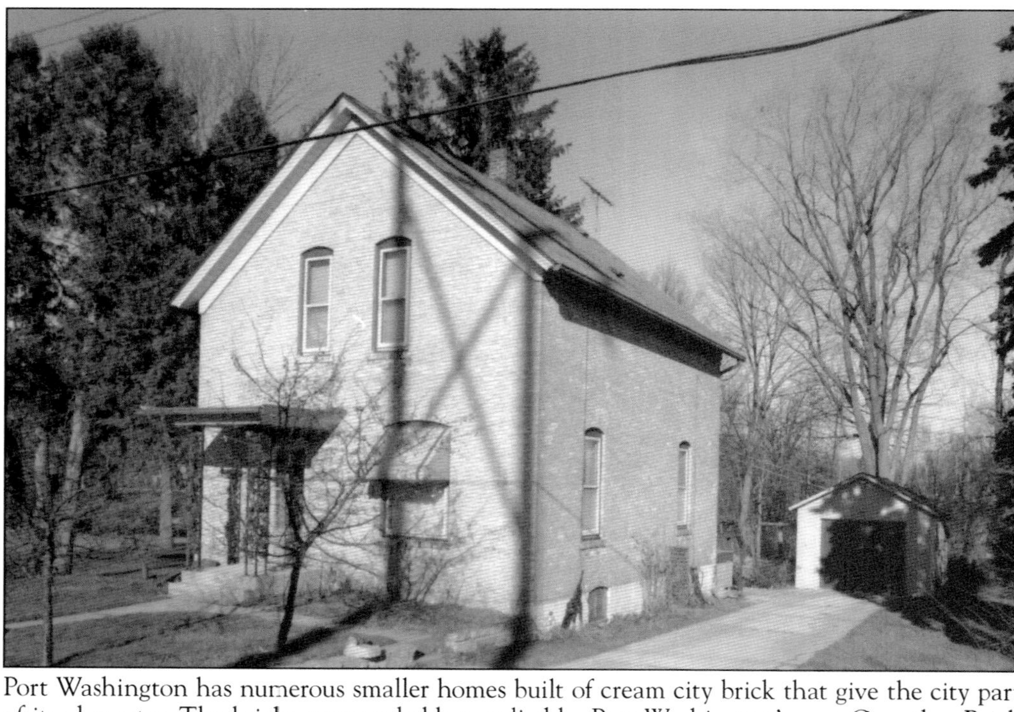

Port Washington has numerous smaller homes built of cream city brick that give the city part of its character. The bricks were probably supplied by Port Washington's own Guenther Brick Company. This home is located at 322 West Western Avenue and was built prior to 1938.

Nine

THEN AND NOW

Every city goes through an evolutionary process and, as in nature with plants and animals, if it doesn't adapt, it dies. Looking through this book you can see the changes that have occurred in Port Washington. Platted originally in 1835 as a residential city, it was abandoned and became just a stopping place along the route to Green Bay. Eventually, in the 1840s, people began returning and Port Washington became a landing place for migration inland. Trading with Native Americans died out, but agriculture and shipping of the city's products increased. Commercial fishing and industry grew and became the focus of this harbor city. Today commerce has left the waterfront, many large industries have closed down or been sold and moved to areas with cheaper labor, and the waterfront caters to tourism and pleasure craft. The city is rapidly becoming primarily a residential/bedroom community. This chapter touches on some of the changes that have occurred.

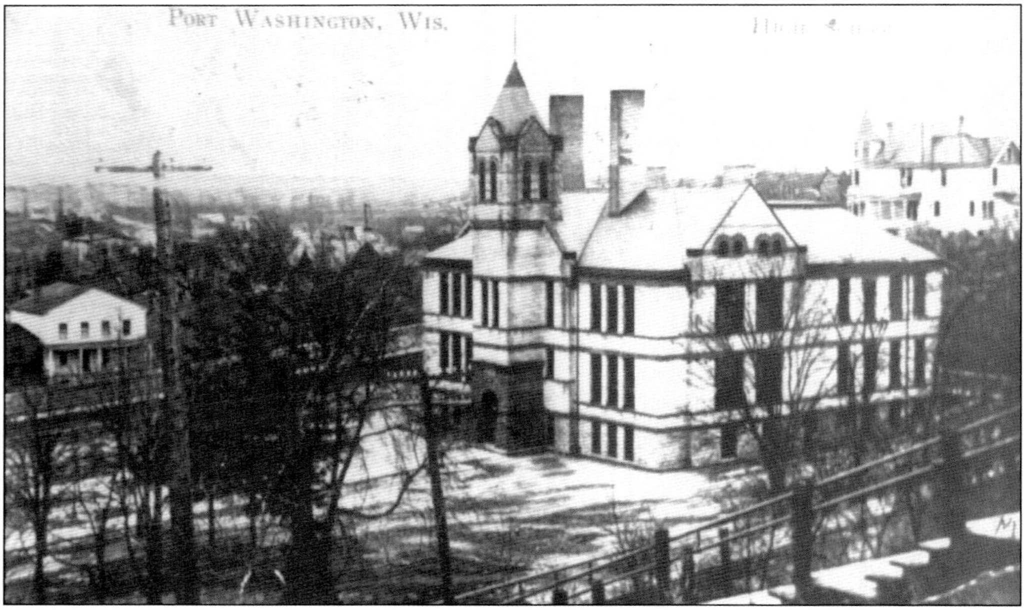

Pictured is the old high school in a photograph taken in 1910. In the upper right corner is the Bostwick House, named after one of the financiers of the Wisconsin Chair Company.

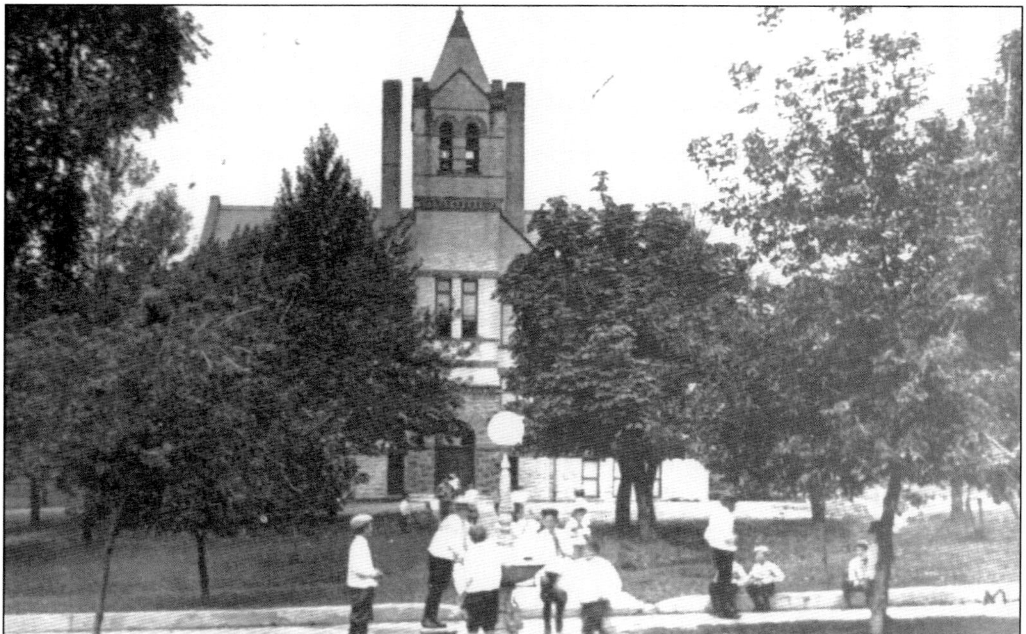

Seen in this 1918 view of the old high school are tree-lined walkways and students dressed up for school. Times have changed. The school burned down in 1989, and the site is now occupied by the Port Washington police and fire departments.

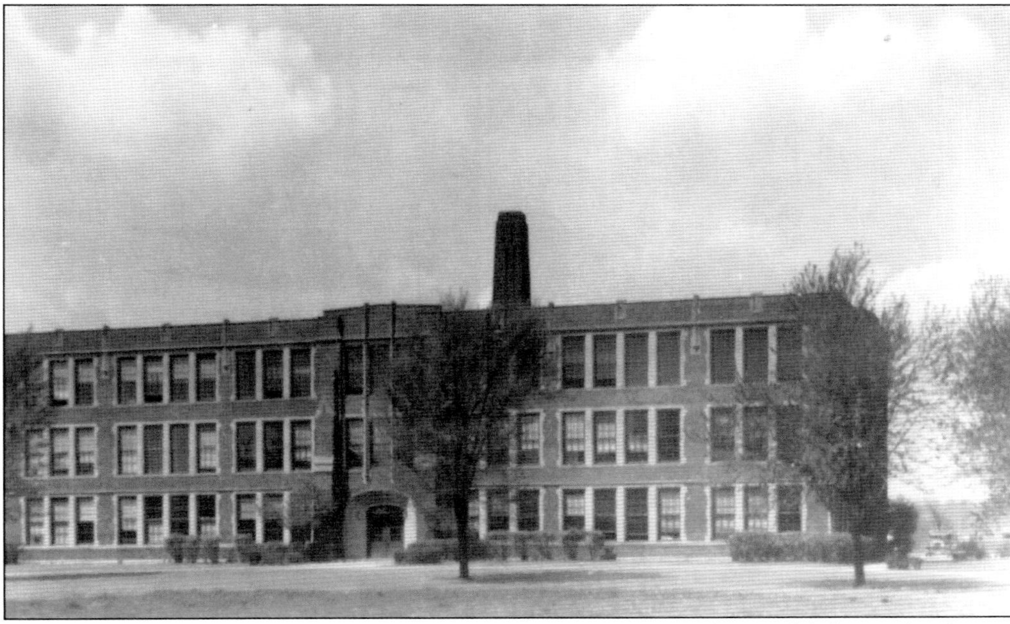

The "new" high school, built in the 1920s, had an actual campus with graceful elms and a classical neo-Romanesque interior architecture.

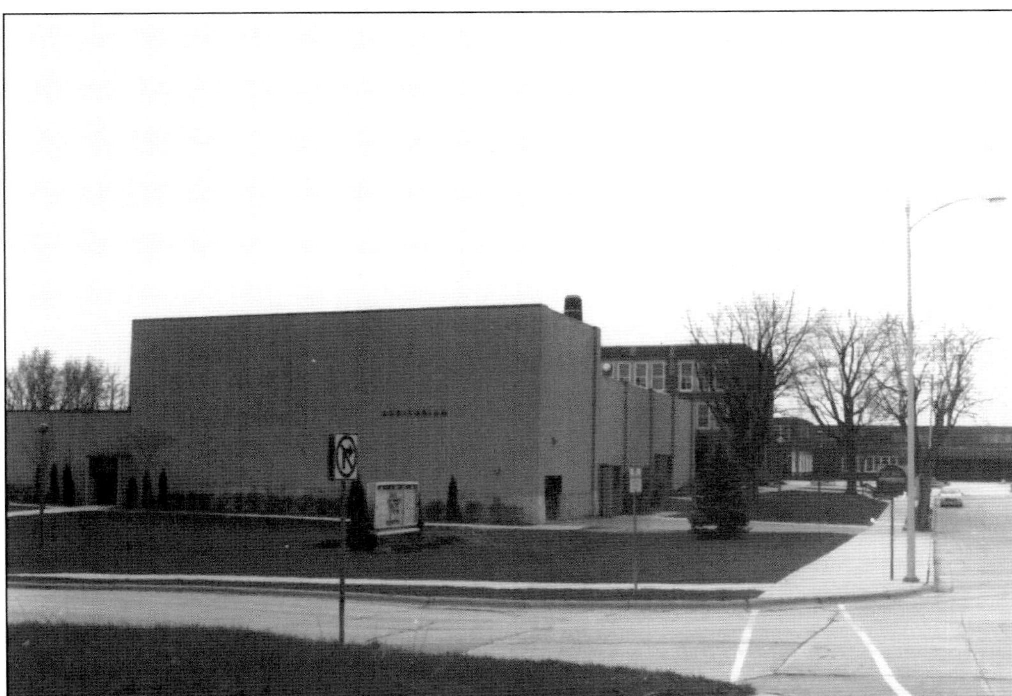

The high school today is barely recognizable due to multiple add-ons and blockhouse economics.

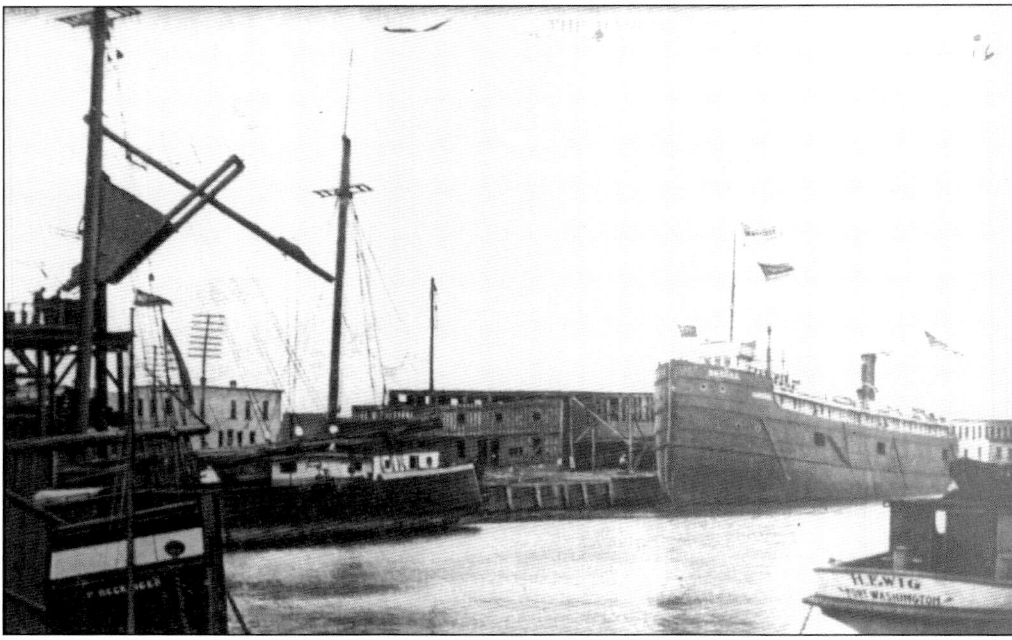

This is the west slip, looking east, with the Ubbink Coal and Dock Company and lumberyard on the left. In the foreground are the fish tugs of local commercial fishermen.

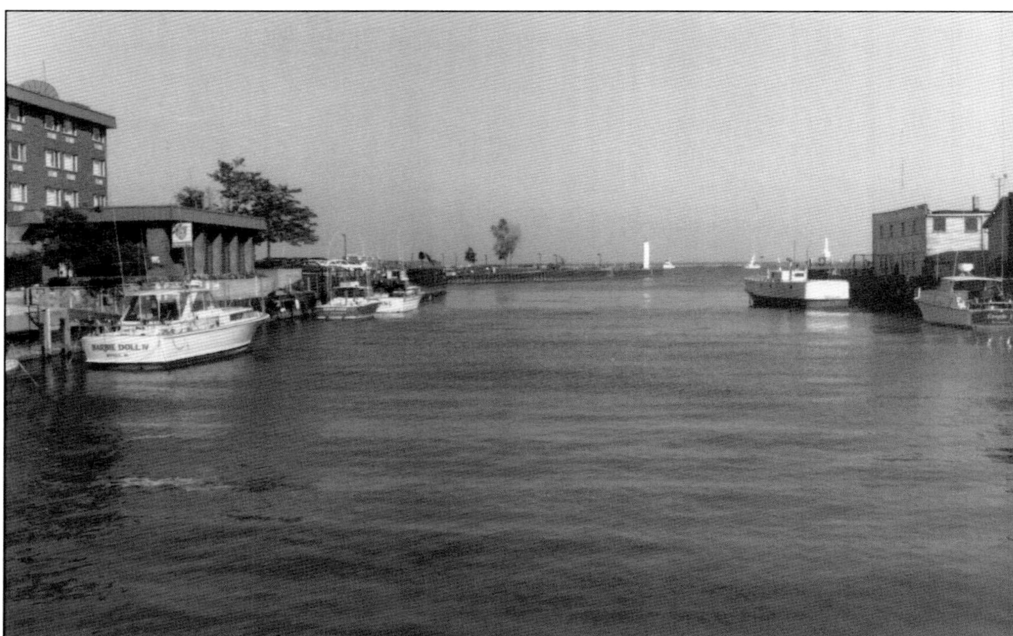

This same area is now a large hotel, the Holiday Inn Harborview, and the slip is surrounded by condominiums and moorings for charter boats.

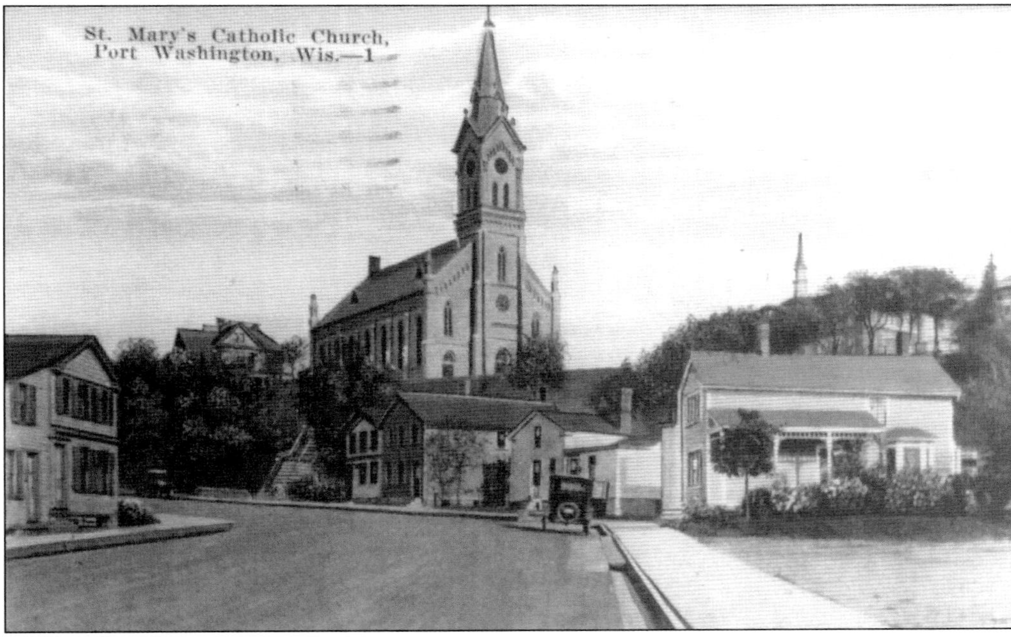

This photograph from 1936 looks north up what today is called St. Mary's Hill, but originally was known as Lighthouse Hill.

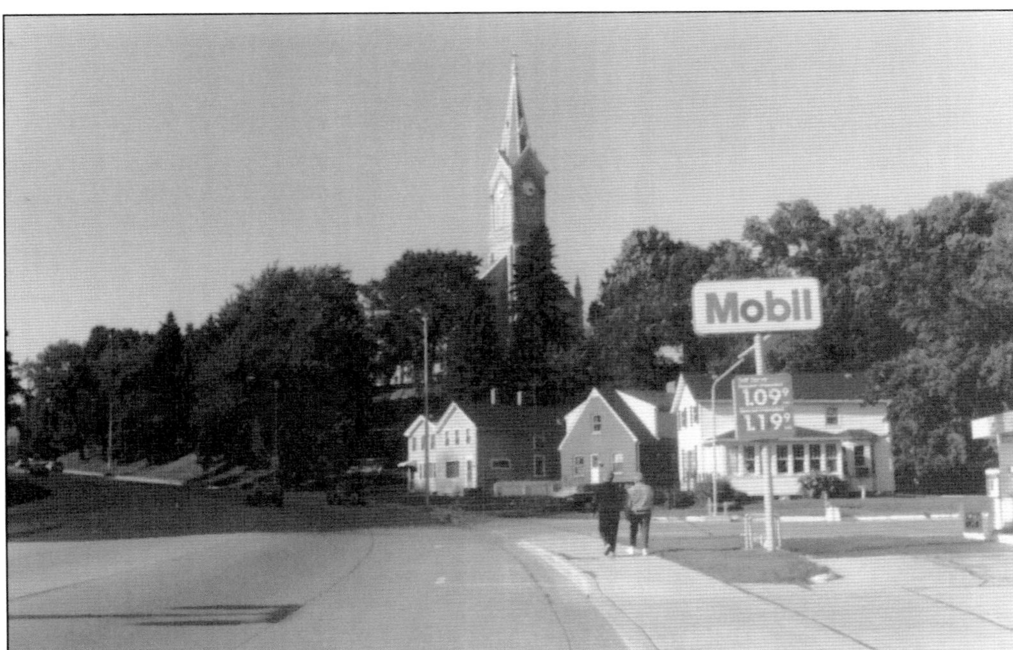

Here is the same view from the 1960s or 1970s. Note how the homes have been altered.

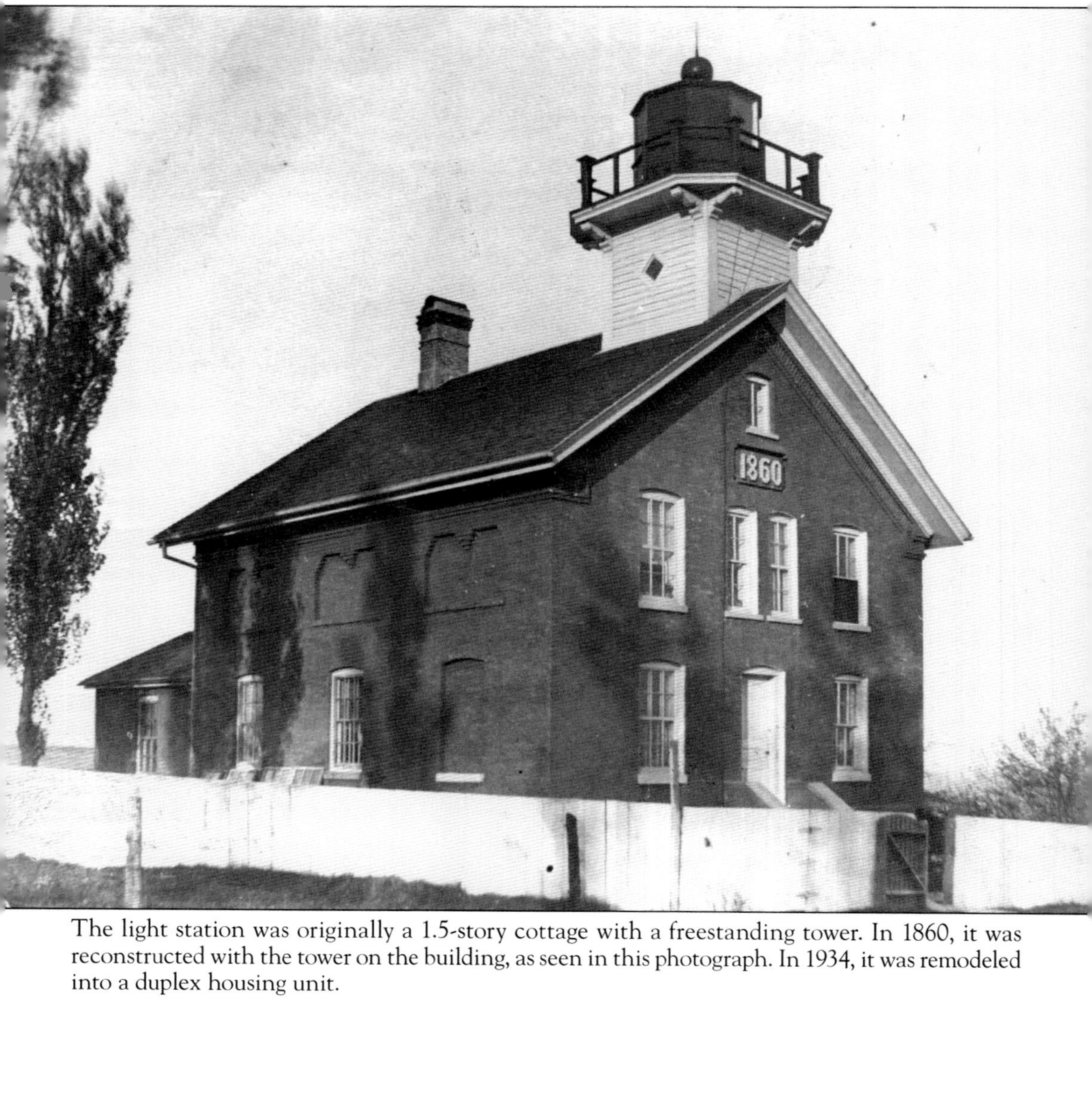

The light station was originally a 1.5-story cottage with a freestanding tower. In 1860, it was reconstructed with the tower on the building, as seen in this photograph. In 1934, it was remodeled into a duplex housing unit.

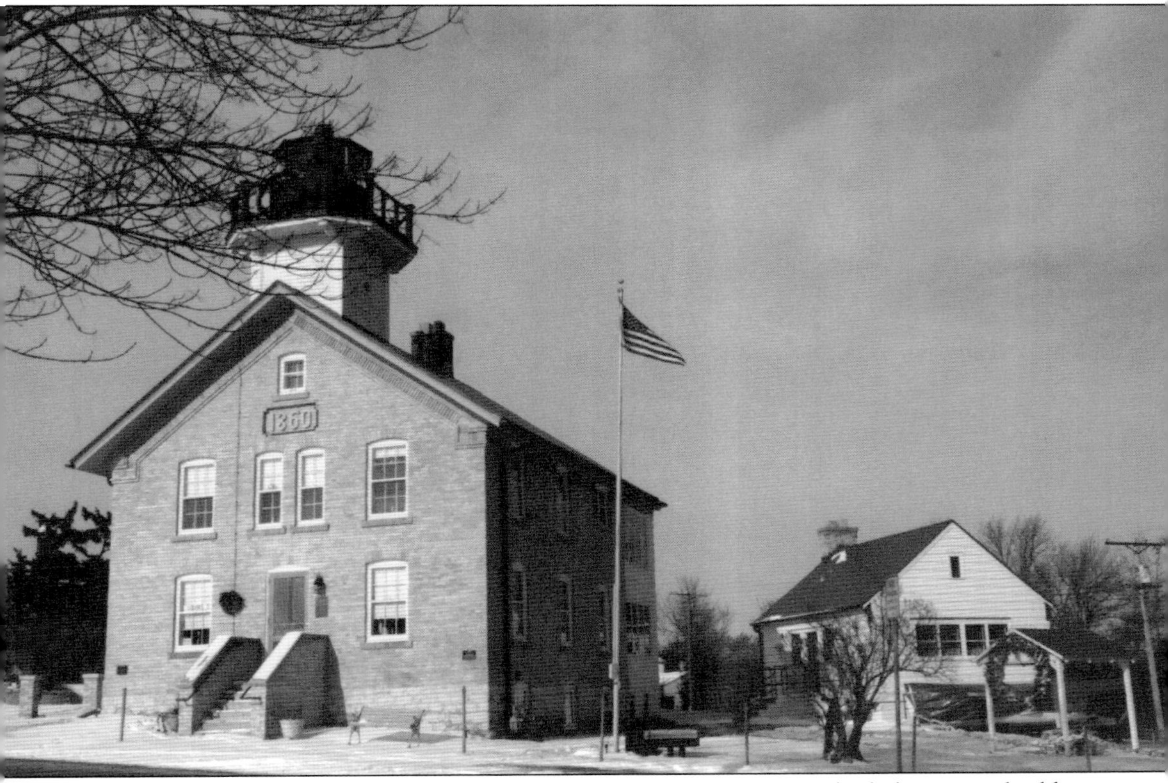

The Port Washington Historical Society made the decision to restore the light station building in 2000. This is how the station looks today.

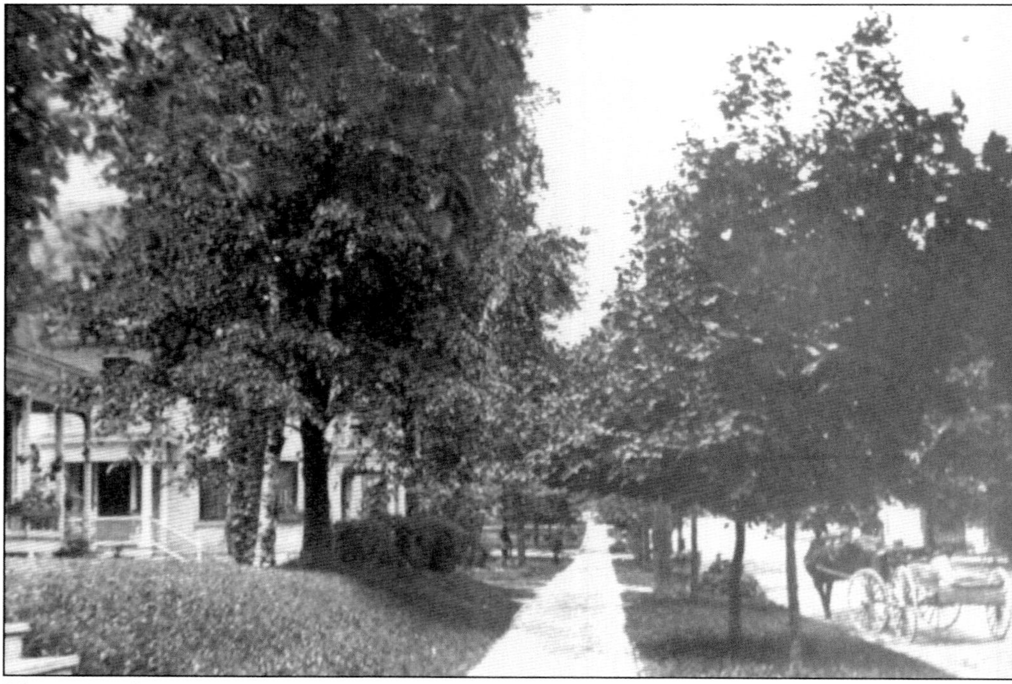

This is South Wisconsin Street, looking north at about 1918. Note the horse and buggy, heavily tree-lined streets, and unpaved sidewalk.

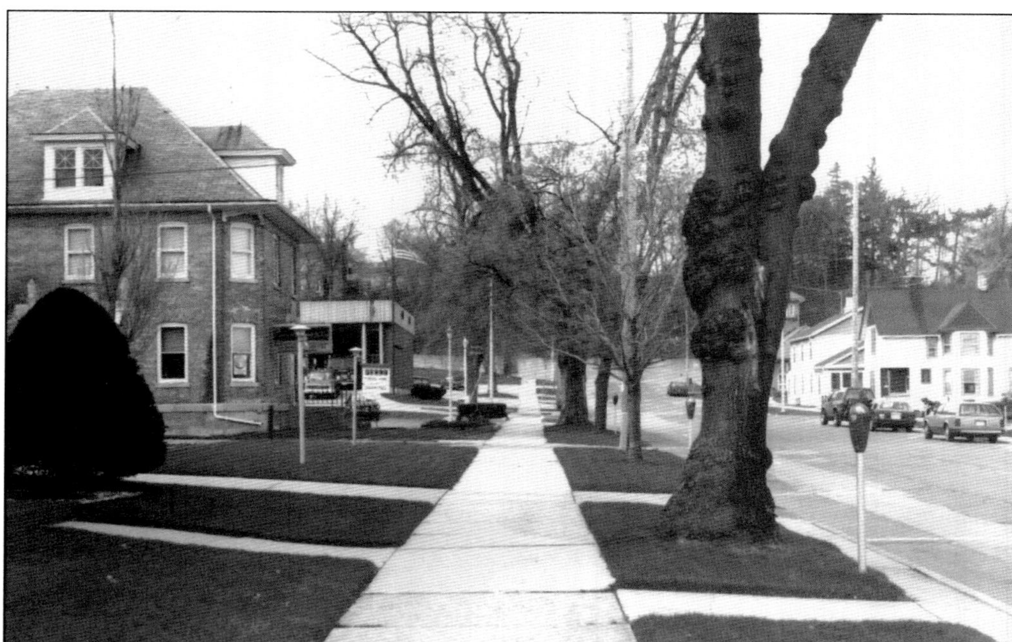

This is South Wisconsin Street today. The trees are gone and many residences have become commercial buildings.

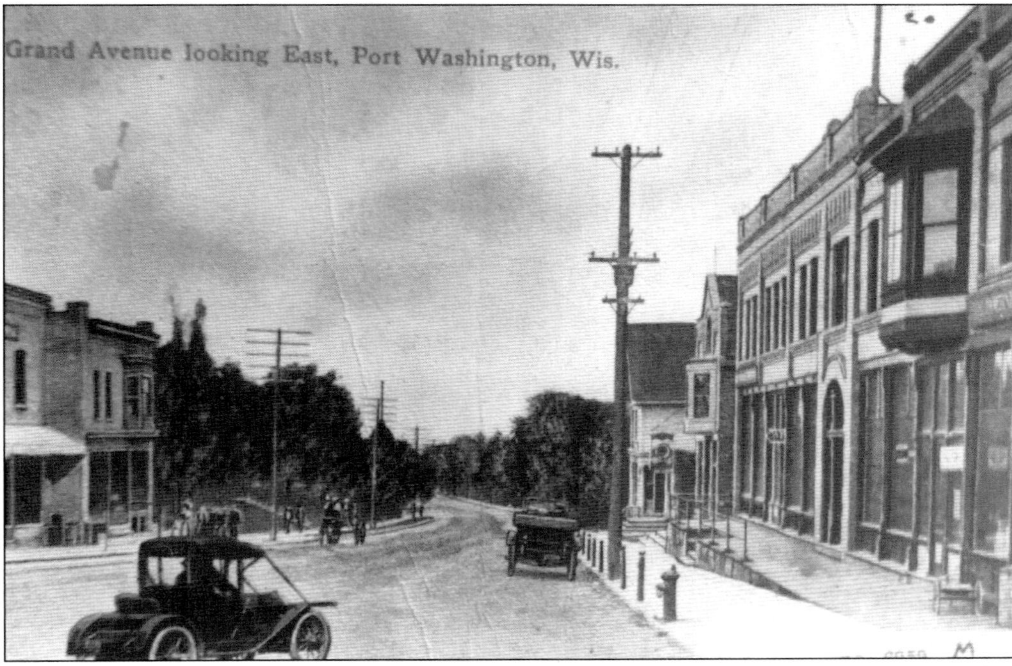

This 1908 photograph of Grand Avenue, looking east toward Lake Michigan, was first published by H. O. Beverung of Milwaukee.

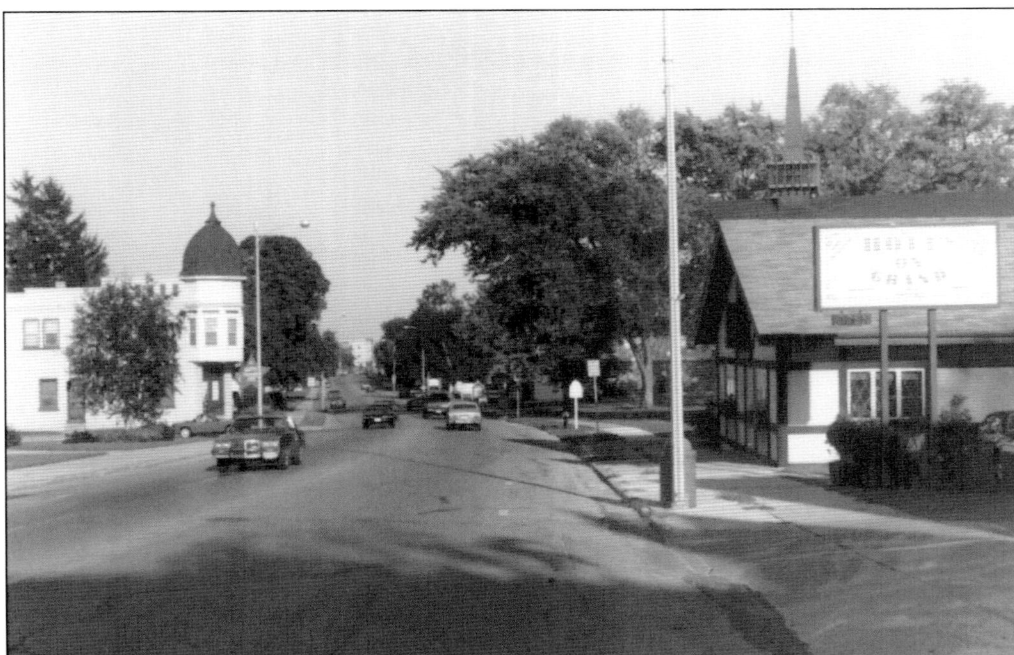

This photograph of the same area in the 1990s shows Holt's on Grand Avenue, at the right, which is now a church center. The domed building on the left was once a saloon. It is now a hair salon, apartments, and commercial space.

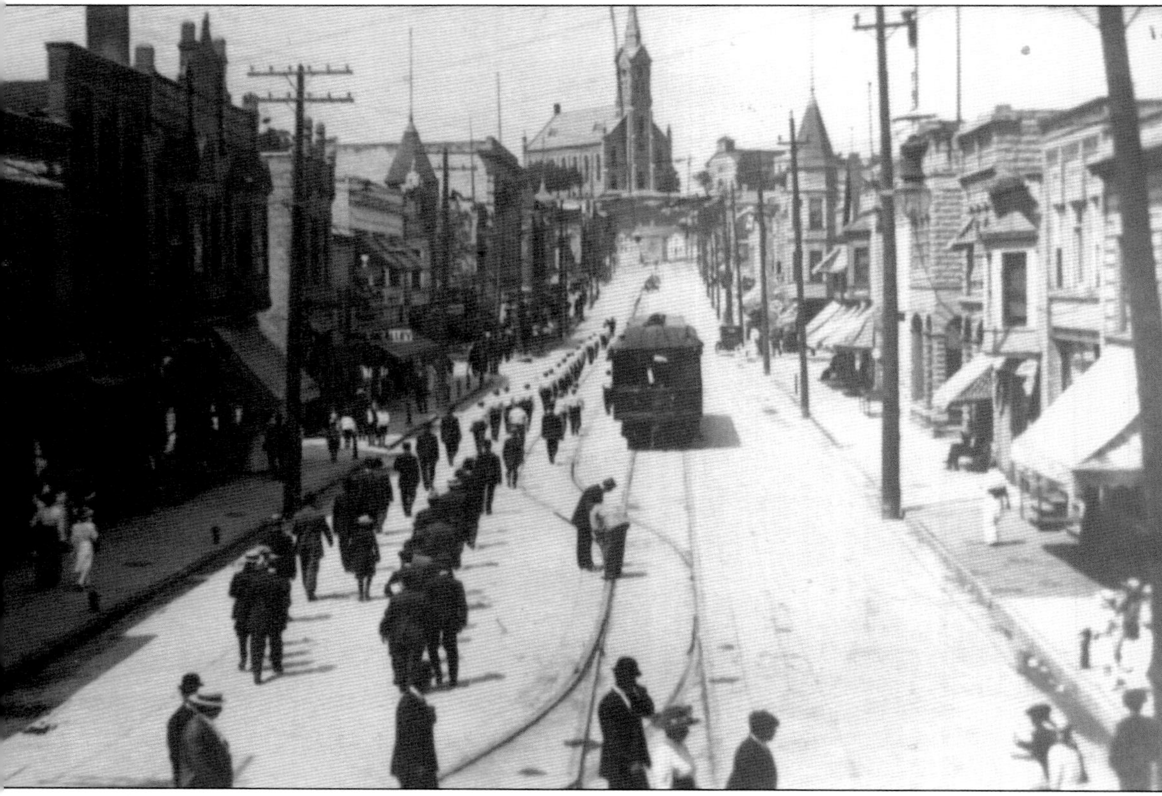

Franklin Street at the corner of Franklin and Grand Streets is shown above, looking north, in the early 1900s.

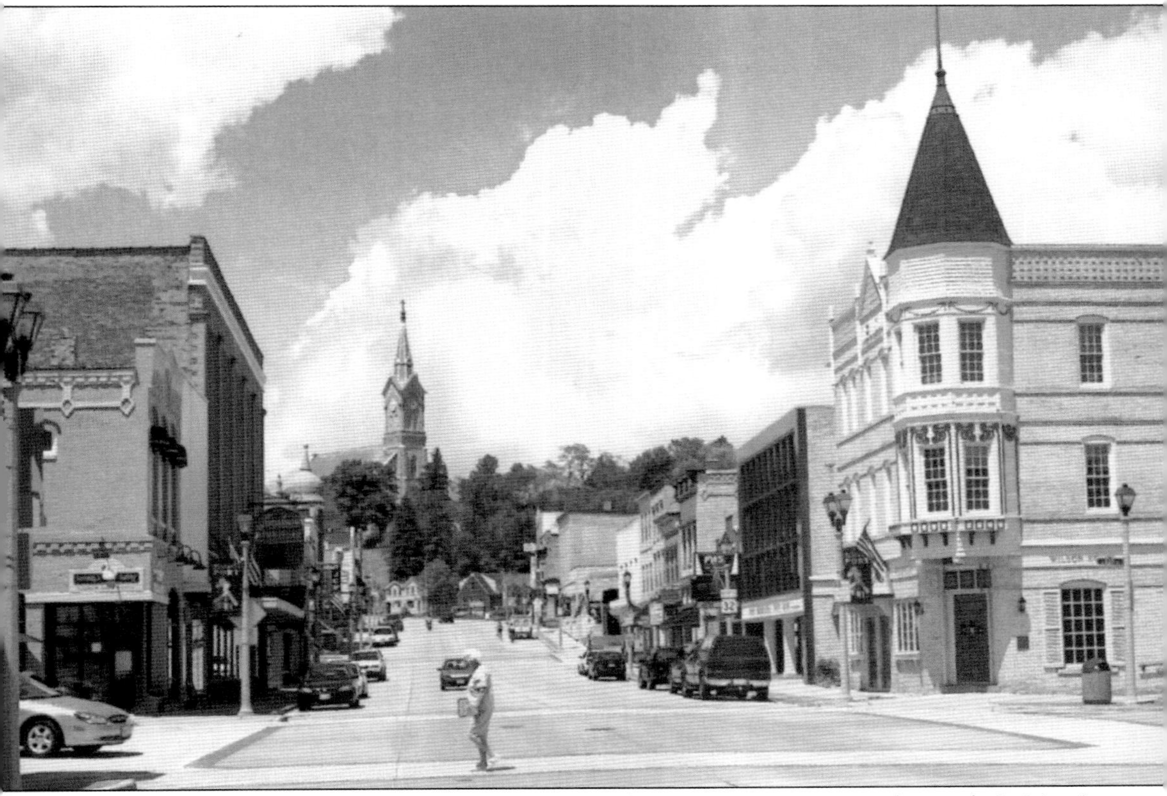

Here is a similar view of the corner of Franklin and Main Streets as it is today, with St Mary's Catholic Church overlooking a busy downtown.

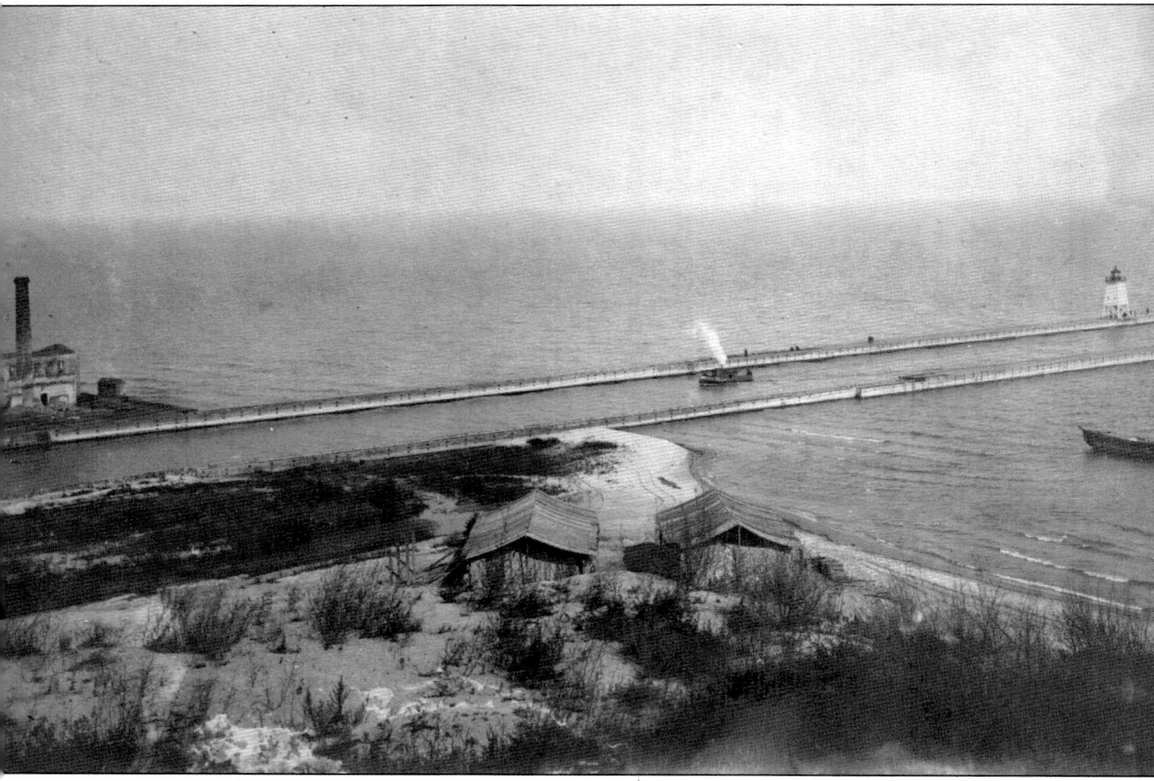

Looking from the south bluff, here is a view of the harbor from around 1897. Note the wreckage of the scow schooner *J. B. Prime,* the remains of the Schramka brickyard, a fish tug coming into port, and, on the left, the Turner foundry.

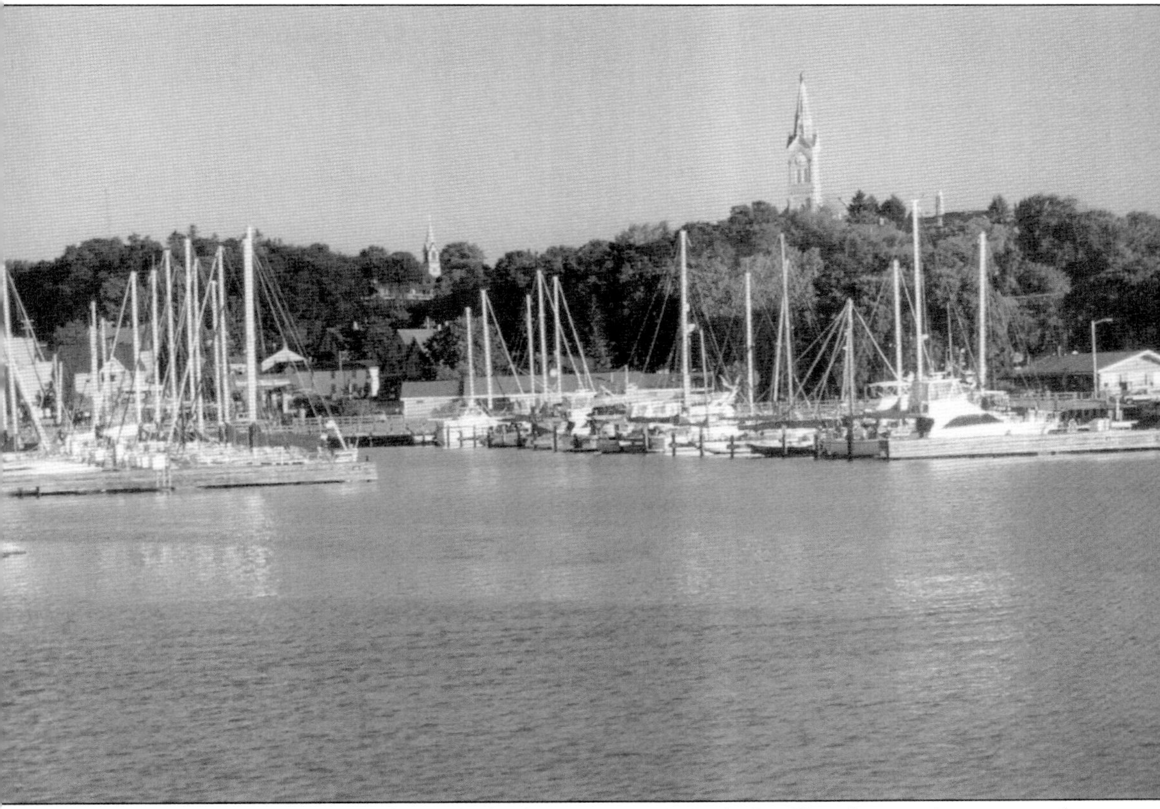

Today this area boasts a 220-slip yacht harbor. St. Mary's Catholic Church is in the upper right, and the steeple seen in the center is the county courthouse.

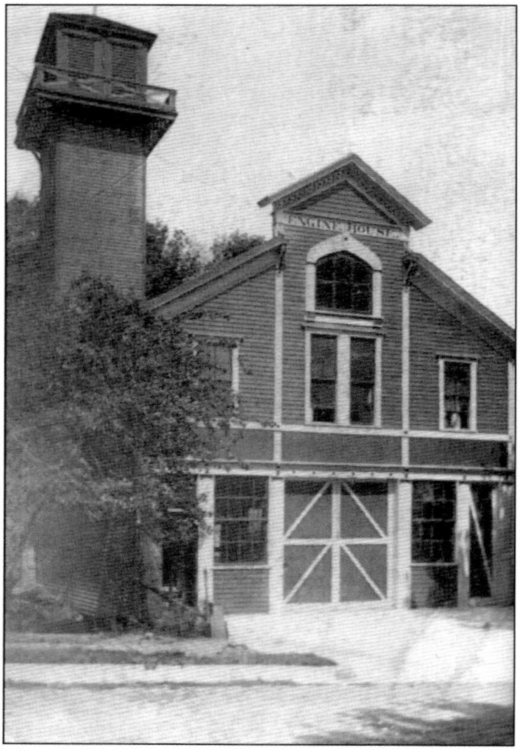

The original firehouse was located on Pier Street. This picture was taken around 1900.

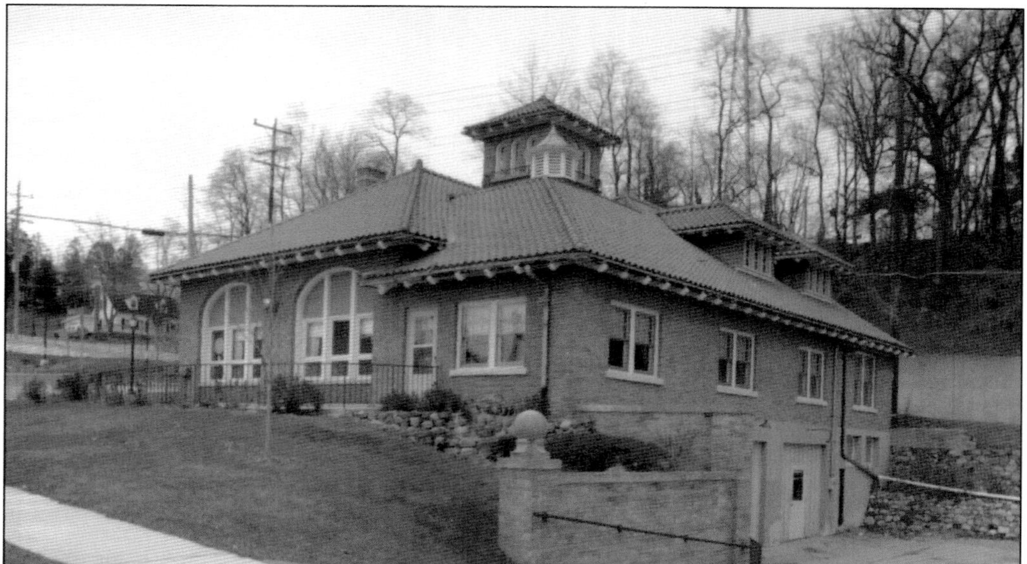

The fire engine house, now a state and U.S. National Historic Landmark, was constructed in 1929 on the site of the 1884 multipurpose wooden firehouse. Architect John Topzant of Milwaukee designed the Mediterranean Revival–style building with tan brick walls, a Spanish tile roof, copper gutters and downspouts, and a campanile-like hose drying tower. It has served as the Port Washington Senior Center since the construction of the present fire and police stations on Wisconsin Street.

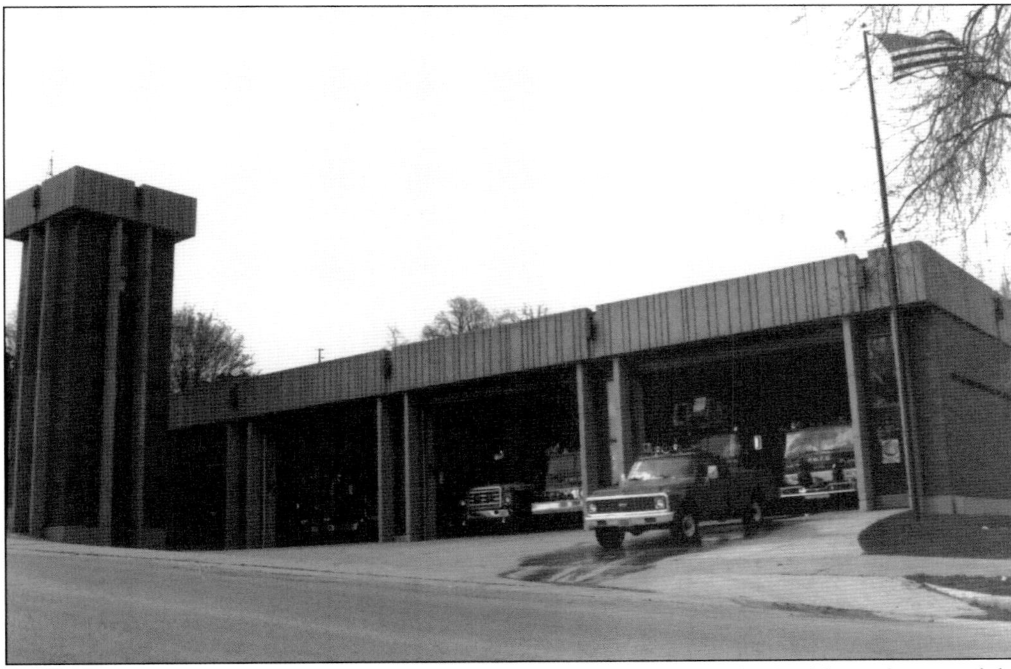

Today Port Washington's fire and police departments are housed in this building, the site of the former Port Washington High School, located on Wisconsin Street.

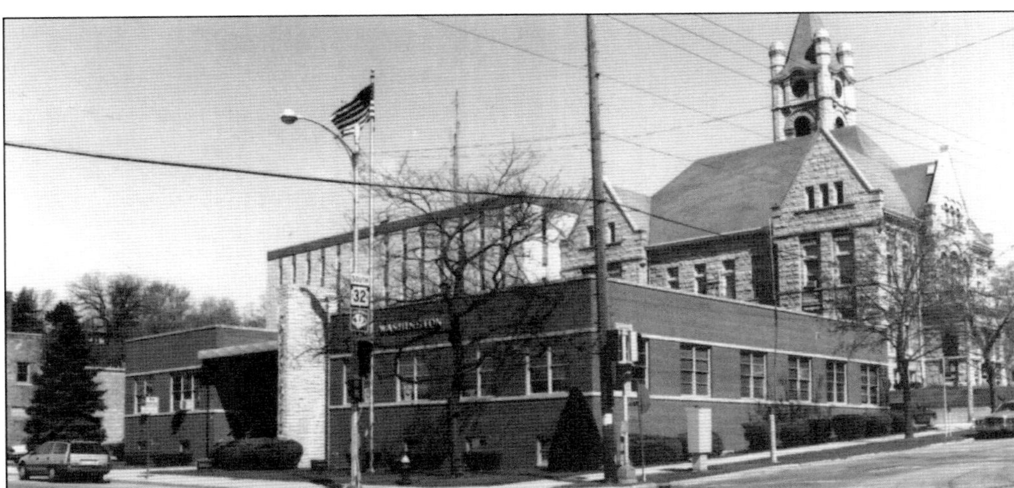

Built on the site of the former opera house, city hall is located on Grand Avenue at the intersection of Grand and Wisconsin Streets.

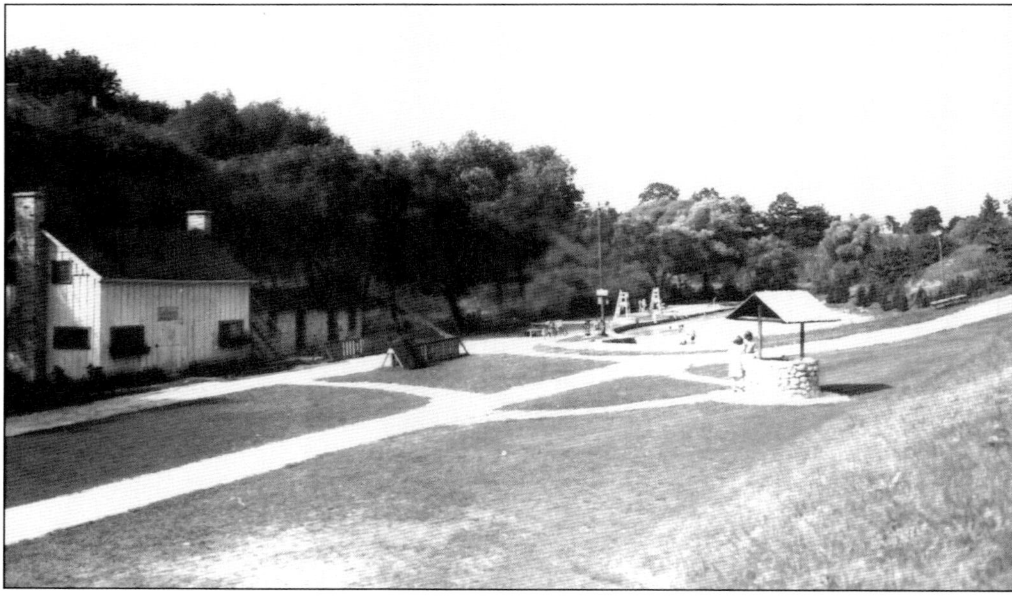

Port Washington once had a very picturesque swimming pond. It was named Guenther's Pond for the Guenther's brickyard once located there. The building on the left used to be a Girl Scout camp. It eventually burned down. On the right is the quaint artesian wishing well, which has since been removed—a victim of maintenance and liability costs.

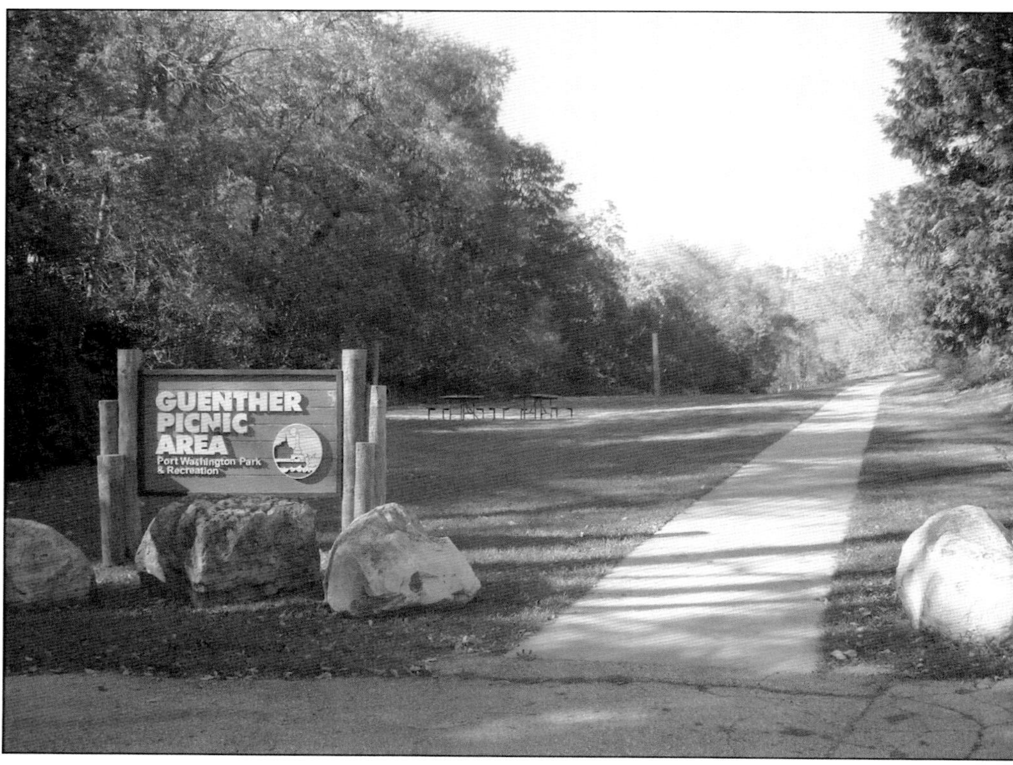

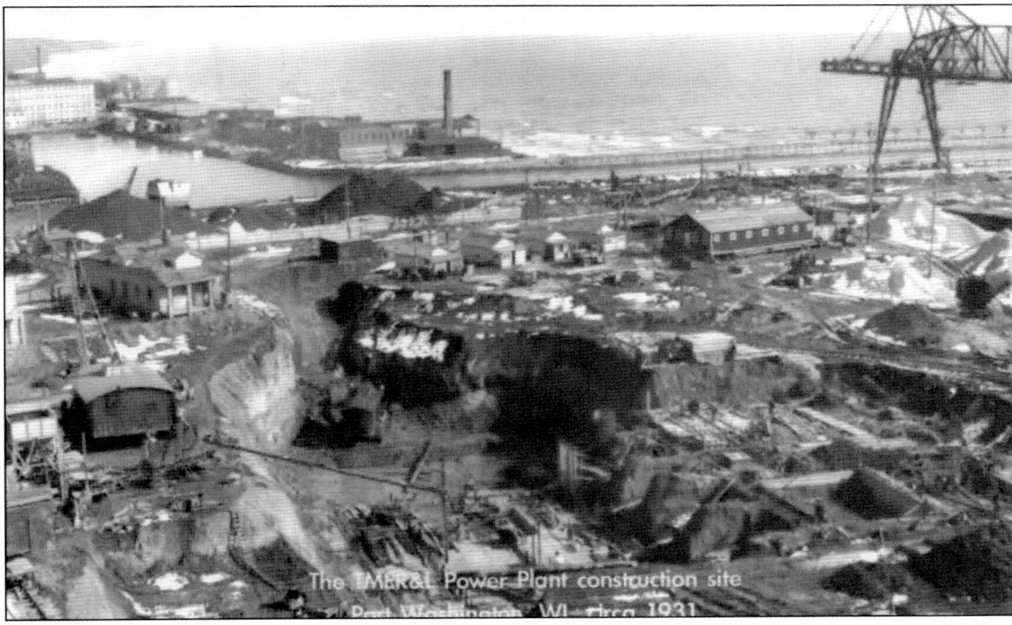

Progress can be hazardous to the topography of the land. By 1931, most of the south bluff was gone and being used as fill for the coal dock. The TMER&L power plant was being constructed on this site. Notice that some of the cottages were kept for housing the construction crews and were later moved or demolished as the building of the power plant progressed.

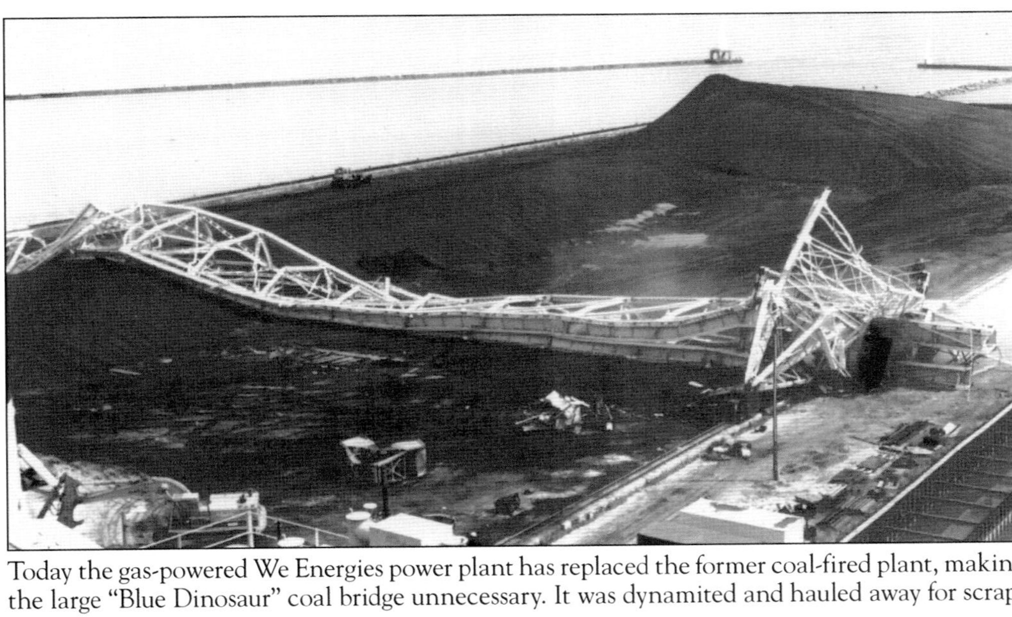

Today the gas-powered We Energies power plant has replaced the former coal-fired plant, making the large "Blue Dinosaur" coal bridge unnecessary. It was dynamited and hauled away for scrap.

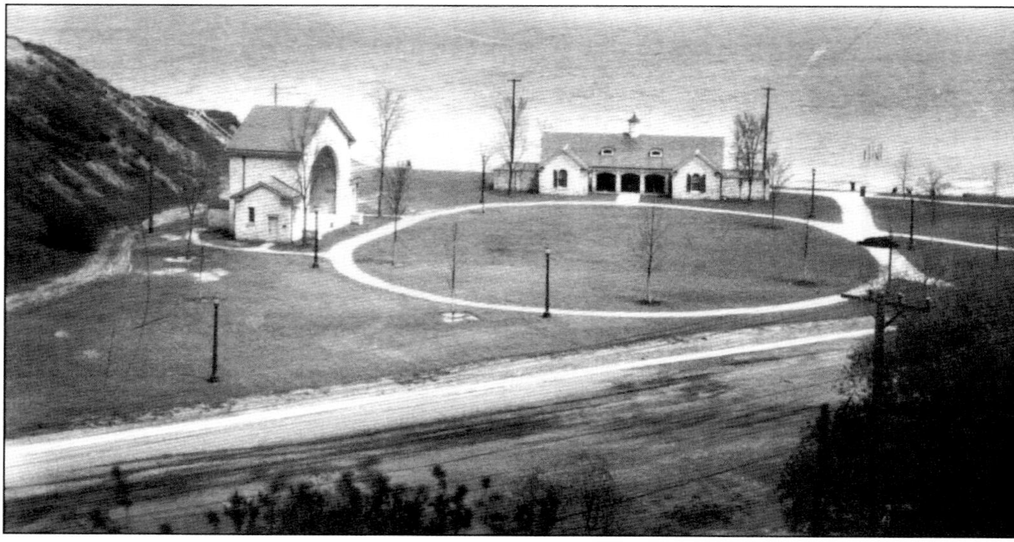

Port Washington's bathing beach was once located at lower Lake Park. The band shell and beach house were constructed with money donated by the Jaenigs. The looping walk is gone. The beach is gone. The band shell remains and is used for evening concerts throughout the summer. The bath house has been renovated and is now the Port Washington Yacht Club.

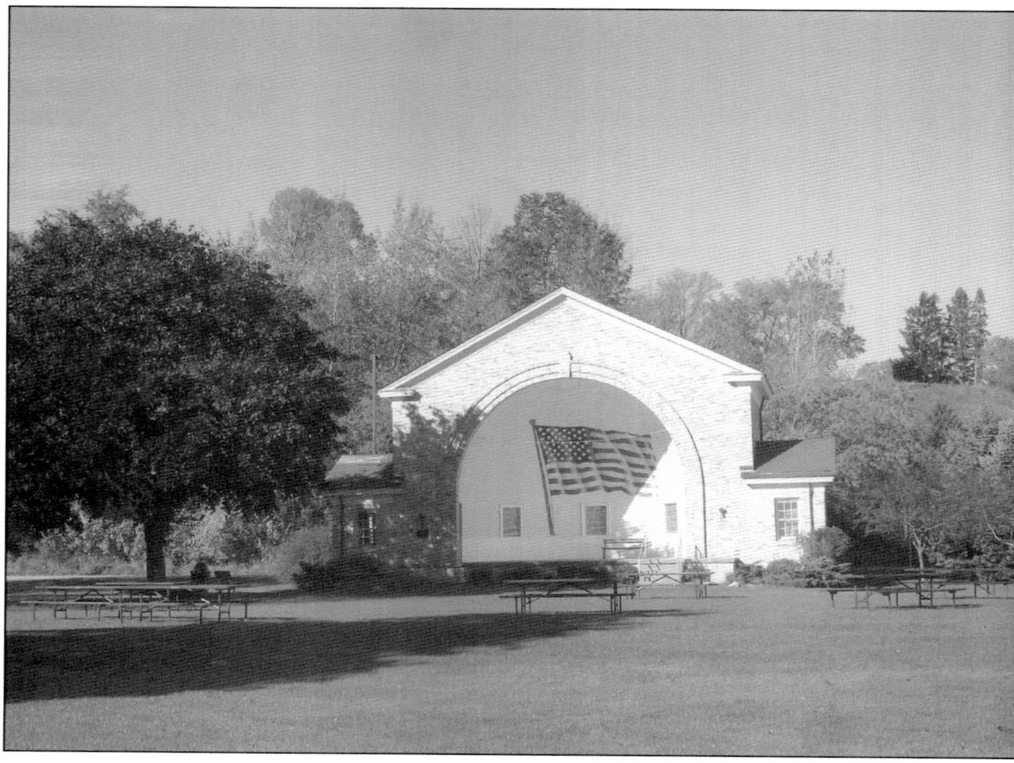

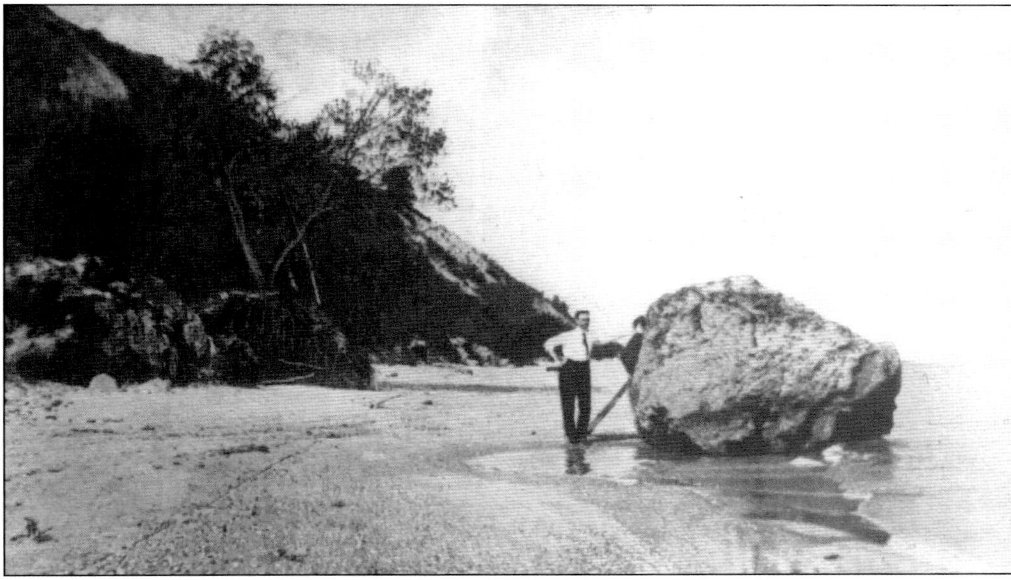

For many years, the "big rock" has been a fixture on Port Washington's north beach. This 400-million-year-old dolomite boulder today is half-buried in the sand and is reduced in size, due to nature and man. Today it is known as "Mile Rock" but is actually only .85 mile from the mouth of the old harbor. It is pictured at right, nearly submerged by the tide.

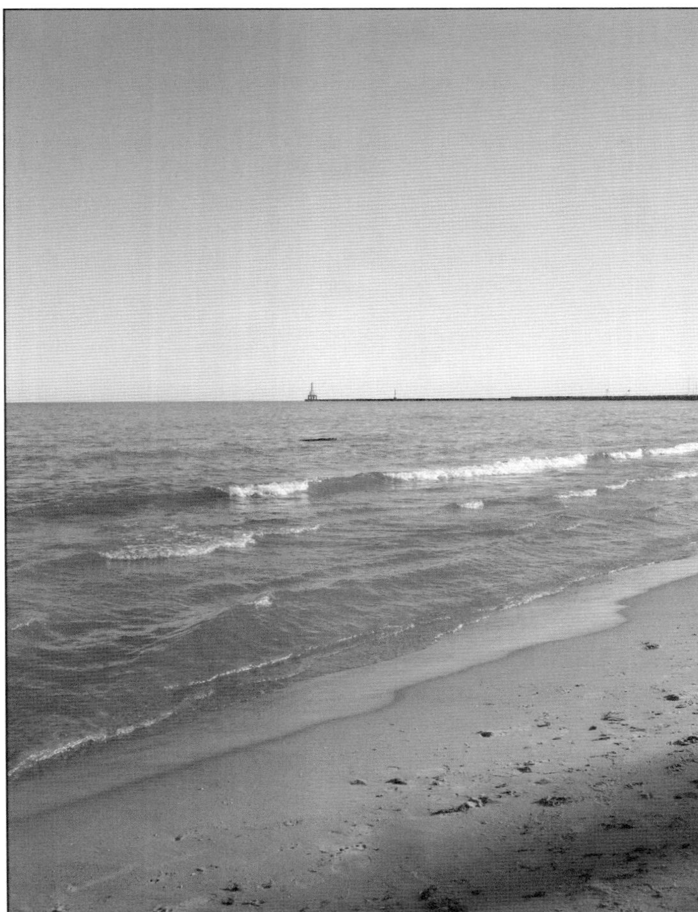

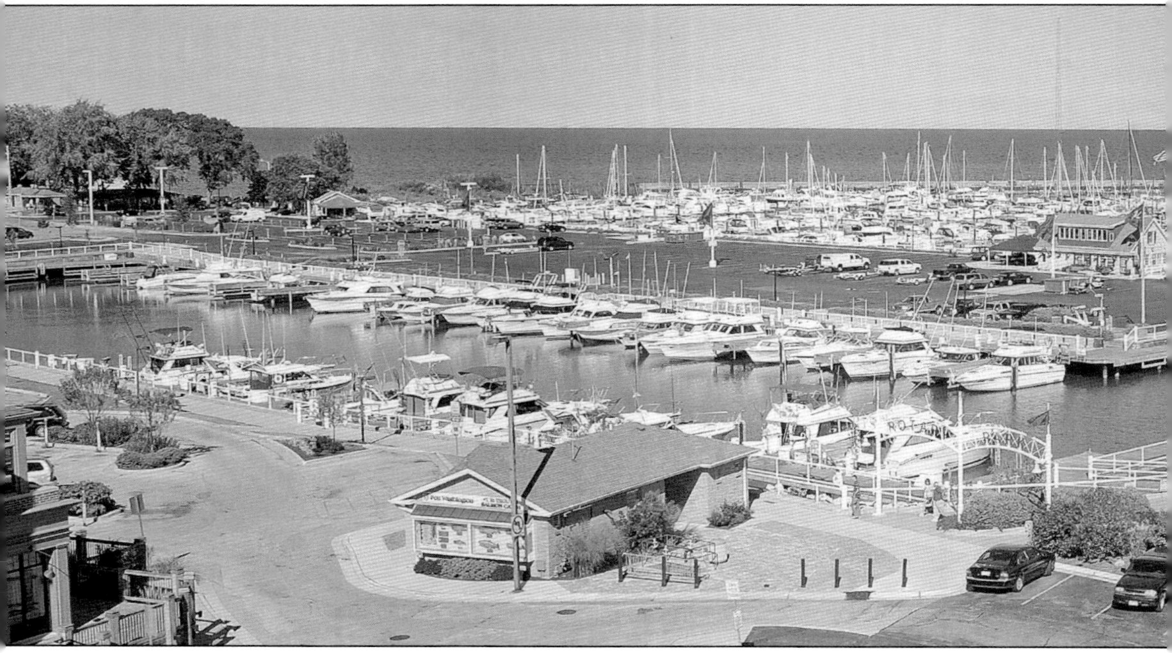

Once a commercial harbor with limited recreational uses, the Port Washington harbor today has one of the best marinas on Lake Michigan while still catering to commercial users. The west slip and the north slip were built before the turn of the century. The outer breakwaters were constructed in the 1930s and the small boat harbor followed in the 1980s. The west and north slips were built before the 1900s, and the outer breakwaters were constructed in the 1930s. The small boat harbor was built in the 1980s. The north slip has since been incorporated into the marina with the creation of a new channel through the peninsula and closing off the south end with fill, which created Rotary Park.

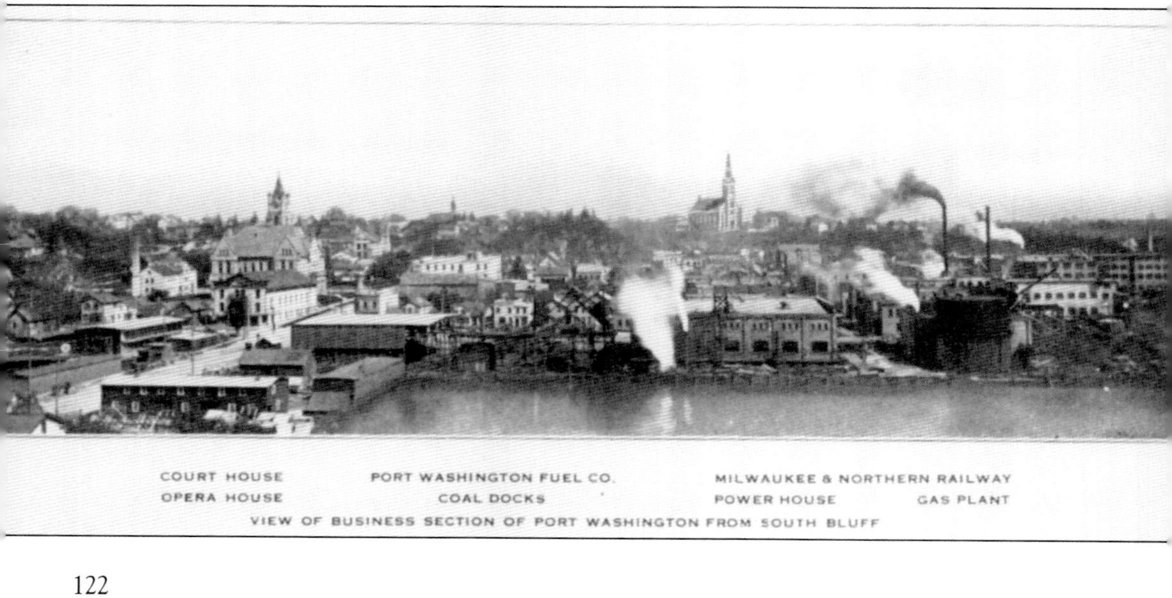

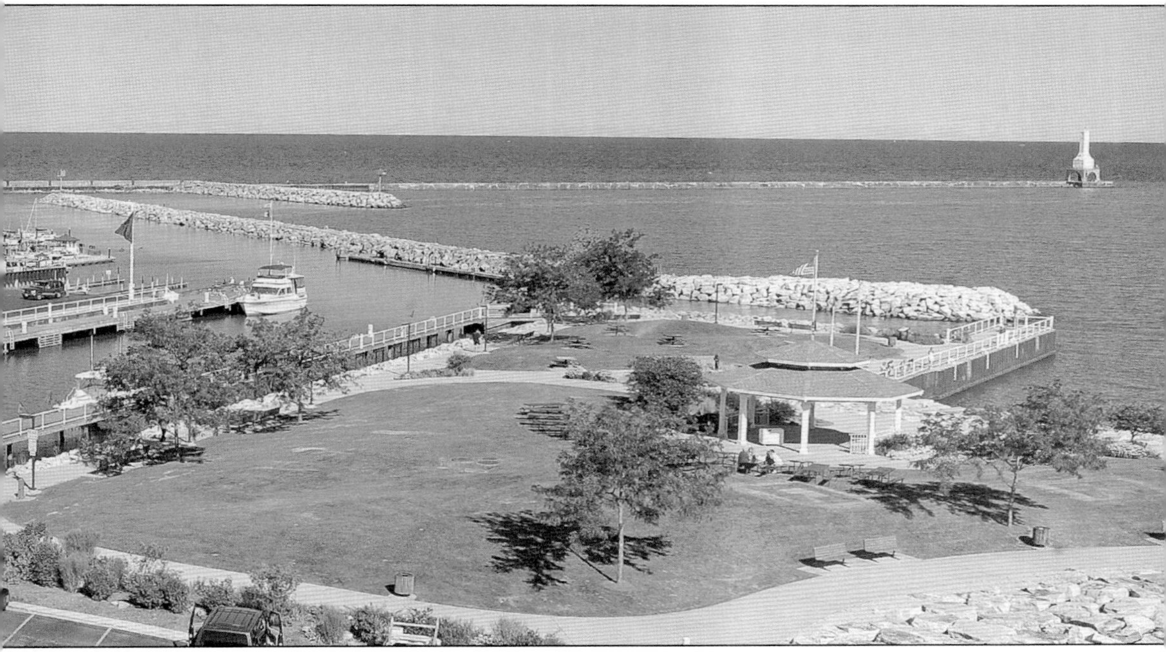

Opposite: This view of the Port Washington harbor, taken from the south bluff prior to 1935, shows the industry that lined the Lake Michigan shoreline in Port Washington. The harbor was of great commercial use, but was of limited recreational value.

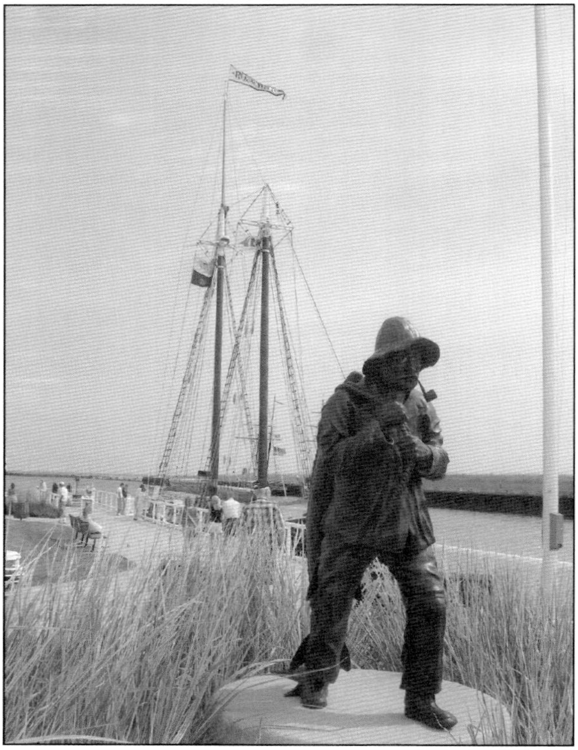

Port Washington celebrated its 175th anniversary on September 2, 2010. In August of that same year, the annual Maritime Heritage Festival featured five tall ships. Pictured at left, behind the iconic fisherman statue, is the *Lynx*, modeled after the private schooners that served America as blockade runners during the War of 1812. Below is the 180-foot-long *Bounty*, which has starred in movies like *Mutiny on the Bounty* (1960) and *Pirates of the Caribbean* (2006).

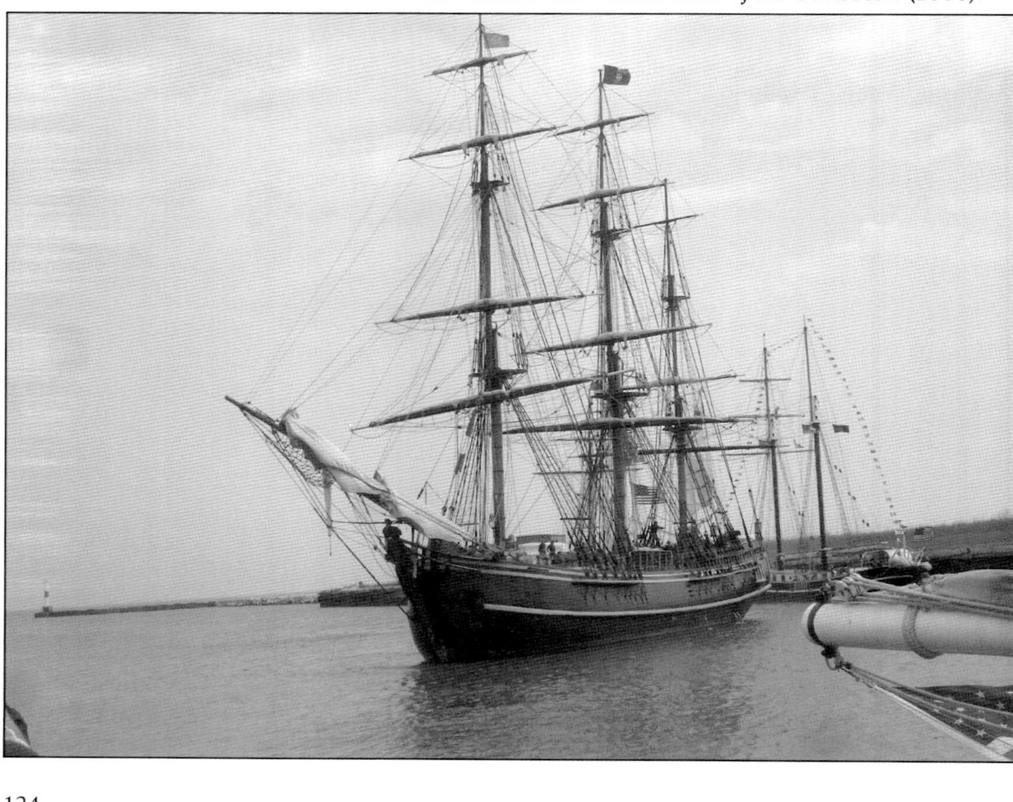

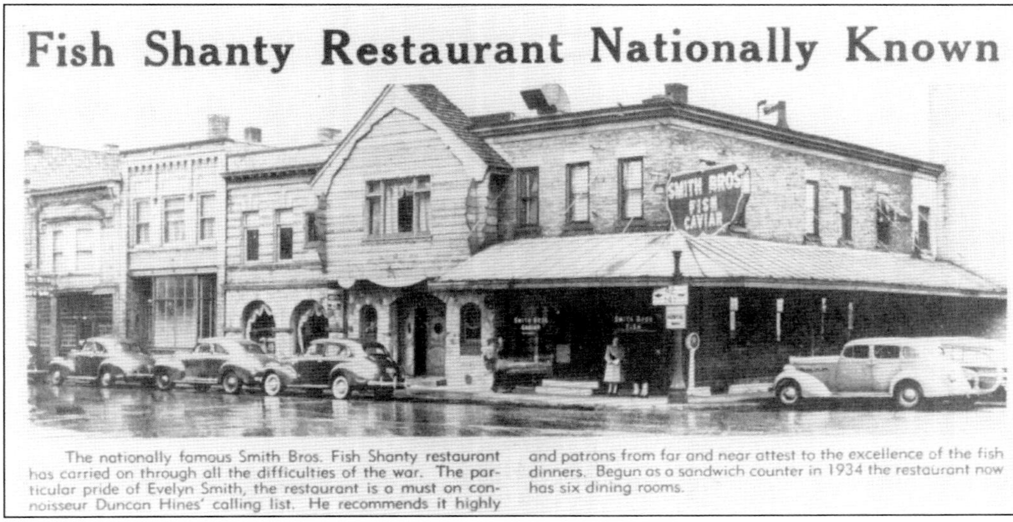

Fish Shanty Restaurant Nationally Known

The nationally famous Smith Bros. Fish Shanty restaurant has carried on through all the difficulties of the war. The particular pride of Evelyn Smith, the restaurant is a must on connoisseur Duncan Hines' calling list. He recommends it highly and patrons from far and near attest to the excellence of the fish dinners. Begun as a sandwich counter in 1934 the restaurant now has six dining rooms.

This old newspaper ad promoted the "nationally known" (Smith Brothers) Fish Shanty Restaurant. The building was gutted by fire twice during its heydey era of the 1930s through 1960s, and in the 1990s was completely remodeled—inside and out. The photograph below is an early 2000 view of the Port Washington landmark. There have been a few architectural changes to the facade since this photograph, and the Fish Market in the lower right is now Smith Brothers Coffee House.

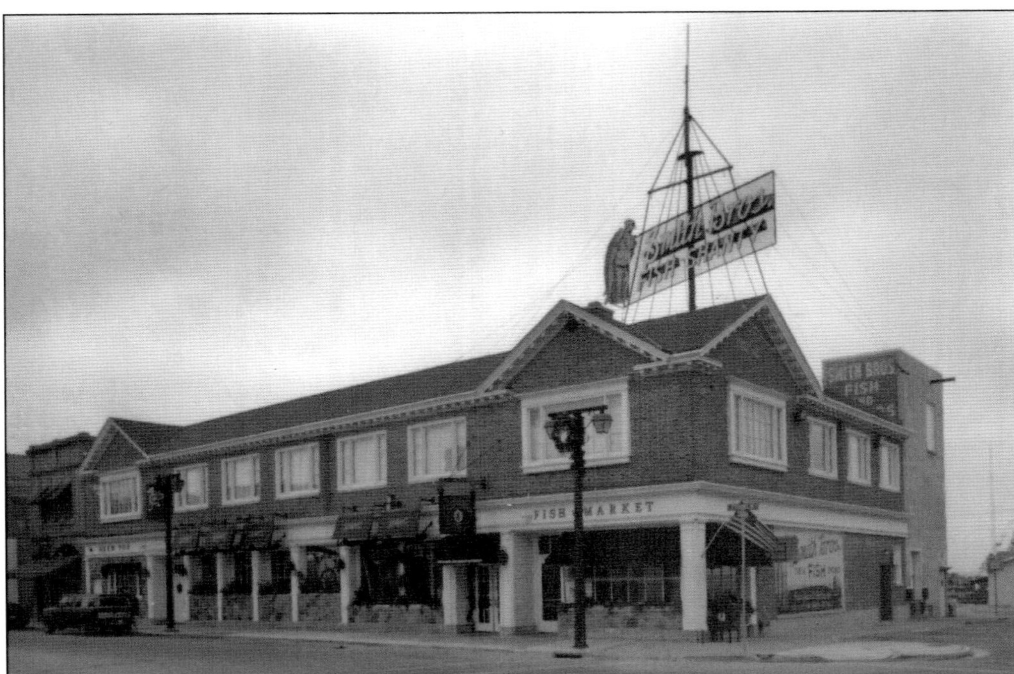

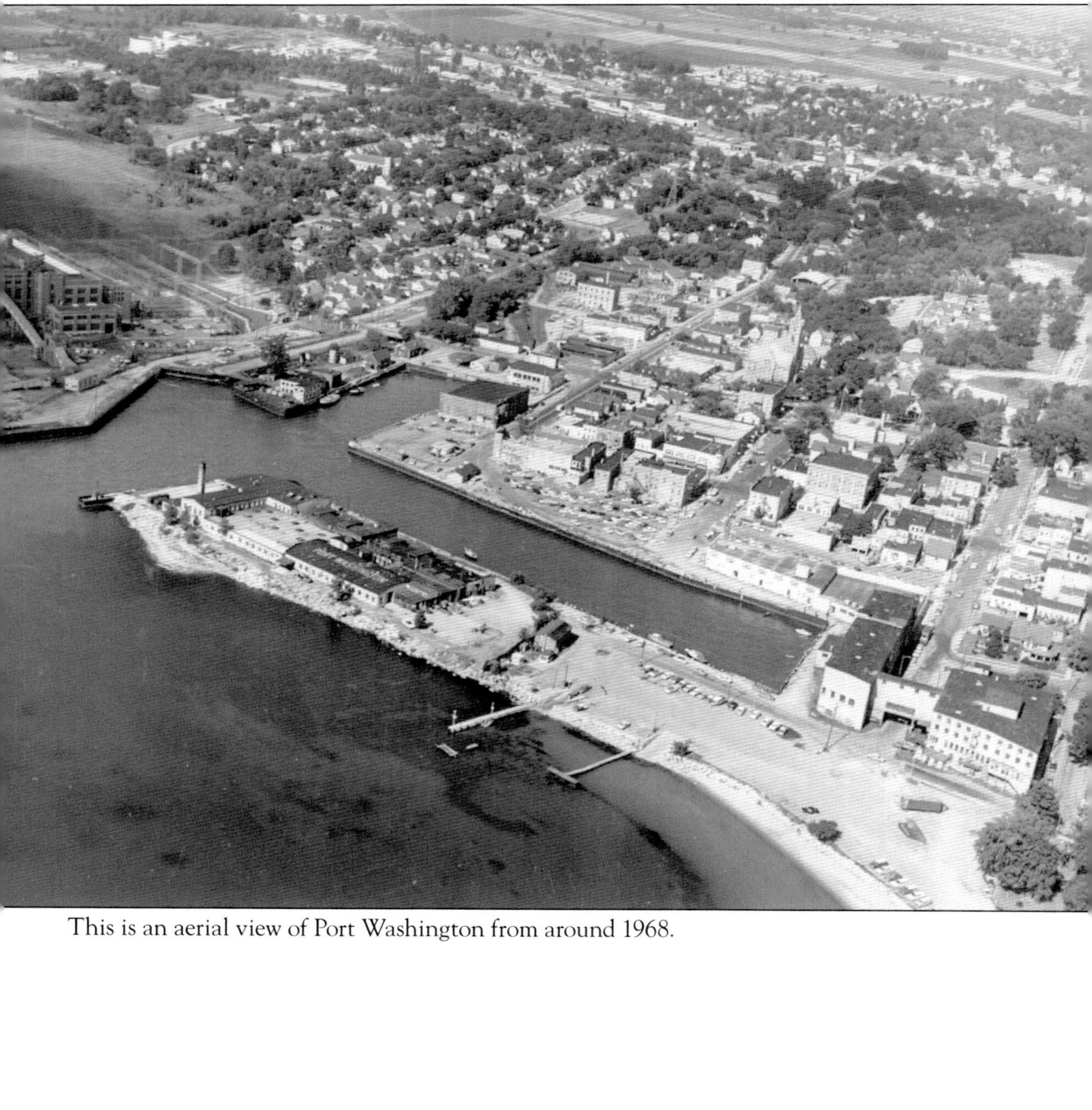

This is an aerial view of Port Washington from around 1968.

BIBLIOGRAPHY

Bruecher, Lawrence. Photograph collection.

Kubiak, William J. *Great Lakes Indians, A Pictorial Guide*, 2nd ed. Grand Rapids, MI: Baker Books, 1999.

Nenn, Linda M. Collection of photographs and postcards.

Ozaukee County Historical Society. *Early Ozaukee County Historical Sketches*. Cedarburg, WI: Ozaukee County Historical Society, 1967.

Ozaukee Press.

Port Washington Businessmen's Club. *Home Coming*. Milwaukee, WI: Burdick and Allen, 1908.

Port Washington Centennial Committee. *Port Washington Centennial: 1835–1935*. Port Washington, WI: *Port Washington Herald*, 1935.

Port Washington Historical Society photograph files.

Port Washington Sesquicentennial, 1835–1985. Port Washington, WI: 1985.

Smith, Richard D. *Out of the Past*. Vols. I–IV. Port Washington, WI: LMN Publication, 2007.

———. Photograph collection.

Wiening, Paul G. *The History of Port Washington Harbor*, Passages.